Helen's Opus 1

Helen H. Anderson

Copyright © 2018 Helen H. Anderson
All rights reserved.
ISBN: 1986319334
ISBN-13: 978-1986319331

I grew up with the piano. I learned its language as I learned to speak.
— Keith Jarrett

Life is like a piano. What you get out of it depends on how you play it.
— Tom Lehrer

The aim and final end of all music should be none other than the glory of God and the refreshment of the soul.
— Bach

PROLOGUE

My writings are for you, with the hope that you will enjoy them and be inspired to also relive parts of your life in story form. As such, this is not an autobiography but rather a collection of stories that I enjoy telling.

My goal was to be honest and put on paper what I remembered. I did, however, struggle as I attempted to tell my story. Probably the most difficult was to write about my hurts and disappointments regarding First English Lutheran Church in Mansfield, Ohio. However in the process of telling the story, I slowly began to heal. What was most enjoyable was to write about my childhood antics, about relatives, schools I attended, and the love of my life, Bert Anderson, who assisted me in growing up.

Each chapter is a stand-alone story and includes the date it was written. In addition, the chapters are not always in chronological order; instead, they meander through periods of my life, just like a conversation.

Scattered throughout the pages are another of my joys—word play. You'll find these tucked in among the pages here and there in order to give relief from just reading about me. Enjoy!

Helen

ACKNOWLEDGEMENTS

We started the writing group "My story, Your story" on February 7, 2012 and we met weekly for several years. I wrote a story almost every week. This book is a direct result of writing, listening, and working with this wonderful group. I am grateful to all the participants for their encouragement, feedback, enthusiasm, and joy. Thank you. Keep telling those stories!

My dear friend, Roslyn Banish, is a professional photographer as well as the author of several books. She planted the seed; she was the first one to suggest that I should write this book. Thank you for your encouragement and sage advice, and thank you for the photographs you took, including the picture of me on the back cover.

When my son David volunteered to be my general editor, I was relieved and very pleased. With his vision and suggestions, I began to see my book taking flight. We worked together in mutual agreement. So, thanks, David, you deserve a standing ovation.

I am grateful to Christina Raymond whose editing skills brought a professional polish to the book and to Michelle Samplin-Salgado whose design skills and artistic sensibility resulted in a beautiful book cover. Any mistakes are all mine.

Finally, thank you to all of the friends and relatives who patiently listened to me read these stories and gave me encouragement and advice.

IT WAS ALL MY GRANDMOTHER'S FAULT

It was all my grandmother's fault. Well, actually I should say my life took off in a different direction when Grandma came to live with us. When I should have been off to college after completing high school in 1945, I stayed home for a year at the request of my parents in order to help care for Grandma, my mother's mother. She came to live with us a couple of years earlier when she no longer was able to care for herself on the farm. During the next few years she became increasingly more confined to her bed and needed care around the clock. Mother would lift her from the bed to a wheelchair several times during the day. She'd bring her food trays, take her to the bathroom, change sheets, rub her arthritic knees with balm, and on and on. The daily laundry was a challenge. It was a day and night job. Mother got very little sleep.

Grandma spoke Swedish with a few English-Swedish word combinations she had learned. I was able to talk with her since I had taken two years of Swedish in high school. I really did not help very much with her care, however. I had plenty of time during this year to play tennis, swim at Lake Nokomis, visit with my friends, and come and go whenever I pleased. Dad also trusted me with the use of the car. But one thing I did do was talk with Grandma and read stories to her from my Swedish text books. This kept her from dozing in her chair so she would sleep better at night. Oh yes, I also was very active in the local Lutheran Church a few blocks from my house.

Let me tell you about my Grandma. She was born in Hörken, Sweden, a very small town in the province of Värmland. In her twenties she left home, came to the United States, met her future husband, Nils Nelson, also a Swede, got married and settled in a small house near Seven Corners in Minneapolis, Minnesota. Shortly after their first child was born, they moved 60 miles north to Milaca to an 80-acre homesteading farm.

As a child my memory of the farm was a two-story, three-bedroom house with a large kitchen, middle room, and sliding doors opening into a living room that was seldom used. Here I often played the phonograph and listened while sitting in a squeaky rocking chair. Attached in the front of the house was a screened porch. My Uncle told me that he would sleep there regardless of the weather. (Remember this is Minnesota.) There was a cellar reached from the outside and often used as a shelter in severe weather. It also was for storing potatoes, home canned goods, and apples. I hated to go there since it was full of cobwebs and had a dirt floor and the beamed ceiling seemed no higher than just above my head. There was a barn, a woodshed, summer kitchen, horse barn, chicken coop, pigpen, and a makeshift shed for the farm machinery. Of course there was an outhouse. A number of big oak trees surrounded the house including an apple orchard that Grandpa had planted, plus a vegetable garden. A few cows, a couple of horses, chickens, pigs, and the farm crops supplied their immediate needs. Their only neighbor was a family living directly across a dirt road. The nearest houses were a mile or more away and it was three miles into town. Horse and wagon was the only transportation during those early years.

A pastor from the main Lutheran church in Milaca would come to preach and hold services at a small chapel in the Bogus Brook area near their home. The pastor would also come to visit at their home. This was a big event for the family. A special chair was designated just for him, and Grandma would remind the children not to sit in that chair, which was most likely polished for his arrival. The pastor conducted the funeral for my Grandpa Nelson in 1929. I was two years old.

There were five children in the Nelson family; one died in childbirth, a girl named Hattie. Herbert, the second child, died of typhoid fever in his late 30's. My mother, Adelia, was next in line. Her name was really Helga Adelia, which she hated, so she chose to be called Adelia or Dee. She left the farm for Minneapolis in her early 20's, worked as a housemaid, seamstress, and personal maid for several influential families. She married my father on June 28, 1919. The fourth son, Edwin, who remained on the farm, was killed in a gun accident while hunting. He was in his late 40's. I remember when Mother got the news of her brother's death. I felt so helpless when I saw Mother sobbing, lying on her bed. I wanted to do something, but I just walked back and forth and felt sad.

So this left Grandma and Arvid, the youngest child in the family, to take care of the farm. When it became apparent that Grandma was failing, she came to live with my family in Minneapolis. Arvid continued farming until he was stricken with a bleeding ulcer several years later. As a result of his not being able to care for the farm, it was sold, and he came to live with my parents, Grandma, and me. I was in ninth grade. A room had been built for me in the attic just before Grandma arrived. It was very spacious. At the far end was my father's den where he kept his guns, hunting equipment, cameras, a bed, plus a desk to handle the work he brought home from the office. When Arvid arrived, the den became his bedroom. It was accessible only by going up the stairs and walking through my bedroom. Arvid always chuckled and teased me when he hooked his door from the inside and said, "Now, you can't get into my room, ha, ha." We always had fun. We had a good relationship, and he always respected my privacy.

My father's parents, William and Anna Hoffman, had come from Västmanland, Sweden and briefly settled in Minneapolis before moving near Milaca, Minnesota, about two miles from the Nelson farm. I often heard the story that my mom and dad first met at ages three and four. When a tug of war over a toy erupted between the two of them, Grandma Nelson said to my father, "Do not cry, Edwin. When you are older you can marry my daughter." I like this story.

The Hoffmans had five boys. My father, Edwin, was the firstborn, followed by Victor, Harold, William, and Arthur. (My mother told me the story that when Arthur was born, and Grandma was told that she now had a fifth boy, she said, "Take him back." I'm sure she must have wanted a girl.) Three sons (Edwin, Victor, and William) left the farm after high school for Minneapolis, and later, all three found employment at the Minneapolis Moline Tractor Company. Arthur and Harold stayed and managed the farm.

My father eventually rose to the position of General Superintendent of the Company. He worked hard and was often away on company business, especially during World War II. Mother was an excellent cook, hard worker, and a marvelous hostess at many dinner parties at our house. She canned everything. Even during the war, when there was rationing, she found ways to always serve tasty and healthy meals. Her sense of humor was especially evident at dinner. Often with pad and pencil in hand, she'd ask each of us, "What would you like for dessert?"

When we gave her our choice she would go to the cupboard, open a drawer and announce, "I'm sorry we're all out of that." This would go on until we chose the correct dessert she had made. I remember Floating Island was often on the menu, plus another she called "The Forgotten Dessert." I asked her why she called it "forgotten". "I usually forgot to add something that should be in it," was her answer.

But now I'm really getting ahead of myself. At this point I need to explain about my entrance into the world. One thing I know for sure is my birthdate—it was on a Saturday, June 4, 1927. Other than that, I know very little except that my birth mother could not care for me and as a result she allowed me to be adopted. At the age of three months, my adopting parents signed the legal papers, and I became the daughter of Edwin and Adelia Hoffman and given the name Helen Rowene Hoffman.

My mother wanted to name me June because I was born in June, but my father strongly objected. His reason was that my Swedish grandparents on both sides of the family would call me "yune." (The "j" is silent in Swedish). He wanted a name that they could easily pronounce, so he said, "Her name must be Helen." Rowene was my mother's choice, having read it somewhere, so this became my middle name. Why my parents could not have children was also a mystery. I never broached the subject with either of them.

Mother said that she told me of my adoption when I was quite young, but true to form I did not remember it. On one particular occasion some children were teasing me about being adopted as we walked home from school. I immediately ran into the house crying telling my mother what these mean kids had said about me. Her response while closely hugging me was, "I told you some time ago about your adoption." No doubt I forgot, or perhaps I really didn't know what it meant. There were times as I grew I would wonder how a mother could give up a child. I guess I was too young to understand.

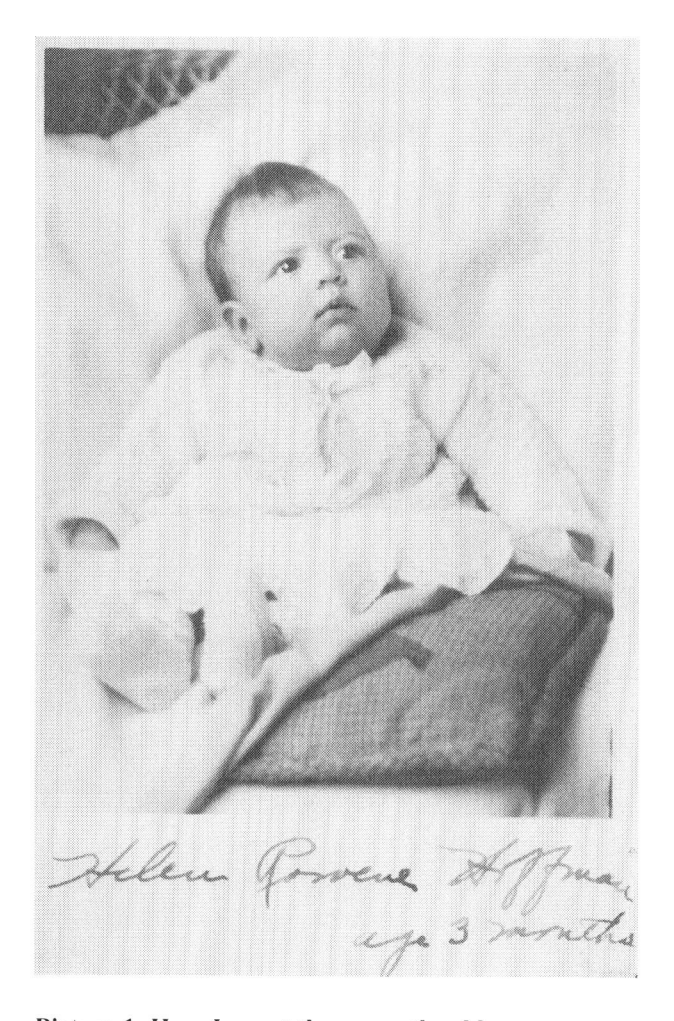

Picture 1: Here I am at three months old

A couple of months before I was to be married, Mother told me a few details about my adoption. She said that she had some papers that I could have if I ever wanted to find my birth parents. During her haltingly difficult attempt to explain, she began to cry. She then showed me a well-worn, brown leather envelope with a ragged ribbon tied in a bow to hold it together—but never opened it for me to see. There were times I wondered if I would ever get to see it.

After my father died in 1973, she brought up the subject again. She said she wanted me to have this information, but that my father was very much against giving it to me since they had promised secrecy to my birth parents. I elected not to pursue it any further. I could see that it was still quite painful to her, and I did not want to cause any hurt. I knew that the reason for the adoption was done in love, and that she and Dad had dedicated me to God, promising to raise me in the faith of the Church. I realized that my life to this point could not have been better. However, when Mother entered a nursing home in 1981, she insisted that I accept the leather envelope tied with that ragged ribbon. I have since opened it a couple of times, but it didn't give me any pertinent information to help locate anyone.

Before my wedding in 1949, Mother sent for my birth certificate to the Hennepin County courthouse in St. Paul, Minnesota. When it arrived I saw that it had no evidence of my birth parents. It functioned fully, however, as a legal document. I've often wondered about my decision for not trying to find my birth parents. Also, I have questioned who do I look like, and do I have any sisters or brothers. At this point I have to leave these questions unanswered.

At this point I must tell you, dear reader, the truth about the opening statement of my story—"It was all my grandmother's fault"—and how this impacted the rest of my life. After my graduation from high school, I wanted to go to college. I was very interested in St. Olaf College in Northfield, Minnesota, since it was famous for its music program and that's what I wanted. This was not to be, since my parents wanted me to stay home for a year.

After a year, it was time to decide where I should continue my education. It was a big disappointment to learn that St. Olaf was available except they had *no* available housing. It was 1946 and many service men and women from Minnesota were given first choice in colleges and universities. As a result, all possible housing was taken. So I went for my second choice, Bethel College in St. Paul, and found that they also had no available housing. But here I realized I could commute. I made application, was accepted, *and this is where I met my future husband!!!*

For the first semester I stayed at home and commuted. In January a dormitory room became available. I moved in. Two bunk beds, four desks, four chairs, and four dressers completed the room. Living with three new girls and trying to study was a challenge. It was convenient to go home every weekend—and of course, I came with my laundry and visited with all my friends while Mother washed and ironed my clothes. Dad would take me back to school on Sunday evening. During the week I treated classes like I did in high school by doing only what was necessary. The midterm exams were difficult and the shock set in. The first marking period brought me up short. Studying now became more intense.

Two times a week all the students were required to attend Chapel. I don't know if the teachers really took attendance but most of us thought so because the school was small enough that it was obvious who was missing. It was soon learned that I played the piano, so I was asked to play for Chapel.

The one who played on alternate days was a guy by the name of Bertil Anderson. He was thin, had lots of black hair, was a veteran, and I watched his hands sail up and down the piano keyboard. When I saw and heard him, I immediately thought, "What a show-off!" Of course this made me practice even more in order to best his playing. One day the school president inquired whether the two of us would like another piano brought in so we could play duets. It seemed like a good idea. This meant we'd have to practice together!!

When we began practicing I was furious because Bert seemed to always be in charge. But as the time progressed I found myself looking forward to these sessions. I thought, "Hmmm …he's really not so bad." At least he played piano. During this time I dated other guys. One date was to a school Halloween party with Jim. Bert was there and was very attentive until he realized that I was with Jim. He told me many times over the years that his actions were quite embarrassing to him.

The duo-piano practices and performances continued and it soon became apparent that Bert was really interested in me. One Sunday he came for dinner to my home. My mother met him at the kitchen door with several bandages covering part of her face and neck. She just had had her thirteenth plastic surgery on her nose. (This was as a result of earlier radium treatments that caused her nose to deteriorate; as a result, she developed lupus, a progressive skin disease). Well, back to my mother. She greeted Bert as though nothing was wrong and welcomed him royally. Of course she had prepared a wonderful dinner and served it elegantly, being careful to keep her head erect so as to not undo the stitches and bandages. Bert often commented on her tenacity in the face of her medical problems.

Grandma Nelson liked Bert immediately. After all, Bert was Swedish. Bert's mother and dad were born in Sweden, so he grew up speaking both Swedish and English. One day he suggested to me that we offer to stay with Grandma so that Mom and Dad could go out for dinner. During the evening a hearty voice came from the bedroom. Grandma called out " Bertil, kom hit." ("Bertil, come here.") When he entered the room Grandma had him bend down to hear what she had to say. "Skall du gifta mej Helen eller skall du bara monkarunt." ("Are you going to marry Helen or are you just going to monkey around?") Her Swedish had become a bit of both languages. Bert did not tell me that he answered yes to her question until much later when he proposed marriage. So Grandma knew of our engagement before I did.

Bethel College was only a two-year school. During my second year, Bert's sister, Ruth, came to study at the school. She also was from Chicago. She and I soon became good friends and told me many Bert stories. In order to pay for part of his schooling, Bert worked at night mopping floors. Ruth and I would sit on the top step and chat together watching Bert as he polished the dining hall floor below. I believe Ruth thought I would make a good match for her brother. Finally he began to be more attentive and we dated frequently.

During these two college years we both studied piano at Bethel with Professor Theodore Bergman. He was very interested in our careers and frequently asked what the next step would be after college. Bert had been in the Navy as an Operating Room Technician. His first choice was to enter medical school. However, when he applied to the University of Minnesota Medical School, he was told that since he was from Illinois (Chicago) he was ineligible; the quota had already been filled by Minnesota applicants. This was a big disappointment, to be sure. The year was 1948.

My first choice was to be a nurse. I applied to Midway Hospital School of Nursing in St. Paul. Everything was in order until I had a physical. The doctor was very blunt. He said "Are you sure you want to be a nurse? With feet like yours I'm not certain you'll be able to do the required amount of walking." (My foot disorder was congenital and no surgical procedures had ever been suggested).

So there we were. Both of us felt lost and "out in left field"! This is when Mr. Bergman came up with the solution. He said, "You can finish your college education at the MacPhail College of Music in Minneapolis, and I will see to it that you both can join the faculty and be assured of teaching positions to help fund college costs." Mr. Bergman was one of the Board Members of the school. This seemed like a logical solution and so plans were made to transfer our credits, and we began classes in September of 1948. By this time we were already engaged to be married.

Bert proposed to me on the front steps of Bethel in May of 1948. I was thrilled. We were a perfect match for one another and had a musical future ahead of us. One Saturday we went to a jewelry store in downtown St. Paul and picked out the rings. He told me much later that he had previously talked with the jeweler about a price range before we got there. However, when I picked out a set that was above that price, he nodded his approval to the jeweler and then wondered how he was going to pay for it.

The next day, a Sunday, at the dinner table of my parents, I flashed the ring towards my mother several times until she finally saw it. "Congratulations," she said, and my father echoed by nodding his approval. Of course it was suggested that a wedding should come after we finished college. We both nodded our agreement.

In the fall of 1948 we began our first semester at MacPhail Conservatory of Music. Both of us took tests to eliminate several classes—ear training, first year harmony, and piano performance. It was thrilling to be immersed in full time music—and life looked so promising. It was obvious to us that in order to graduate in two years we'd have to take classes in the summer. We began performing duo-piano concerts, and also became a part of the Carillon Singers. I sang alto in a sixteen-voice choral group with Mrs. Edith Norberg as director, and Bert was the accompanist. The height of our success was winning the national title of Choral Singers held in Chicago. The prize was being the featured group in the evening at the Soldiers Field in Chicago together with the Chicago Symphony Orchestra.

Bert lived in a third-floor room on Pleasant Avenue. No meals were included. In order to save money he walked a couple of miles to school each day. Naturally he was invited to my house for dinner at least two times a week. I also had use of the family car. Mother would occasionally do his laundry. It became increasingly difficult for both of us to attend school during the day, teach in the afternoon and evening, and fit in time to practice on our own and together.

Towards the end of the first semester, we began talking about getting married. We felt life would be much easier. Tentatively we thought about a wedding over Labor Day weekend. At dinner we proposed this option to my parents. Of course the discussion was met with disapproval, but when we seemed a bit resolute they finally agreed. Later that evening my father informed Bert when and if we married before I graduated he (Bert) would have to assume my tuition for my senior year. With only $300 in the bank and his own tuition to pay, this presented a new wrinkle in our lives. But we were determined to make it work. Our plan seemed so logical to us.

Summer school was intense. We both had five classes five days a week for six weeks. There were times in class when I would make lists of what needed to be done for our wedding, and with half an ear listen to the professors. There were tests, performances, finding time to practice individually and as a two-piano team, and we each taught piano to at least eight or more students per week.

Our wedding on Friday, September 2, 1949 (Labor Day weekend), was held at First Covenant Church in downtown Minneapolis. I remember waiting with my father to hear the cue "Here Comes the Bride" at the Chapel door.

February 18, 2014

GLADYS

One of the most important events in my life was to have a friend that I met for the first time when I was nine months old. Our neighborhood was typical in that most residents were Scandinavians of some sort, or Germans, and I remember one Catholic family. At three months of age I was legally adopted. The year was 1927. My mother suggested the name June, since I was born in June. My father did not approve. He wanted the Swedish relatives to be able to pronounce my name. Thus, I was named Helen. I'm sure the neighborhood was aware of this new baby in the Hoffman household. I suspect that's typical of neighborhoods, especially for a first born.

One day a visitor came and knocked on the door, asking to see the new baby who had arrived in the house on the corner of 44th Avenue and 53rd Street in Minneapolis, Minnesota. She was two years old and her name was Gladys Osterberg. She began walking in front of me in my highchair. She stopped, looked up and said, "Can you walk? See I can walk," and proceeded again to walk around the chair.

This initial act was the beginning of a friendship that is still thriving after 89 years. The three-year difference in our ages made no difference. For all intents and purposes, she became my sister. Naturally I did not realize at that time that we would remain very best friends through the years. To this day, as I write this story, we frequently talk about all the good times we had. We have visited in one another's homes even when miles have separated us.

Gladys was the youngest of six children. They lived a half a block from me with their mother and father in a small house. At one point Gladys' father deserted the family and her mother had to go to work. It became Gladys' job to make dinner each evening and share in the housework since everyone had a day job. I believe my mother was sensitive about these conditions, and also aware that it would be good for me to have a sister. She was right. It worked! My parents were pleased to include Gladys on family vacations, sleepovers, and for meals. Gladys and I were inseparable. Sleepovers, birthdays, church, family vacations, meals—she was always a part of the family.

Mother was often inventive in our playing. Gladys and I remember fondly how she filled two wash tubs with water in my front yard and let us splash around in our bathing suits as we pretended to be swimming. She also hung blankets over the clothes line in the backyard for us to set up housekeeping. Gladys and I remember how we pretended to be sleeping when we heard Patty coming. Patty would look into the tent and shout at us, "I know you are just pretending to be sleeping." We were trying to be quiet until she left. It was difficult.

The front porch of my house became a favorite pretend play area for Gladys and me. With a doll buggy and small tea sets, we set up housekeeping. Gladys would be the nurse and take care of me and my baby. Mother would often come with cookies and milk. One summer we went to church camp for a week. My mother told Gladys to take care of me since it was my first time being away from home. I was twelve and she was fourteen.

Gladys' brother, Oliver, was very artistic, constantly producing plays for us to perform. Some of the productions were held in my basement and others in a friend's garage. Tickets were usually one cent, or sometimes the kids got in free. Some of our costumes were found in my mom's attic. She was a collector and shared whatever we asked for. One day Gladys, Oliver, and I dressed up in long dresses, and one of us was privileged to wear a pair of mother's "golden slippers." Of course, we sang "Oh, Those Golden Slippers" as we paraded around the block.

When one of my baby chicks died, a funeral was held in my backyard. Gladys and I sang "Jesus, Loves Me," and Oliver preached. We shed a few tears as we lowered the little box containing the deceased chick into the hole that Oliver had dug. A prayer closed the burial service.

On occasion when my mother would go shopping, she would set the table for Gladys and me. When we came home for lunch there would be sandwiches, fruit, and dessert ready for us. Also, there would be a dime or quarter under each plate. She always trusted Gladys and felt I was safe when we were together. I remember feeling grownup even though we were still in grammar school. Mother's words to Gladys were again and again "Please look after Helen."

Gladys and I loved to sing. Our local pastor asked us to sing at the burial of a young child. We were nine and seven years old and very nervous because of the seriousness of the occasion. I gave the pitch to begin—started too high, and we got the giggles. We composed ourselves and started again. The pastor was complimentary and thanked us for singing and told us that God loved little children. His words made us feel better.

Through the years it was great to have such a dear friend; actually, she felt like my sister. We served as Maids of Honor at each other's weddings. She was always at my birthday parties, many sleepovers, lunches, dinners, and family vacations. At this point we now must rely on phone calls and the postal service, since she lives in Minnesota and I in California.

In June 2013, Gladys and her husband Bob celebrated their 60th wedding anniversary. I longed to be there but called with my regrets, and then called the next day to hear the full story. Most recently I telephoned to wish my dear friend a "Happy 92nd Birthday." Again we shared memories from so long ago.

Even though we are legally not sisters, looking back you'd never know it. We were always together. So what is the verdict? I leave it up to you, the reader.

January 24, 2017

GRADE SCHOOL MEMORIES

It was a five-block walk to my grade school. There were no buses. Everyone walked the distance in all kinds of weather. When it was below zero, Mother would dress me warmly and added a woolen scarf around my head that covered my mouth and nose. Minnesota winters could be brutal. I remember going to school when it was close to fifteen-below zero. I was one of only two students in my grade that came that day beside several teachers and the principal. I think we were sent home before we took off all our outer garments.

Minnehaha was the name of my grade school. Sometime in the course of my school years, we were told the name came from Henry Wadsworth Longfellow's poem entitled "Song of Hiawatha." I remember memorizing the poem… "By the shores of Gitchi Gumee, By the shining Big Sea-Water, stood the Wigwam of Nokomis, Daughter of the Moon Nokomis…" (That's all I remember.) Nokomis was the name of my junior high school (also a part of the poem), and I attended Minnehaha Academy for senior high school. Longfellow's original house occupied a prominent setting, not far from my house; it was painted yellow, and is now used as a public library.

In addition, Hiawatha was one of the main streets that led directly to downtown Minneapolis. About six blocks from my house was Minnehaha Park, a lovely large area with lots of picnic possibilities, a large covered stage, and trails to follow. To this day it still has several statues depicting Minnehaha, a young Indian girl. One lovely statue is placed near the stream that courses toward a large and beautiful waterfall in the park. There were days when my friends and I would dip our toes in the stream, attempt to cross over to the other side on a series of rock shapes, or walk the trail alongside the stream as it flowed and emptied into the Mississippi River. There we explored some empty caves, daring one another to go further into its depth. Someone, usually the leader, would suddenly scream and we'd all run out pretending to be afraid. Actually, I was afraid.

My kindergarten memories are non-existent. I remember nothing. However, one thing I am sure of is that on my first day, Mother would have dressed me in my best dress, polished my shoes, added a bow to my Buster Brown haircut, and walked with me, most likely with a tear in her eye. She probably told me to mind the teacher, and also how to behave. Funny—her advice continued all through my school life, and, come to think of it, even after I was married.

My first grade memories are a bit clearer. One day in class we were told that at the end of the week, at about noon, there would be a solar eclipse. We talked about it during the week, what it was—that it did not happen every year, and that we would be watching it through smoked glass. On that Friday I remember standing at the window looking through a piece of smoked glass and being warned by the teacher not to look directly at the eclipse because it would damage our eyes. It was hard to wait until the eclipse actually began, and it was spooky when the sky got dark.

Another event I recall was when the students in grades 1-6 were examined by a dental hygienist to determine if he or she had any signs of tooth decay (cavities). If there was none, a gold star headband was presented to the cavity-free child, together with a certificate. When all the testing had taken place those fortunate ones that were cavity free would don their gold star headband and along with our teachers, join in the "Dental Gold Star Parade." All the honorees would parade around the block carrying banners and flags. This was a good way to encourage good tooth care. This was also before the introduction of fluoride. It must have worked because my dentist found my very first tooth cavity when I was in my late twenties.

For Mother's Day we drew pictures of our choice on white paper, pasted it on colored paper, decorated it with crayons and attempted to print our name. Sometimes we were allowed to make cutouts using the snub nose scissors. When I arrived home carrying this precious present behind my back, my mother would attempt to steal it from me. It was a game, of course, and I would hide this precious gift in my room until Mother's Day. The same routine was repeated at Thanksgiving, Christmas, Valentine's Day, and Easter.

Living in Minnesota, the weather often became a factor that would prohibit students from using the outdoor playground. When this happened the gymnasium on the first floor became our playground. The younger students would play games such as "Ring Around the Rosie," "Farmer in the Dell," and "Duck, Duck, Goose." At other times upper grade students favored "Dodge Ball," volley ball, and a series of exercises and relays. There were ropes on the wall that allowed us to attempt climbing hand over hand.

Quite often we had special events when guests would come to our school to perform for the entire assembly. We all sat on the floor in neat rows facing the stage. The principal would introduce the program and give orders concerning our responses and behavior. One delightful show that I remember so well was a man who portrayed the story of "Rumpelstiltskin." Our stage at Minnehaha School was not very large, but with a few props and quick changes of costumes, this gentleman had us all believing and following the story. The characters were the imp, the King and Queen, and a young maiden who was given the task of turning straw into gold. I remember all the students trying to guess whether the fair maiden could guess the imp's name. I still can see it clearly in my mind's eye. The answer came from a lowly worker in the court who found the imp singing a song in the woods around a fire and revealing his name in one of the verses. His name was Rumpelstiltskin! The court worker came back to tell the young maiden and the mystery was solved.

No doubt we all remember how a teacher would give directions as we left the room, be it at the end of the day, or when we were going to the gymnasium. In a loud demanding voice she would say, "Line up in a straight line, please." An additional admonition was "Please remember, no talking." Bess T. Plummer, the principal, stood against the wall observing our behavior as we passed. When we entered the gymnasium there would be marches playing over a PA system. One day the principal asked if I was able to play a march for the assembly. I said yes—and did so from fourth through sixth grade. Many times I would invent new march tunes, which presented no problem. It just had to be a march rhythm.

My dad played the violin—mostly self-taught. During the day when he was at work, I would pick up his violin and try to copy what I had heard him play. One of Dad's favorite violin pieces was "The Blue Bells of Scotland" by Arthur Pryor, adapted for violin from an original Scottish song. The form of the piece was "theme and variations". The violinist would play the melody through once and then several adaptations of the original melody would follow. It was fun to make the bow bounce up and down and pretend to be a real violinist like my father. More often I would accompany Dad on the piano when he played.

In the sixth grade an opportunity came to have violin lessons at the school. My mother agreed to let me take Dad's violin without his knowledge. The lessons were very basic and each took about twenty minutes. The teacher would give me examples to practice at home. Sometimes I preferred practicing the violin more than my piano lessons. Mother insisted I do both, of course. About four months later, parents and friends were invited to a concert at the school. As the orchestra filed into the gymnasium I walked in with the members of our small orchestra with Dad's violin tucked under my arm and sat down in the honored first chair position. Why did I deserve first chair? The answer is easy. I was the only one in the violin section who had had lessons. When my father saw me come through the door with a violin tucked under my arm, he turned to my mother and said, "What's she going to do with that violin?" He was really surprised to learn that it was his violin. Later, when he saw that I enjoyed playing the instrument, he became my teacher. Unfortunately it did not last too long. It took a lot of patient practice and I found that practicing the piano was really more enjoyable.

I have several report cards from grade school that my mother had saved. It is interesting for me to read what kind of student I was. In third grade Miss Smith wrote the following: "Helen is an earnest, conscientious and willing worker. She is neat in her personal appearance and in her work. She has confidence in her own ability so makes a good leader. Helen is pleasant at all times, shows growth in her work, however her addition and subtraction combinations need strengthening."

The last statement submitted by my teacher, Miss Smith, is very interesting to me now. My mathematical skills have not improved that much. It makes me wonder if I ever learned the essentials and the necessary building blocks and the teacher never saw what was happening. I wonder why not. Could it have been a lack of interest or daydreaming on my part? To this day I often find myself counting on my fingers for some problems or grabbing a pencil and paper. I'm glad that in this day and age there are iPhones with calculators. I'm also thankful that it did not affect my sons. They both have highly skilled jobs: One is a computer engineer in California, and the other manages a large New Jersey Heating and Plumbing store. Both use math throughout the day, using a variety of mathematical solutions that are far beyond my level.

Looking at my fourth through sixth grade report cards—they are pretty good. The letter "S" was used for all subjects indicating "Satisfaction." There were no indications that I had any problems with math. What happened? Maybe I fooled my teacher? I've heard about adults who have gone back to school and found the answer that was lacking in their early education.

In sixth grade the report card had five categories: Social Studies, Language Arts, Written Language, Mathematics, Music, and Art. Under Music, Miss Daugherty wrote: "Is showing special ability in music, (piano, chorus, violin)." I can easily see now how my future was shaping up—just like the song, "She Shall Have Music Wherever She Goes."

Today the method of learning by rote is not used as much as it used to be. But in my childhood memory, it became a strong force for learning. Addition, Subtraction, and Multiplication flash cards were used—in fact, used every day. I'm certain rote exercise gave me a basis for learning the "numbers tables" (1-12 as they were called). It is still stuck in my brain. Also with regard to spelling—there were classroom spelling bees, and spelling words to write as part of our homework. I'm also grateful for the early teaching of Phonics. I often use this method when I question the spelling of a particular word. I can usually sound it out and if not perfectly spelled, at least it comes close. Of course today "spell-check" or a click on Google on the computer is a quicker method. Let a machine do the thinking. Maybe this has become an excuse rather than using memory.

Penmanship seems to be another lost art. In grade school it was somewhat painful at the beginning to practice beautiful writing. The teacher had us hold the pencil or pen in a special way (the third, fourth, and fifth fingers touching the paper, and the thumb and index finger holding the pencil) as we drew circles round and round. She would walk up and down the row checking that we all followed her instructions. Then we started writing letters of the alphabet on tablet papers. The "As" reached the middle line, the "Bs" touched the top line, etc., and this practice continued every day. I guess it worked for at least no one has any problem reading my writing. I'm wondering when it became an unnecessary addition to the curriculum? As I observe young peoples' handwriting today, most of it is written backhand. Students would argue that it's faster, and furthermore, who cares whether it is beautiful? I have letters written to my grandmother from her father in Sweden. It was pen and ink on beautiful thin paper (size 8.5 x 11) and folded in half. Since it took a long time, maybe months, to reach her in Minnesota, words and content had to be well thought out. No wasting of words. Who knows, maybe it would be the last letter ever received.

Once a year our grade school would ask the students to collect old newspapers and bring them to the school on a selected day. Hemp ropes were handed out ahead of time for neatly tying the papers in bundles. Each grade would have an outer section around the ball field along the fence. It was a great competition to see which grade gathered the most. It was measured by weight on a scale in a truck. The scene was electric with excitement as students pulled wagons with their bundles, and parents driving to the spot and unloading their trunks. Some students walked and valiantly carried a couple of bundles along with their books. Later in the day a ceremony was held in the gym to award the prize to the wining class. What was the prize? I don't remember.

My mother was a firm believer in autograph books. She bought one for me and in it I collected the names of all my grade school teachers over the years. Some wrote little sayings or a bit of advice to continue being a good student, and sometimes a comment about my musical ability.

My music career began in 1931 at the age of four with Mrs. Matilda Olsson Soderlind. Lessons were 50 cents for one half hour. My first recital was held on December 5, 1931 at the Leamington Hotel, Third Avenue at 10th Street in Minneapolis, Minnesota. Until the age of 13, all my recitals were held once a year at this hotel. My dearest friend, Gladys, would attend together with my family. I always was happy to have her next to me. One time she and I went to explore the bathroom in the hotel before the recital began. We were fascinated with the beautiful pillars, gorgeous long draperies, and bathroom sinks that looked like marble, and faucets that shone like gold. There was an echo affect in this cavernous room, and we were not aware that our voices could be heard outside the room.

I remember being nervous about my piano performance—there were the ever-present "butterflies flying around inside my stomach". Of course I wanted to play well. I guess it was to make my parents happy and of course it felt good to receive praise from others. It took a few years to learn to satisfy myself, which meant to practice correctly with intention. But I had to start at the beginning with recitals.

At my first recital I played three pieces:
    "Up the Hill and Down the Hill – Williams
    "The Yellow Butterfly" – Corinne Bowen
    "The Red Butterfly" – Corinne Bowen

It must have taken less than 30 seconds to play, and I was finished. There was applause, the bow, and the return to my seat—and the inward sigh of relief. For every recital, just before I got up to play, I could count on my father clearing his throat. Mother said that he would position himself (get comfortable) and with his pencil check off each student on the printed program when they had finished playing. He would always compliment me on my playing, and give me a hug or a pat on the back. Not true for my mother. She often would remind me of my mistakes—but when I think about it now, she had heard my pieces over and over when I was practicing. I guess she knew my songs as well as I did. Father always encouraged me to continue practicing.

March 25, 2014

PLAYTIME GONE WRONG

Every house in my neighborhood was different. No house looked like mine. Some were two stories, some had dormers, and others had porches. However, three things we all had in common was a front yard, a public sidewalk, and a boulevard with a curb next to the street. Everyone took care of their front yard and their boulevard. My father was upset with the amount of weeds taking over our boulevard so he began turning over the soil, sowing grass seed, and covering it with straw. He then placed a steel pipe in each corner and strung wires around the entire area. Our house was on a corner lot with a street sign that read 44th Avenue & 53rd Street. This sign stood on one of the corners of our boulevard.

The street sign to some of us kids was an object to be climbed. It was a trick to see how fast one could reach the top and slide down while someone did the timing. It was my turn and I shimmed up quickly. However to be the winner, I came down fast and landed with one of the steel pipes jammed into my thigh. I don't remember it hurting as I ran to the front door calling for my mother. I do, however, remember her expression when I showed her the open wound. It was sheer panic. She literally threw me on the bed, hurried to the bathroom and came back with a bottle of "red stuff" and threw it on my leg. There was no 911 to call, and my father had the car, so in a panic she ran outside. She saw a parked car up the street. It belonged to a man who was painting inside a house. She pleaded her case, and he offered to drive us to a doctor.

Mother sat in the backseat holding me on her lap. She told me later that she envisioned at any moment that the wound would erupt in severe bleeding. We arrived at the doctor's office and the kindly gentleman driver carried me upstairs. I remember crying not because of pain but of fright. The doctor cancelled his waiting patients and attended to my wound. I remember him clipping the last stitch and telling me that I would be fine as he was attaching a large bandage.

Back home I laid on the sofa nursing my wound. When my dad came home from work and learned what had happened to me, he immediately went outside and took down the steel pipes. I think he suffered from some guilt—another kind of wound. This one didn't need a bottle of "red stuff".

May 1, 2012

PERFECT PITCH

I've had it all my life. No, it is not a disease. What I'm talking about is the actual ability to hear the exact notes of a scale being played or sung. Perfect pitch, or more correctly called "absolute judgment of pitch," is an attribute that can be very useful or drive you crazy. What is it? The dictionary describes it as "the ability to immediately identify by name a musical sound or sing any tone at will." It is often characterized as being inborn, but I believe it also can be acquired by training.

I remember distinctly when I learned that I had this ability. I think I was about four years old. A piano tuner who came to our house suspected that it was one of my gifts, so on one occasion he gave me the ultimate test. He had me sing a note. Then he asked me to find the same note on the piano. I identified it correctly each time, and by this test and a few more tests, he recognized that I did indeed have perfect pitch. At the time it never occurred to me that it was something unusual, but Mr. Carlson, the tuner, strongly stressed that I should have piano lessons. Mrs. Matilda Olsson Soderlin became my first piano teacher.

The ability to hear a pitch and know what it was, or to pull a wanted pitch from memory became very useful at times. For instance, it made memorizing music much easier. Hearing the notes in my head made it easy to play or sing them without music. One of the dangers was to depend on my hearing instead of reading the actual notes on the page. Fortunately my teacher suspected what I was doing and trained me to read notes.

Let me tell you of one instance when having perfect pitch proved embarrassing and made it impossible for me to perform. A group of young people from my church were giving a program at another church, and I was to play a piano solo. I was fifteen years old. As I stood to walk to the piano, I noticed that the piano was an ancient variety. This should have given me pause, but I sat down to begin.

The moment I set my hands on the keys and began to play I knew I was in trouble. It was an old upright piano that had not been tuned, maybe ever, and as a result had drastically lost its true pitch. (By the way, middle "A" on the keyboard should always be tuned to 440 vibrations per second, and the rest of the keys tuned in relationship).

As I began playing the correct keys, I heard distinctly conflicting tones. What I heard and what I was playing did not match. I had a dilemma. I couldn't continue since my hands wanted to play the notes that I heard and not the notes I knew to be true. Finally I stood up, apologized, and tried to explain why I could not continue. The questioning looks that I saw while standing there were riveting. There were no smiles—mostly stares as they tried to figure out what I was saying. As I returned to my seat, I was sure people thought I was grandstanding.

All through my life having perfect pitch has been a valuable tool, especially when teaching piano. I could walk away from the piano and still determine whether the student was playing the notes correctly. I would often demonstrate my ability of perfect pitch much to their amazement. It also has been thrilling to be able to know when an operatic soprano has managed to reach that thrilling high "C", or follow in my head the notes played by a symphony orchestra or the Beatles. Also in the many choirs/choruses that I have sung in, I was often the one to give the beginning pitch. No pitch pipe was needed when I was around.

One of the disadvantages of having perfect pitch is when a soloist, instrumentalist, or choir/chorus do not perform on pitch. It grates on my soul! But now as I've grown older my perfect pitch ability has begun to change. At this point I am not always so sure of myself. I'm close, but not always "dead on." It could have something to do with a bit of hearing loss. Oh, well, I'm grateful for the time I had, and furthermore, who needs to be perfect all the time anyway?

August 12, 2014

HOW I LEARNED THE SWEDISH LANGUAGE

When the Swedes first came to America, a good number settled in Minnesota, either in Minneapolis, or neighboring St. Paul. Both sets of my grandparents came to Minneapolis. This same pattern was true in other large cities such as New York and Chicago. It was obvious that their reasons were to be with fellow Swedes where the stores and butcher shops catered to the needs they had in their homeland.

When I was quite small, I began to hear the Swedish tongue spoken by my grandparents and parents. My tiny ears heard the lilt of the language and it found a storage place in my brain. Also I figured out that if my parents didn't want me to know what they were talking about, they would switch into Swedish. That made me more determined to learn the language.

When I was approximately five or six years old, I remember hearing my parents talking to one another after they had gone to bed. A long hall separated my bedroom and their bedroom. One evening when I was in bed, I called to my mother, "Mama, how do you say curtain in Swedish?" She answered, "gardin". A little while later I questioned, "How do you say bed and rug?" The answer came back, "säng" and "matta". As I kept inquiring about several words and my parents gave me the answer, somehow it began to make sense. Many times I could determine the nature of their Swedish conversation, and listened more intently if it appeared to be a secret or especially if it was something about me.

In senior high school, Swedish was offered as an elective course. I jumped at the opportunity knowing that I already could speak and could even read it rather easily. My thinking was basically, "What an easy class—I'm certainly going to do well." This was true as we began learning the alphabet with its three extra letters after the letter Z: Ä, Å, Ö. I knew these three extra letters from my mother's first Swedish language book that had a whole page devoted to the alphabet. I had read it and said it many times. Ä, Å, Ö. My Swedish class had five students. At graduation in June, one of the students became Valedictorian, another Salutatorian, still another was very bright, and then there was one other student and me. Both of us had to work really hard to keep up. However, I did learn a great deal of pertinent Swedish language skills that proved helpful on trips to Sweden in later years. In addition, Bert and I were able to use the language when it became necessary to keep some information private. Isn't it interesting that we became copy cats of our parents in using the language just as they had previously done many years before?

April 15, 2014

LIFE ON THE FARM IN THE 1930's

During the summer it was a yearly activity for my mother to go for two weeks to help her mother (my grandmother) with general housecleaning. Of course, I had to go with her. Grandma lived on an 80-acre farm in Milaca, Minnesota 60 miles north of Minneapolis. It was exciting for me to be on a farm. My two uncles, Ed and Arvid, lived with my grandma. I watched them milk the cows; even tried it, but when the cow kicked the pail I gave up. I walked with the family dog to round up the cows in the pasture, and to ride atop the hay wagon as it headed for the barn. It was fun each day to go with Grandma to collect eggs. I still remember the chicken coop smell, and how to watch where I walked. There were three horses in the barn, one old and two that were workhorses. When riding, I always had the slower older horse. (No saddle or reins). A pigpen behind the barn completed the menagerie. That area had its own peculiar odor. Sometimes my mother would allow me to take the "slop bucket" out to the pigs. Oh how they loved this treat!

After the evening meal and the chores were finished, my uncles, Arvid and Ed, would entertain me with games. This took place at the kitchen table with a flickering kerosene lantern in the center since there was no electricity. We played word games, did tricks with numbers, and they told me many stories and fables. A favorite was Paul Bunyan and his blue ox named Babe. After all, Paul Bunyan was said to have lived in Minnesota! I've actually seen this bigger than life statue of Paul and Babe in Bemidji, Minnesota. It was quite impressive. Another was Big Claus and Little Claus. The most exciting stories were my Uncle Arvid's personal close encounters with mad bulls. I could listen to these tales over and over.

A telephone hung on the wall. The family ring was two short rings and one long. Several families were connected on one party line. It was fun listening to their conversation. It was like being a spy. My mother often cautioned me about being a snoop, and after a considerable time listening, she would insist I hang up. The outhouse was a short run out the backdoor. It had two holes with a Sears catalog for use. This worked fine during the day. At night, however, a white porcelain jar was provided in each bed room. I never could figure out why the jar had a lace-covered lid. Everyone knew what it was, and what it was for.

Every summer my Uncle Ed hung a swing for me in a sturdy oak tree in the front yard. A strong rope with a couple of knots was looped around a sturdy branch. Then a wooden seat was added and was adjusted for me to sit on. This swing gave me a great deal of pleasure. I loved to pump myself to daring heights and jump to the ground on the upswing.

A summer kitchen was connected to the main house by a short concrete sidewalk that afforded me a bit of roller-skating. This small building had three screened windows. At each window a wooden cover was held up by sticks to let in the air and lowered in case of rain. Many delicious meals were made on a wood burning stove including breads and desserts. A cupboard held the necessary tableware. Outside was a washstand attached to a tree that held a washbasin, towel and soap. My uncles would wash before a meal, and it didn't matter that the water splashed when they rinsed. A sturdy pump afforded tasty cold water with a tin cup for common use. Coffee was always available accompanied by fresh cake or sweet buns. I fondly remember my grandmother sitting outside the summer kitchen peeling potatoes, apples, and onions or shelling peas for our dinner.

A short distance down a dirt road was a river. It was called Rum River, since it made many turns like a drunk. I would take my fish pole equipped with hook, line, and sinker and a can of worms that I had dug. Most often my catch would be very small bullheads. Uncle Ed had warned me to be careful in handling the fish since they had stingers that could pierce your fingers. I remember returning with a couple fish, telling my uncle that I was careful—I had used my foot to hold the fish until I got the hook out. I was barefooted!

One day I brought home a tadpole. Grandma gave me a square tin pan that I filled with water and added stones for the tadpole to hide. I wasn't sure what tadpoles ate but I was hoping to see it turn into a frog and watch it jump out of the pan. That never happened.

In this fishing spot the water was quite calm, a perfect place to swim. I joined with several neighborhood kids during several summers. It was a common sight to see turtles, snakes, and frogs. Later we would pick off bloodsuckers (leeches) that had attached themselves to our arms and legs. When I reached the age of twelve, this whole scene freaked me out and I never went swimming there again.

Approximately a quarter of a mile down the road lived a family that had a daughter named Miriam. During my stay at Grandma's she and I would visit regularly. I learned to ride a bicycle with her help. We also would play photographer. The camera was an egg-crate top. The snap of the handle took the picture and the picture was processed on a stone grinder by pedaling the spinning wheel. The final result was a likeness torn from a Sears catalog. When playtime was over we walked together down the road toward her house and stopped at a little bridge where a tiny trickle of a stream wound its way to Rum River. This was halfway. There we talked and when we finally parted, we waved to one another until out of sight.

A short distance from our swimming hole was some strategically placed rocks. These different sized rocks were intentionally laid in order to cross the river to some lush pasture. Often the cows would find their way to this area by wading through the water. Arvid and I used the rocks to get to the other side and together with the dog we got the cows moving and headed them towards the barn. More than once I slipped on those rocks. The dog was the most agile and with tail wagging he would patiently wait for us and then do his job of rounding up the herd.

It was necessary to take several milk cans to the creamery in town. I rode along with my uncle. He called the creamery man by name and their conversation usually was about the weather, politics, or a joke. Sometimes if it was necessary for my Uncle to wait, I was allowed to walk to the ten-cent store. I remember on one occasion buying light colored nail polish, and when I got home painting my nails in the privacy of my bedroom.

I'll never forget the taste and smell of cow's milk. For me, one sip and that was it. The milk was always slightly warm, and I refused to have it in any shape or form. I honestly cannot remember what I drank instead, since my favorite breakfast was a bowl of oatmeal. I also remember Mother opening the oven door and smelling the aroma of a freshly baked coffee cake. This was on an old cook stove fueled with wood. As I look back it was truly amazing how baked items were timed and/or baked without a thermometer. A hand quickly thrust into an oven was the only thermometer. How they did it is still puzzling.

A dog and many cats were a natural part of the farm. The dog, a Collie named Sport, had special duty to keep the cows traveling from the pasture to the barn and back again to pasture. Sport, the dog, was fun to chase and hug. One incident I will never forget was how my Uncle Arvid stopped Sport from chasing chickens. He took a hen that Sport had killed and tied it around the dog's neck. I remember screaming and crying "You can't do this!" After a couple of hours he untied the dead chicken. It worked. Sport stopped chasing chickens. The cats kept mice and rats at bay and were very skittish. They would only appear during milking time in order to get a taste. My uncle would squirt milk directly from the cow into their waiting mouths, and then leave a small dish for them to finish. Even then I would try to pet one of the cats but was rarely successful.

A mailbox stood near the fence opening to the house. Grandma's address was RFD, Route 5, which meant Rural Federal Delivery. I noticed that the mail truck was driven from the right side in order to reach the mailboxes. Mail arrival was a special time—everything stopped, except for Sport, who loved to give chase.

There were no washing machines. All the wash was done by hand. Big tubs of water were heated on the stove, carried outside, and with a scrub board leaning against the side, the items were scrubbed and then rinsed in the second tub. Long clothes lines were strung across the yard and even the heavy quilts were hung to dry. One had to depend on good weather and a drying breeze. It was an all-day event. I realize now how strong my mother must have been to complete this chore.

The memories of these experiences over the years have given me much pleasure and insight. I am grateful for catching a glimpse of what it took to run a farm. It was a never ending seven days a week hard working job. Uncle Arvid told me that during the Depression they had everything except money. With a vegetable garden, an apple orchard, eggs, and meat from pigs, cows, and chickens, they were well fed. For coffee, sugar, and flour, a trip to town was necessary. They were grateful and thanked God for what they had. And now, today, I thank God for being a witness to farm life in the 1930's.

Picture 2: The Nelson Farmhouse in Milaca

August 14, 2012

MORE THAN JUST A FARMER

My father's two brothers, Harold and Arthur, stayed on the farm, while the older brothers, Victor, William and my father, left for Minneapolis to pursue better jobs. Harold and Arthur not only took care of the many chores on the farm, but also saw to the needs of their mother and father, my grandparents. Grandpa was getting on in years, as was my grandmother, but they did what they could. I remember seeing my grandpa feeding the livestock and chickens, and Grandma over-seeing the kitchen.

Harold had a leg that for some reason caused a limp. To my memory I never asked about it. I knew him as a happy person with a hearty laugh. Arthur also had a problem—I believe I was told that his thyroid affected his speech and brain function, but I never knew why. However the two of them carried out the necessary duties of manning the farm.

Inside the house against one wall of the kitchen stood a heavy iron wood stove that had four burners with lids that could be lifted revealing a fire beneath. There was a rather large oven, and a well filled with water. The water provided warm water for dishwashing and hand washing. I could never figure out how the correct baking temperature was determined as I watched Grandma put her hand in the oven and said that it was ready. The cakes and pies were always perfect. A rather large box against a nearby wall contained wood with which to stoke the fire. Across the room was a counter with shelves beneath. On top was a pump to provide water, and a basin and towel within reach. Of course there was a pantry, a marvelous invention to house all the necessary items of food and such. I could always find several kinds of cookies in there.

Grandpa's bedroom was on the first floor. It was a tiny room with a single bed, a chair, and a small dresser. He napped often. After he died, the room was never used. The rest of the family had bedrooms on the second floor.

In the dining room was a heavy round dining table surrounded by four or five chairs. This table was used mainly for special events such as Christmas and birthday celebrations, and for guests who attended Grandpa's funeral. Friends and family would wind their way around the table to select from choices people brought for the occasion. An array of flowers from Grandma's garden occupied the center. The kitchen table became a work station for making pies, cakes, and bread, and was then cleared for the next meal. Of course there was always afternoon coffee and something homemade no matter what else was going on.

One of my fondest memories was seeing the decorated Christmas tree in the front room. It had real candles waiting to be lit on Christmas Eve. Alongside the tree was a pail of water—just in case.

On Christmas Eve at my childhood home in Minneapolis, I was anxiously waiting for the signal that it was time to open the presents. However, dinner had to come first. I dreaded this meal. It was a Swedish tradition to serve Lutefisk covered with a cream sauce. Lutefisk was cod that had been dried by soaking it in lye. Several weeks before Christmas the fish would be soaked in water, changing the water many times to remove the lye. This meal was relished by the family (not me), but I knew the presents were waiting to be opened, so I endured.

Finally we finished dinner, cleared the table, and went to the living room. Just as we began opening gifts the telephone rang. My dad answered and came back to tell us some news. I knew that it was not good news by his somber appearance. There had been a fire—it was Grandma's house. It had burned to the ground. He left that same evening to drive sixty miles to the farm. I remember it had been snowing heavily. Mother and I were very concerned about his safety.

By the time my father arrived, Harold and Arthur had rescued some furniture—the heavy iron stove, some bedding they had thrown out the windows, a couple of chairs, a table and some other useful items. They often talked about the adrenaline that gave them super strength to save items during the fast moving fire. A decision was made to have Grandma Hoffman leave the farm that night and come to stay at our house. Harold and Arthur stayed and began setting up housekeeping in the milk house, a small structure near the house. It had no insulation, only a cream separator and assorted farm equipment inside. A potbelly stove was installed for heat. The remaining things scattered on the lawn were eventually stored in a shed. It was determined that the cause of the fire was burning flower boxes from Grandpa's funeral, causing live embers go up the chimney setting the roof on fire.

In the spring, plans were made to begin building a new house, this time with electricity and more modern equipment. Thank goodness plans were also made to include a pantry where I would once again find those delicious cookies.

Harold had several talents that should be noted; he was not just a farmer.

1 – He was a constant reader who loved history and politics.

2 – He was an artist and drew pictures of birds and animals for me. Often, I would receive a hand written note that would include a picture of a bird or animal that he had drawn in one of the corners of the letter.

3 – He was a debater. He most often could be heard loudly discussing politics with my father: My dad was a staunch Republican. Harold was equally an immovable Democrat praising the current president, Franklin Delano Roosevelt.

4 – He was a poet. Now and then Uncle Harold would write to me and sometimes send a card for my birthday. These cards often included a pen and ink drawing. The following poem included a hand drawn picture of a black crow with the caption "it is so, it is so". This framed poem now hangs proudly on my wall in my apartment. I'm glad I saved it, for it is a portrait of an uncle who cared enough and took the time to gladden the heart of his young niece.

DEDICATATED TO HELEN AND MUSIC

Rural Life

When the day's toil is over
and when I get thru with my chores,
I sit down and read, about Foreign wars.
The only music we have here is when grandpa snores.
Last night I dreamed I was a rich man and lived in a town,
woke up in dismay, when the clock began to pound.
Jumped out of bed and milked like a hound.
Out and shoveled snow, and broke road to town.
So stick to your music, and you can wear silk.
You could not do that if you had cows to milk.
Well, this is enough of this tale of woe.
but it is true, it is so – it is so.

Your Uncle Harold
Dated – Feb. 21, 1940

May 22, 2012

AND THEN THERE WAS ARVID

Arvid was my mother's youngest brother. Since she was the only girl in the family it became her responsibility during the day to look after "little Arvid." When he misbehaved, her mother would scold her and say, "You who are older should have known better." She always got the blame for Arvid's misdeeds. This pattern continued until she finished high school and decided to leave the farm to work in Minneapolis. Arvid, and his brother Ed, stayed on the farm with their mother, my grandmother.

Subsequently Grandma came to live with us in the city when her life became more difficult. At that point Arvid was alone to do the farming since Ed died in a fatal gun accident several years earlier. Finally, the day came when Arvid could no longer work the farm because of illness, so he, too, became a part of my family. As a result my Mother, by her own mother's long standing order, once again resumed the job of seeing to Arvid's care. I was thirteen.

Arvid and I got along famously. He would help me with my homework, especially math. After the evening meal we would wash and dry the dinner dishes. Before we began he devised a plan to see who should wash and who should dry. He held three toothpicks in his fist. He said that two were short and one was long. The long one indicated wash and if it was drawn, you were destined to wash. Neither one of us liked to wash because it included scrubbing the pots and pans. For three days I was the dishwasher until I demanded to see all the toothpicks. You guessed it. They were all long.

He taught me to play checkers. We did crossword puzzles and played card games. He took me to see a Globe Trotters basketball game. He was a really good handyman and could fix anything that was broken and build anything that was needed. He became a handyman for several neighbors. He also told many wild stories about bulls he had encountered when living on the farm. I told him he should write a book about his bull stories. It was my idea to call it "Full of Bull". I was certain it would be a big seller since his stories were exciting.

Neighboring children were always in our yard entertained by Arvid. One little girl who lived across the street wouldn't allow anyone to sit on his lap. She'd say in a strong voice that Arvid's lap was her lap.

Arvid also enjoyed playing tricks on my girlfriends. Evelyn was mortified when retrieving her coat in the bedroom found a stick pierced through the material. She couldn't believe it! Her new coat! Arvid stood in the background gloating about the trick. Finally he confessed and showed us all how it was done. The stick was in two pieces with a needle stuck on one end. This allowed him to place one half of the stick inside her coat and then add the other stick outside and push the sticks together. The only one not laughing was Evelyn.

After Bert and I married, we moved to an apartment. Arvid continued having fun with unsuspecting friends and family. He usually had a joke. After my father died, Arvid was a big help to my mother. He would take her to the grocery store, the bank, and the post office in his old Ford car: I mean really old! They were quite an attraction in the neighborhood. While he was waiting for my mother to finish shopping, Arvid would answer questions about the age of his car. Mother still continued to anticipate and fulfill all her baby brother's needs.

One winter Mother became ill. At this point I began seriously thinking she is going to need more care. She and Dad had made a reservation several years before at the Augustana Home in Minneapolis. It was an ideal residence; a part of the Lutheran Church. One day the director called my mother to say a room was available. At this point Mother's world began to fall apart. As she and I talked I realized that she was unable to think clearly. She wondered about selling the house, what about Arvid, and would I come and help? When I told her yes, she reluctantly decided to move.

Remembering once again her promise to her mother to look after Arvid, she insisted he had to move to the same place so she could continue to see to his care. With this news Arvid's world fell apart. He found it very difficult to see why he couldn't remain in the family home. After all he was the man of the house after my father died. He could easily take care of himself, he said. Well, finally after much agonizing conversation, (mostly shouting), they agreed to move. Mother moved first. Arvid followed in two months.

One day I received a call from the Manager of Augustana Home. She was trying to understand why my mother locked herself in the bathroom for several hours. She wondered if I could give her a clue. I promised to call her when and if I had an answer. Actually it didn't take long. In my mind it became clear. Mother had complained for several weeks that she was annoyed that she had no time for herself. She said there were people constantly in and out of her room, mostly caregivers, asking question upon question or making suggestions as to what she should be doing. At one point Mother had said to me "I never have a moment to myself." As I saw it, in her own home she had the privilege of going to her bedroom and closing the door. There she found peace and quiet. There she would read her Bible and pray. At Augustana, she had no place to escape. Thus she found peace and quiet in the bathroom. When I called back I explained my theory. It gave the manager a possible thread for action.

Mother died two years later. Arvid remained at Augustana. To say he did not get along with the residents was a huge understatement. He was uncooperative, and caused a great deal of disturbance among the residents. What was the outcome? He had to move! This made him very, very angry. Since my mother made me promise before she died that I would look after him, it now became my responsibility to see to his care. Fortunately a lady who had been taking care of his finances came to the rescue. She found a senior facility for him—a private home that housed six people each with differing health problems. Arvid would have his own bedroom. Reluctantly, Arvid moved in. The residents ate together in the dining room, rarely speaking to one another, and immediately after the meal disappeared to their respective rooms. I kept in contact by telephone and correspondence.

I made numerous trips to Minneapolis from Ohio to see Arvid and each time it was obvious he thought everything that was happening to him was my fault. This made our visits very uncomfortable. I remember bringing a scrapbook I had put together hoping that it would bring certain memories to mind. It had photos of his deer hunting trips, the farm, cottages he had built, and pictures of the family. He made no comment. When he became ill at one point and was hospitalized, it was determined that he would have to be moved to a full care facility. It was obvious that he had begun the slow process into dementia. The last time I visited him I saw a significant change in his appearance, and he either didn't recognize me or refused to talk. I was never sure.

A year and a half later I got a telephone call that Arvid had died. I immediately called the mortuary in Milaca, the town where he had lived. I knew he was to be buried in the family plot. A date was set and my husband made roundtrip plane reservations to fly to Minneapolis. We rented a car for the 60-mile trip to Milaca. The month was January. The temperature in Minneapolis was ten degrees above zero, about a 40-degree difference from Ohio. We drove north to the mortuary in Milaca, took care of the paper work, and then followed the hearse to a small cemetery near the old farm where Arvid, my grandmother, and my Mother had lived. As we stood in deep snow with a howling wind swirling around us my husband had a short burial service. One of Arvid's close neighbors saw us as we were gathering and came. A lovely gesture, I thought. I soon began to realize I was finally taking care of the promise I had made to my mother to see to the care of her brother, my uncle, Arvid. The deed was now done.

Total trip plus car rental was $1,200. On our return flight, we were pleased that we were able to take care of business, but agonized over the $1,200 we could ill afford. I contacted Arvid's lawyer asking if we could be reimbursed for at least part of our travel expenses. The answer came in a formal letter a couple weeks later stating that Arvid had told him since I was an adopted child I legally was not a part of the family. That hurt.

Picture 3: Uncle Arvid

At this point, however, it's good to remember all the good times I spent with my favorite uncle, his jokes and all his many bull stories.

April 29, 2013

A GREAT FOURSOME

A trio of three friends often has jealousy problems—two against one and the alone one feels left out. But a group of four in my case succeeded and lasted for several years. It began in my early teens. There was Gladys, Marion, Laura, and me, and we lived within two blocks of each other in Minneapolis, Minnesota. We were not exactly the same age. Gladys was the oldest, then Laura, followed by Marion and me.

Birthdays were special celebrations for the four of us. The three with un-birthdays made the choice of what to do and where to go. For the birthday girl our destination was always kept secret. This took extensive conversations and finally a decision was made. On one occasion the four of us rode the streetcar downtown to a tea house. It was a rather small room with five or six tables for four. Following some light tasty goodies with cups of tea, a woman walked through a beaded curtain and sat down with us. She was dressed in a gaudy costume with a wide colorful band around her head. She spoke softly and explained the process. She asked us to swirl the last drops of tea in our cup and turn the cup over on to our saucer. She would then read each of our teacups and tell our fortune. The birthday girl's cup was read first. I remember we all sat wide-eyed trying to catch every word. It was difficult not to believe what she said.

For another birthday the four of us went to a bowling alley in downtown Minneapolis in a rather seedy section of the city. As we entered the building we walked through a pool hall to the back in order to take the elevator to second floor. I remember feeling a bit uncomfortable as I eyed several unsavory characters leaning on their pool cues watching us. Once we had the right bowling ball we lined up and began the game. During the evening I noticed there were young men as pinsetters. I don't remember whose idea it was but one of us began putting notes in one hole of the bowling ball before letting it sail down the alley. We never got the notes back. We all thought it was quite daring. Our next idea was to try bowling with the opposite hand. This caused a riot of laughter, especially when Laura fell.

An additional memory was getting together for a Christmas party. This, too, was just the four of us, and it was a gift exchange. Gladys' gift for each of us was long matching flannel nightgowns. Of course we put them on and took many pictures sprawling across her bed. We couldn't stop laughing.

Since we did so many things together our lives continued getting together until there was an engagement and then marriage. As you might suspect we became bridesmaids for each other. Laura married first, and then Marion, who had moved to California where she met and married a great guy. We had a personal shower for her with a wrapped gift from each of us that we opened, rewrapped, and sent to Marion with our love. I was married next, and then Gladys. We all continued to keep in touch but it was not quite the same.

Am I glad to have these memories? Of course. Unfortunately, of the original foursome there are only two of us remaining. Gladys still lives in Minneapolis with Bob. They've been married for fifty-one years. Bert and I made it to forty-four.

November 18, 2014

ANOTHER QUESTION—TB

Before my first birthday in 1928 my parents brought me to see both sets of grandparents. Their farms were approximately four miles apart. It must have been a thrilling day for Mom and Dad to show their new member of the family and for my grandparents to get to hold and examine their new grandchild. I wonder if I cried or fussed? Little did I know as I grew that the two farms would be a significant factor in my life. When my maternal grandmother asked my mother what they had named me, she said, "Her name is Helen." Grandma responded, "Helen, that's a nice name." She then asked about my middle name (Rowene) and responded in a serious questioning tone—"What kind of name is that?" Of course the conversation was in Swedish so she pronounced my middle name as Roveen, and then added, "What kind of name is that?" My four grandparents spoke only Swedish.

As I grew up, I was carefully and lovingly cared for, but my general health was always a question. I was given the best choices in everything (so my mother told me), and I was a normal growing baby. At about age three, however, I was hospitalized with pneumonia—actually, double pneumonia, I was told. My dad kept track of my daily temperature on a grid, (I have a copy), and he later in life told me repeatedly about the oxygen tent that covered me to help me breathe. All of this trauma must have been very difficult for both of them. I remained in the hospital for over three months. Perhaps they even questioned as to whether I would live through this sickness. Finally I was released and returned home and my mother became my "round the clock" nurse. I remember being in bed or on the couch and mother feeding me, and trying to get me to a normal weight and good health. She would often hold a peeled apple and with a spoon scrape the softened fruit and place it in my mouth. There was always oatmeal, milk, and orange juice, and on occasion, one of her specialties, a sugar cookie. All of my meals were accompanied by her reading a book. My two favorites were *The Little Red Hen*, and *The Three Little Pigs*.

One of the residuals from being immobile for so long was the loss of my ability to walk. Little by little I regained mobility. But I wonder to this day if all of this played any part in my ongoing foot problems. Over the years I have seen many chiropodists and podiatrists, and wore Dr. Scholl's shoes until I was seventeen years old. Also, a considerable amount was paid for arch supports, pads, and lotions. As I grew older I was forced to take a daily spoonful of cod liver oil. "It is good for you," Mother said. I shiver even now as I think about the taste and smell.

The first indication I had that I was being kept from the truth about my hospitalization was when the school I attended began giving tests for TB (Tuberculosis). A small scrape on the arm and with some sort of serum this test was used to diagnose the disease. If there was no reaction one was cleared of any possibility of previously having TB. On the other hand, if a rash appeared this indicated that the TB germ was still prevalent. Of course the kids in school would look at each other's arms. My reaction was very positive; no hiding the fact. I remember trying to hide the big ugly red blotch on my arm. It was impossible. When the kids saw it they began teasing me and would in a singsong voice say, "Ha, ha, you have TB," and repeat it until I started to cry. At home my mother would insist that it was not TB but the result of the pneumonia I had earlier. I gave that answer the next day to my teasing classmates but I don't think they bought it. It was all so confusing. Do I believe my mother who says it is pneumonia, or do I believe the rash on my arm strongly indicating TB?

The real truth came in a letter I received in 1957 when we lived in Rock Island, Illinois. It was from a doctor who was doing research about TB, especially those who had the disease as a child. This information came as a huge shock to me. I shared it with my husband and then answered all the questions and mailed it back. In addition I wrote in my response that I never knew for sure that I had had TB and had wondered about it. There was no response from my return letter. I never told my mother about the letter, but I did wonder why she wasn't able to face up to the truth. There may have been a stigma pertaining to having TB and maybe she did not want to face it. Thus it was a secret.

Well, the truth about whether I had TB or did not have TB can only be answered with apologies to Shakespeare from one of his famous statements,

"TB or not TB: that is the question."

I leave the answer with you, dear reader.

September 5, 2014

FINICKY CHILD

As a child, describing me as "finicky" would be an understatement. For example, choices of foods depended on several things. How it smelled and how it looked was a good reason not to find out how it tasted. No chiding by my parents did any good. I just refused. Also if one food touched another food, it was dead. One day my mother presented me with a plate that was divided into three sections. In fact all of us got the same kind of plate. Interesting, I thought. Did it help my situation? Not really but at least the foods were not touching.

It was a Sunday noon meal and nothing interested me except the chicken, a drumstick that I could pick up. The vegetables and salad were left untouched. This time my parental discipline came down hard with the words, "You will sit here until your plate is empty." Everyone left. I was alone at the kitchen table. They even took my dog, Birdie, into another room. I sat for a few minutes, of course feeling sorry for myself, but suddenly I had a plan. On the drain board at the sink were old newspapers. Perfect. I took a couple of pages, opened them up, scraped my food on top, wrapped it tightly and hid it behind my back as I left the kitchen. I must have shouted, "I'm done eating," and headed for my bedroom. I placed the food package in my dresser drawer deep under my clean clothes.

One day a couple of months later, Mother and I were straightening the items in my dresser. You guessed it. She found my newspaper package and said, "What is this?" I had completely forgotten that it was there. She opened the package slowly, looked at the shriveled vegetables, and I was convicted on the spot. To this day I'm not certain if she admired my creativity and was withholding a grin, or thinking of a discipline that would be appropriate. At any rate I think I got away with it.

One other food incident comes to mind. This time it was tomato soup. To me it smelled funny. Again I was forced to sit at the table until it was consumed. It was impossible for me to think of a way to get rid of it. I sat and sat, and sat some more. My parents had left the table and were on the front porch reading the newspaper. After a time, it seemed like hours, Mother came in, saw that I had not touched the soup. She grabbed the soup bowl and ordered me to leave the table. I wondered what my punishment would be. In a few minutes she called me back to the kitchen. There at my place at the table was a bowl of oatmeal. Now this I could eat. In fact, to this very day I have oatmeal for breakfast almost every morning.

August 5, 2014

DEER HUNTING VACATION

It was on the farm that my father learned how to handle a gun. The love of hunting continued through-out his life. I remember seeing him polish his guns that were stored in a locked knotty pine cabinet in our attic. He also did skeet shooting on many weekends. I loved to watch and hear him call "pull" as he raised his gun to "make a killing". In preparation for deer hunting, several weeks before the trip, he would dress in his hunting gear and go for long walks. He would keep a steady pace for about an hour, and arrive home with rosy cheeks and a big smile.

One year plans were made to take the family deer hunting in November. I had to be excused from school, and was given homework to complete. Our destination was Lake Kabetogama, in Minnesota, twenty-seven miles south of the Canadian border. A two-wheel trailer pulled behind our car was piled high with equipment, and securely covered by a tarp. My dad was the driver of our family car. Inside was Mother, my Uncle Arvid, and me. Mr. Hemming, his wife, two children, and his brother were in the second car. We started out before dawn since the trip was over 300 miles. There was a considerable amount of snow on the ground.

En route we came to the top of a hill that descended to a stop sign where we had to turn either right or left. To my dad's surprise the road was surprisingly icy. Dad applied the brakes which immediately caused the trailer to jackknife. Dad spun the steering wheel from right to left, then left to right and again right to left. I was aware that we were intermittingly sliding on two wheels. We all leaned in the opposite direction to help keep the car up right. Finally the car righted itself, and we slid to a stop a few feet beyond the stop sign. At first it looked like we were going to go over an embankment. We all breathed a sigh of relief after one minute of absolute fright.

We arrived to the campsite late in the evening, unpacked, and settled down in a large three-bedroom log cabin. The next morning after breakfast the men began making preparations for the next day's hunt.]An island across the lake was their chosen destination. A couple of toboggans were packed with tents, bedding, food, guns, and cooking utensils for their three-to-four day stay. Each man had creepers on their boots and the lead man would be testing the ice and giving the signal when it was safe to walk. It all sounded so dangerous to me. My mother suggested we all pray for their safety.

In the meantime those of us who stayed in the cabin had our duties. We children had homework while the women prepared meals. In the afternoon it was either playing indoor games or playing in the snow. I remember finding an old run down toboggan. I remember how much fun it was as we raced down a snow covered curved driveway edged by tall spruce trees. The problem was to avoid a collision. It was below zero so that limited our outdoors time.

It became obvious to me that the women were anxious about their husbands as they often looked through the window for any evidence of their return. Finally, on the fourth day someone spotted them in the distance and shouted, "Here they come". As they came closer I saw several deer stretched out on top of their gear. It was a great reunion and the feast the women had prepared smelled and tasted so good. The men didn't smell so good, but their stories were exhilarating.

The next day everyone helped pack for our early departure the following day. The deer were strapped to the top of the two cars and the cars and trailer were now less crowded.

Back at school I was asked to tell about my experience in the north woods. As I recall it appeared to me that the students were a bit jealous because I had had time off from school. But as I told the story I felt like an explorer on the greatest adventure of my life. However, I kind of remember that I used a bit of exaggeration.

October 29, 2012

MY FIRST DOG

As a child it was not easy to keep begging for a dog and being told no. However, the story about my first dog came about in a strange way. But first you need to know the following:

My father was raised on a farm in Milaca, Minnesota—sixty miles north of Minneapolis. On the farm, he grew up learning the facts of life, shooting a gun, and game hunting with his brothers. He was the oldest of five boys. (No girls.) After he graduated from high school he left for Minneapolis and worked for the Street Railway Company. Subsequently, he was hired at the Minneapolis Moline Tractor Company and rose, after many years, to an executive position. Every year he would set aside time in the fall to go hunting for ducks, pheasants, or deer. This story is about pheasant season. Also he needed to get in shape, so he said, and began walking in the neighborhood dressed in his hunting clothes.

The car was packed with all the necessary equipment and he and his brother, Victor, left to hunt on a friend's farm for the weekend. Mother always worried about his safety, but she and I prayed that they would be safe.

It was Sunday afternoon and I heard the familiar sound of my dad's car pull into the driveway. They were home! Before I could reach the back door, the door opened and in came a beautiful brown and white dog—a Spaniel. Wow, I thought. Where did this dog come from? While petting and hugging the dog, my dad stepped through the door. I looked up to question him about the dog and was shocked to see his face covered with little white patches. As Mother and I listened, he told us what had happened.

The men were lined up, he said—seven or eight in a row with a dog in front of them to raise the prey. All of a sudden the pheasants began to fly upward, and the men raised their guns. Just then they heard several shots. The shots came from some men within a short distance coming towards them. It was completely unexpected since it was private property. My dad told me he knew he was shot—it felt like someone had thrown a handful of marbles at close range. He said he leaned over, put his hands over his eyes, knew that he was bleeding, and waited for a minute or two. When he lifted his hands he opened his eyes and knew that he could see and immediately thanked God. He was taken to the hospital where all the buckshot was removed from his face and upper body except one shot was left under his left eye. The doctor explained it was better to leave it where it was.

But how does the dog fit into this picture? After the initial shock, Mother and I began to realize that Dad thought if my mind was taken up with a new dog, I would better understand the story that he was about to tell. Even though I was sorry that he had been shot, I was happy he lived through it, and I was thrilled that I had a new dog. Later there were times when I sat on Dad's lap, and he would let me feel the buckshot under his eye. I would hug him and say thanks, Dad, for giving me Birdie, my wonderful dog—and her four new puppies that came several weeks later.

Picture 4: Birdie and her puppies

March 6, 2012

THE GREAT DEPRESSION

I entered the world in 1927, and my life was dependent entirely on my mother and father. Looking back, I know now that I was safe and all my needs were met. In 1929 a huge change took place in the United States, and I was oblivious to what the world soon called The Great Depression. During those years some changes in our living conditions were made but I was never aware that we were suffering. For instance, to save heat a blanket was stretched across the divide between the living room and dining room. The heat registers in the living room were closed, which made a big difference in the use of coal, thus saving money. Our family life now centered around the dining room table. In the morning before my father went to work, I could hear him in the basement getting rid of the "clinkers" in the furnace and adding coal for the day. Coal was delivered to our basement through a small outside window. The coal pile was kept in a special closed off section of our basement. Mother attached pieces of cotton cloth to the heat registers in order to minimize the amount of coal dust blowing into the rooms. In the winter my day usually started by standing in front of a heated oven to get dressed. Milk had already been delivered, and the cream that formed on the top was poured off and saved for coffee and cooking. Mother made hot oatmeal and occasionally I had an orange cut in slices for breakfast.

Mother was a good baker. The 20-pound bag of sugar rested on top of the cool attic steps. It often was my job to get a cup or two for her recipe. During the summer she canned many kinds of food that were stored in the basement fruit cellar. Our meals were fairly complete. When ration stamps were issued, she would plan wisely. Both grandparents had farms sixty miles north of Minneapolis, so we had eggs, and chicken. Beef and pork were available at butchering time. During the winter Dad would go deer hunting. The local butcher would make packets of various cuts of venison that my parents would generously share with relatives and friends. I really never liked the taste of venison.

Life was really like the book *Everything but Money* by Sam Levenson. How to pay the mortgage, insurance policies, piano lessons, groceries, utilities, etc., and fill our church envelopes each Sunday was a puzzle. Because the banks had a poor reputation or none at all, mother hid money in the underside of the upright piano that stood in the living room. She severely cautioned me not to tell anyone. Mother handled the money and gave my father an allowance. His needs were meager. He often rode the streetcar to work to save on gas for the car. He was fortunate to have a job that lasted throughout the war. In a school math class we were required to keep track of our money. We had to list our expenses and savings and it clearly told us whether we were spendthrifts or savers.

Mother made all my clothes. I envied girls who had store bought clothes. I never realized that it was good to be unique. I remember when silk stockings were for sale at the department store. Most often there were long lines waiting to purchase these highly desired items. As careful as I was to put them on, it was so easy to get a run, and mother knew another stocking became unusable when she heard me groan. One year at the state fair I watched a gentleman use a handheld tool that repaired a stocking run. Of course he convinced me that I had to have it. No matter how I tried to do what he had done, I could never make it work. Then there were those garter belts and girdles and the struggles to get them on. I never liked them especially when it was a hot and humid day.

We knew nothing about pizza, frozen foods, TV dinners, or microwaves. Popcorn was made in a pan on the stove. There was no freezer in the old icebox. Ice was purchased in a nearby ice store and carted home in a wagon. Occasionally an ice truck would drive down the street. How well I remember the pan under the icebox spilling over. "All hands on deck" was the call to help mop up.

For fun we kids had favorite games. Kick the can, Run Sheep Run, Ante Ante Over, Who Will Draw the Frying Pan, etc. Indoor games were plentiful. My favorites were jigsaw puzzles, paper dolls, or drawing pictures. Once in a while someone would have a comic book that we'd share. A blanket over a card table made a wonderful tent in the living room. In the backyard a blanket thrown over a clothesline would keep me and my friends occupied all afternoon. By the way, did you ever know of any mother who tore up the carpet in the hallway and replace it with linoleum so her daughter and girlfriend could roller skate in the winter?

For the most part my parents did not discuss the problems of the world. Oh, the usual blame game about the sitting president, or the local politics were discussed, but never to the degree to make me fearful. My friends and I knew that it would be fruitless to ask for money so we manufactured our own fun and dreamed of a time when we had money of our own. After some eighty years I now have money of my own—but I still wonder if it is going to last until the day comes when I do not need it anymore.

January 14, 2015

TONSILS

One definition of the term "rite of passage" is any important act or event that serves to mark a passage from one stage to another. For me it was an event that happened when I was sixteen years old. My "rite of passage" involved removing those fleshy lumps at the back of the throat, called tonsils. Most of my friends already had their tonsils removed. Now it was my turn. I began to wonder what good are tonsils. My father tried to explain that tonsils were a part of the lymphatic system and that they manufactured germ fighting white blood cells. All I could think about was why my tonsils were diseased and weren't doing their job. And so the date was set for the operation. There was no turning back.

I arrived at the hospital with Mother and Dad. They gave me moral support for days before the operation, and even more when I was being prepped for the operating room. To my surprise, after I had completed all of the pre-op, I was wheeled to the surgical wing of the hospital and into the operating room. There I was told to sit in the surgical chair! Oh, something must be wrong. Why am I sitting up and not lying down? The nurse fastened my wrists to the arms of the chair, a towel was positioned around my neck and a facemask was placed over my nose and mouth. I felt trapped. The doctor arrived, smiled, and looked directly into my eyes, and greeted me. He pulled up a chair, sat very close as he tucked his knees in between mine. The surgical instruments were in full view. There was no turning back.

The face mask was removed and a large needle quickly passed my eyes as the Doctor injected something inside one side of my throat—was it Novocain? No stopping now, I thought. A nurse standing alongside the doctor smiled. I assumed it was a smile since her eyes squeezed together behind her facemask. The doctor worked quickly and the nurse followed with forceps to daub the blood. At one point I opened my eyes and saw the bloody forceps and exclaimed, "Is that my tonsil?" My voice sounded as though I was talking through my nose. I saw them both smile. When the operation was over I was wheeled back to my room, and was told I would spend the night.

In the morning a nurse came with a pan of water and gave me a quick sponge bath. When she finished she handed me a wash cloth, and explained it was to finish my bath. Not quite sure what to do, so I washed my face! The doctor came to see me and said it all went well, and that I was free to go home. He assured me that after five days the soreness would be gone. Yes, I ate lots of ice cream, and sure enough, it was true. The soreness was gone on the fifth day.

It became clear some time later that this event in my life was truly a "rite of passage"—an important event that served to make a passage from one stage to another. I was tonsil free. That's all I cared about.

April 16, 2013

PUZZLES, PUZZLE ME

What is the force that draws one toward solving puzzles? Is it the thrill of being able to solve a problem, or is it just a way to avoid something.

For me I find working on puzzles a calming effect that brings my scattered thoughts to ground zero. While working on a puzzle, I often find an answer to a personal problem that I have not been able to solve. Somehow the two coincide. Another way for me to accomplish the same thing is playing the piano music of J. S. Bach. Bach's music is structured so that one must pay complete attention to the running notes in each hand that intertwine in a calculated way. The pianist must give full attention to the notes on the printed page. There is no way to ad-lib. In so doing the answer to something that was previously puzzling seems to come to the fore.

In a bit of Google research, I was absolutely amazed how many types of puzzles are listed. For me the most common puzzles are the crossword, jumble, and Sudoku, found in the daily *Press Democrat* newspaper, plus my computer games. These puzzles have become a daily routine for me.

But now let's look at a particular type of puzzle: the jigsaw puzzle. Two jigsaw puzzles in our library are continually in progress until completed. Oh that glorious feeling to put in the last piece! Soon other puzzles are chosen, perhaps a 500 or 1,000 piece puzzle, and the puzzle solvers begin anew. I will often look to see if the chair is vacant, and sit down limiting myself to one hour. I am also drawn to the puzzle in the evening and am forced to leave when my head begins to bob with sleep.

Recently I began to wonder when jigsaw puzzle solving began. I learned that the inventor was John Spillsbury, born in London, England in 1767. He was a mapmaker. One day he decided to attach a map to a piece of wood and then cut out the different sections. This later became a tool to teach geography in the schools. Colorful scenes began being used by puzzle makers but the pieces were different shapes from what we see today.

The top of the box or a picture layout inside the box becomes a valuable tool in solving a puzzle. The next step is to lay out the frame. One does this by finding all four corners and then adding the straight edge pieces to complete the frame.

Sometimes it is helpful to sort by color. It is exhilarating to return later to a puzzle and see that someone has actually made progress. Occasionally a piece is placed in error.

Never in my mind would I have guessed that I would love to work on jigsaw puzzles. It is really puzzling to me, for sure.

October 1, 2013

MY MOTHER'S FAMILY STORY

My maternal grandmother was born in 1855 in Northern Ställberg in Västmanland, Sweden. In her twenties she left her homeland for the United States aboard a sailing ship. Her belongings were placed in a small wooden trunk that her grandfather had made for her. On the rounded cover her name was plain to see. It said: LOUISA HAGER, spelled out with nail heads. I can only imagine what thoughts and maybe tears accompanied the making of this trunk. As he pounded each nail I'm sure he was certain he would never see his granddaughter again. She came to Ellis Island, and then on to Minneapolis, Minnesota where she had relatives.

There she met her future husband, a swede named Nils Gustaf Lax (later changed to Nils Gustaf Nelson). They married and lived in a small house near Seven Corners in Minneapolis. Soon their first child was born, but unfortunately she died at an early age. Her name was Hattie. She was buried in Layman's Cemetery on Lake Street in Minneapolis. Soon after, Walfred, a son, was born and died at nine months and also was buried in Layman's Cemetery.

When free homesteading properties were made available, they made a decision to move sixty miles north to Milaca, Minnesota to an 80-acre farm. My memory of the farm in the 1940's is a simple two-story house, a good sized barn, a woodshed, summer kitchen, horse barn, chicken coop, pigpen, a makeshift shed for farm machinery, and of course there was the necessary outhouse. All this took time, effort, and years to complete. Grandpa was a stonemason by trade. He built the barn with stone walls that supported the upper structure. The surrounding landscape afforded all the big and small boulders needed. A goodly number of oak trees surrounded the house including apple trees that Grandpa planted, plus a good-sized garden. A few cows, two work horses, chickens, pigs, and the farm crops supplied their needs. The only items purchased from town were coffee, sugar, flour and salt. It was three miles to town. Horse and wagon was the only transportation during those years.

A pastor from the large Lutheran church in town came to hold services once a year in a very small church near the farm and to visit in their home. This was a big event in their life. My mother said that a special chair was dusted and polished and designated for the pastor, and no one was to use it until after he left. Grandpa

Nelson died shortly after my second birthday, in 1929, and the funeral was held in their home by the resident minister.

By now there were four children remaining in the Nelson brood. Herbert, the third child, died of typhoid fever in 1912 at the age of 24 years. My mother Adelia, born in 1892, was next in line. She left the farm for Minneapolis in her early 20's, worked as a housemaid, seamstress, and personal maid for several influential families. She married my father, Edwin Hoffman, on June 28, 1919, whom she had known as a neighbor in Milaca. My grandmother told me about how my father and mother first met. As a three and four year old, they got into a squabble and a tug of war over a toy. When Grandma went to see what the fuss was about, they were both trying to take possession of the toy. Grandma settled it by telling my father, "Don't worry, Edwin, when you grow up you can marry my daughter." How did she know?

The next child was a son, Edwin, who stayed on the farm for many years, but unfortunately was killed in a gun accident while hunting. He was in his late 40's. I remember the telephone call that came with the details of his death and the shock my mother suffered at the time. I didn't know what to do and felt helpless as she lay on the bed with a cold cloth over her eyes. The incident had to be investigated to determine whether it was an accident or suicide. The investigation took a long time but was finally declared an accident.

And then there was Arvid, the baby of the family. My mother often told me that it was her mother who gave her the responsibility to look after him. She often resented the task because if Arvid misbehaved, it was she who was blamed. Her mother's usual words were, "After all, he is so little and you are so much bigger." The task of looking after him continued all through Arvid's life since Grandma was always concerned for him since he never married.

My grandmother and Arvid took care of the farm for many years following the death of Edwin. But it finally came to the point that it was necessary for grandma to leave the farm as her health was failing. She came to live with us in Minneapolis and was given my bedroom. A space in the attic was made into a bedroom for me. Arvid continued to work the farm until he was stricken with a bleeding ulcer several years later. The farm was sold and when he was released from the hospital, he came to live with my parents, grandmother, and me. I was in the ninth grade.

At the far end of my newly acquired attic bedroom was my father's den where he kept his guns, hunting equipment, cameras, and a desk to handle the work he brought home. There also was a single bed. The den became Arvid's bedroom. It was only accessible by going up the stairs like I did, and walking through my room and into his room. Arvid always chuckled when he hooked his door on the inside and announced to me, "Ha, ha, now you can't get into my room." We always had a good relationship and he respected my privacy.

Grandma died in 1942 and was buried in Milaca, Minnesota in the family plot. Arvid then moved downstairs to Grandma's bedroom that was now vacant. Mother again had the responsibility of looking after the welfare of Arvid.

February 25, 2014

WHAT WOULD JESUS DO?

It was a bitterly cold day in Minneapolis. There was snow on the ground and the temperature hovered close to zero degrees. The sun was partially hidden. As usual, mother was in the kitchen making some kind of dessert and some kind of bread, perhaps caramel rolls or plain white bread. I often watched her culinary efforts because it gave me a chance to lick a bowl or stir something. I was about seven years old

A short while after breakfast there was a knock on the kitchen door. When Mother opened the door, there stood an older gentleman with a fairly healthy beard, and poorly dressed for the season. He wore an old stocking cap, mackinaw jacket, boots, and woolen finger mittens. He was holding a hedge clipper. Mother greeted him and asked what he wanted. Could he do some work for money, perhaps trim the hedge, he said. She questioned him and then invited him to step into the kitchen out of the cold. Times were hard and work was scarce. The entire nation was experiencing difficulties; after all, we were still in The Great Depression.

She told him to wait a moment while she made a phone call to my dad at work. She and my dad agreed that this man would be permitted to trim the hedge. We lived on a corner lot, which meant on the street side the hedge ran the entire length of the lot. And on the avenue side the distance was much shorter. He would have a big job. Mother gave him permission to do the job and then offered him a hot cup of coffee and a caramel roll just newly out of the oven. He thanked her in his gravelly voice, finished his coffee, and headed outside to begin his work.

Soon it was nearing lunchtime. As she looked out the window she could see that he was busy at work and making progress. His breath was like steam pouring from his mouth as he breathed and exhaled the cold air. Mother was certain that he must be cold and hungry by now. He had a good start on the work, so she called him to come in. She hung up his jacket, made a place for him at the kitchen table, and she and I sat down with him for lunch. He was pleasant, didn't talk much, but ate everything that was put in front of him.

When lunch was nearly over, he mentioned that his feet were very cold and it was good to be inside for a while. I could see that Mother had an idea. She got up, went to the basement and came up the stairs with a medium sized tub. She filled it with warm water and placed it in front of him. She then knelt down on the rug and began to unlace his boots and remove his stockings. I remember that his stockings were very wet. She placed the stockings to dry near the oven. He put his feet in the warm water and with a bar of soap she washed his feet, carefully drying them with a towel. She then put some kind of healing lotion on to soothe his aching feet. A pair of Dad's heavy socks replaced his own.

Later that afternoon when he had finished the job and Mother had paid him and given him some "goodies to go," I was curious about what had just happened. I asked her the question, "How could you do what you just did for him? You didn't know him and he smelled". Her answer was simple. "If Jesus could wash people's feet, I certainly should be able to do the same." This was one lesson in Christian love in action I never forgot.

John 4:11 *"Beloved, if God so loved us, we also ought to love one another."*

Matthew 22:45 *"Then shall he answer them, saying, Truly I say to you, Insomuch as you did it to one of the least of these, you did it to me."*

May 14, 2012

NYAH NYAH NYAH

As a child I found teasing difficult to handle. I remember when kids teased me about being adopted. How they actually found out eludes me to this day. My guess is that they probably overheard it from their parents. Did parents think it was degrading to be adopted? I wonder. The teasing really pointed to a bias that was hard to challenge. When it happened, my only reaction was to cry and run to my mother for comfort and the assurance of her love, and also to be reminded that I was chosen and a gift. Each time the teasing occurred she would once again tell me about my adoption at three months of age.

Another example of teasing came when Charles Lindberg's baby was kidnapped and was front-page news. It was March 1, 1932. It wasn't the actual story of the child, but rather the reported kidnapper, a man named Hauptman. This resulted in teasing since my last name was Hoffman, a name sounding similar to Hauptman. The kids would taunt me saying it was *my* father who stole the little Lindberg baby. Again each teasing would prompt me to seek the consolation of my mother.

A third story of teasing was about having TB. I actually did have TB as a child, but my mother continually told me it was a severe case of double pneumonia. For me the TB test in grade school produced a big red blotch on my arm that indicated a positive reaction. Because of this the teasing became intense. The kids would point their fingers at me and say, "Nyah, nyah, you have TB." Mother would console me and again remind me it was really pneumonia—double pneumonia!

Growing up I was taller than most girls my age, and also some of the boys, which was the cause of many comments in school and church and by visitors who came to our house. I remember some friends of my parents came for a visit. They were from out of town. I was seated in the living room. Not long after they arrived, one lady said to me, "Helen, stand up so we can see how tall you are!" This made me so annoyed that I refused to leave my chair during their entire visit. I decided no way was I going to cater to their bad behavior.

Teachers would always call my name first when lining up for something and say, "Helen, you stand in the back. You're the tallest." Many times my assigned seat in class was at the back of the room. The teacher must have thought the students wouldn't see over me if I was in the front row!

Another teasing that I hated concerned my first boyfriend. His name was Vernon. Some friends of my parents were relentless teasers. Whenever they talked about my boyfriend they would call him my "jellybean". I didn't like it. In fact, it went one step further one evening when they came for dinner. During the evening they presented me with a nicely wrapped gift. When I opened it, inside was a small wooden wagon filled with brightly colored jellybeans. He and his wife laughed heartily and looked directly at me for my reaction. I wanted to crawl under the table. This time my mother didn't come to my rescue. Could it be she thought I should start laughing with the teasers? It took me a long time before that ever happened. Today it's much easier to be teased because I've matured and can accept teasing as a joke—well, at least, most of the time.

December 8, 2014

HE CALLED ME "PATSA"

It was my dad who called me Patsa. I never knew what it meant, and never heard it before, or read it anywhere in literature, and I'm not sure if I am spelling it correctly. Could it be spelled Potsa? But when my dad said it, I always felt loved and cared for. I could hear it in his voice. My earliest memory is seeing him standing at my bedroom door having just arrived home from work. When I was in bed with some kind of illness like chicken pox, pneumonia, or bronchitis, there he'd be, standing with his hat in his hand, the scarf still around his neck, and a smile on his face. He then would greet me by saying, "Patsa, how you doing?" This would always be followed with another admonition, "Be sure to keep your feet warm." Interestingly enough he never called me Patsa if someone other than a family member was around. This made me think that Patsa was an endearing word meant only for my ears.

I have done a bit of research trying to find the word Patsa on the computer but nothing gave me a definitive clue, except for the following: In the book *Applied Industrial Mathematics*, problems are described using two characters called "Potsa" and "Skinny." Maybe Potsa was slang for "chubby," as in comparing someone to a little pot. I'll bet he thought of me as a little chubby when I was a baby, and that description certainly was true.

My memory tells me that he stopped using this nickname as I approached my teen years. Perhaps to him Patsa was only to be used for a child. Whatever, I thank my dad today that I still can remember him using a loving tone of voice and greeting me with this loving sounding name. Thanks, Dad.

All this got me thinking about nicknames, especially historic figures, well-known athletes, and singers. Here's a very short list. Can you give the answer?

"The Velvet Fog" (Mel Torme)
"Old Blue Eyes" (Frank Sinatra)
"Old Hickory" (Andrew Jackson)
"Old Blood and Guts" (General George Patton)

I know the list could go on and on. Perhaps it's time for someone (maybe you) to walk down memory lane and think of more nicknames of important people. Or answer the question, did you have a nickname as a child and has it lasted to this day?

September 30, 2014

SIXTH GRADE

As a sixth grader, it was now only two months until graduation. In preparation for this auspicious day our entire class went to visit our next school, Nokomis Junior High School, grades 7, 8, and 9. (Most of us would be attending this school in September.) When we arrived we were met by Mr. Maas, the school Principal, and ushered into the auditorium where we listened to an explanation of what we were about to see. I'm sure all of us were anxious and a bit apprehensive, wondering how we were going to master this big, three-floor maze.

We followed him through the halls peeking into classrooms, wood shop, the sewing and cooking rooms, cafeteria, the music room, gymnasium, and a quick look at personal lockers standing like sentries in the hall. The school looked enormous as I compared it to our grade school. The principal also stressed how we must walk in the halls and stairways. Certain stairs were for going up and others for going down. He explained that this was necessary in order to handle the flow of traffic walking from room to room. How would we keep all this information in our heads until September? And how would we find our lockers and not be late in the five minutes allowed to travel from one class to another?

Once we were back at Minnehaha School we discussed all the information together with our teacher, and as you might expect, there was lots of excited talk in small groups. Technically we really had to put off thinking about it for we had work to do before finishing the sixth grade. One thing that occurred to me was that the younger students looked up to us big sixth graders. This was going to change at Nokomis, as once again we'd be on a lower level looking up to those big ninth graders. It was a scary thought!

Graduation was in June. We were now free! The ceremony included awards and lasted for what seemed hours together with picture taking, hugs, and signing autograph books. Our class picture had been taken outside on risers a month ago. Of course I was told to stand on the back row because I was so tall. I hated this. But there was no denying it. I was 5' 9".

What came next? A summer filled with fun with only a few thoughts of junior high.

GOOD FRIENDS, GOOD FUN

Hazel and Clarence were often at our house for dinner usually ending with a noisy card game of Flinch. Clarence was a party animal. He loved to laugh, so unlike his wife. Hazel could be pleasant but the reverse was more often true. When they were at our house, Hazel would stand up and announce in a demanding voice, "Come on, Clarence, it's time to go home." Clarence would ignore her and then the battle began. We often stood around the piano singing some of the old favorites while Hazel stood with her arms crossed. My Mother would try to soothe her temperament but finally Clarence would give up and they would leave.

On another occasion my mother learned that Clarence had had all his teeth pulled and new dentures put in immediately. She knew he would be very uncomfortable but thought it would be fun to stop in and greet him. On our way to the car she picked a bouquet of sweet peas in our yard, put them in a mason jar, and we were on our way. As we stood at the door knocking, a weak voice said, "Come in." Clarence was seated in a chair wrapped in a blanket. He spoke softly saying that he appreciated our thoughtful gesture and the sweet peas. He said that Hazel was at the neighbors, would be home soon, and would call my mother. Not long after we got home the telephone rang. Mother answered assured it was Hazel and said "Sweet peas." The caller responded, "What a wonderful thing to say when answering the telephone." It was a minister from her childhood calling to make contact after many years. It was obvious that he thought she had said, "Sweet peace". Did she tell him otherwise? Of course not! This story was told many, many times, especially to Clarence after pain had subsided and the new dentures were working. Hazel only managed a weak smile.

Clarence died in his late 60's, and Hazel found it nearly impossible to continue. I wonder if life could have been different for her if she had tried the well-known theory of a glass half full?

December 10, 2013

ATTICS I HAVE KNOWN

My childhood home in Minneapolis had an attic. Not surprisingly, it was above the main floor. The entire area was unfinished except for sturdy flooring. Two light bulbs hung from the ceiling gave inadequate light. Much of the floor space was covered with lots of stuff. I remember several trunks, lots of antiques and seasonal clothes, Christmas decorations, and an assortment of furniture.

The dictionary describes not only this kind of attic, but also two others: garrets and lofts. These two types also rest on the top story of a building. In my mind I think of a garret as a space with an artist at an easel, holding a pallet with an assortment of paints, and natural light coming through a window. This is where a dedicated artist attempts to create a masterpiece. On the other hand, I associate a loft to be in a barn where hay is stored.

My grandparents' barn had a crude ladder leading up to the hayloft. My father told me about the hay loft he knew so well when he was a child. He said when unsuspecting city kids would come for a visit, the farm kids would place some hay covering the ladder opening. As they began playing and chasing one another, the farm kids avoided the opening, and laugh heartily when one of the city kids would unsuspectingly fall to the ground floor. "No one was hurt," he said, "except for one's pride," he added.

I remember when I was able to climb the ladder and explore this somewhat spooky place. But later when the neighbor kids came we'd play tag or hide and seek. My uncle had attached a rope to one of the beams. What fun it was to take turns to swing and jump and land in the soft hay. These images are imbedded in my mind, and I like thinking about them.

The attic in my house in Minneapolis was above our two-bedroom bungalow. The stairway was very narrow and the steps shallow. There were two windows. One faced east and the other west, and there was lots of space for storage. My mother was a serious collector. There were picture albums, huge trunks and assorted luggage, old letters, vintage valentines, newspapers with important headlines, all my report cards, and every dress I wore on succeeding birthdays. She kept her wedding dress, circa 1919, and Grandma's shawls from Sweden. This is only a short list.

I remember if anyone came and needed an item for a treasure hunt, she'd run upstairs and return with it. A group from the local church came asking for a dressmaking dummy. They knew mother had to have one since she sewed her own clothes. Before handing it over, however, she covered the form with one of her robes. She was told when they returned the dummy that some of the kids had said "Hello, Mrs. Hoffman" as they passed by her form at the party. How did they know who it was?

The attic was a grand place to explore, but unbearable during the heat of the summer. Any searching had to be done in a hurry. A clear remembrance for me was looking out the west window during a rainstorm, marveling at the lightning and listening to the crashing thunder. Also, reading a book with raindrops tapping on the roof or window seemed surreal.

One day in Jersey City, a young girl named Margie came for a visit. She was a member of our congregation, and often was our son's babysitter. Suddenly through the window I saw black clouds appear with the threat of rain. I excused myself saying that I had windows to close in the attic. As I started to leave she asked if she could go with me. "Of course," I said. As we entered the attic, she turned to me and said, "So this is an attic." She had never seen an attic before, since she had only lived with her family in what was called "The Projects" (low rent housing).

Grandma Nelson came to live with us. She had to leave the farm when she became less and less able to function. I was thirteen. Preparations were made before she arrived to have a bedroom built for me in the attic since Grandma would be occupying my first floor bedroom. My new room was quite large, at least two-thirds of the area. I loved it. The other third, in front of the attic, was my father's den. My room included a dormer with two windows facing south. More windows to watch storm activities, I thought. With my furniture in place, the first night was thrilling as I lay awake looking through the windows. The moon, sometimes covered with passing clouds, I attempted to see the "Man in the Moon". I also loved to watch the changing scenes and seasons, especially when it was snowing.

So what happened to all the many treasures that occupied the original attic?

There was space made available under the eaves accessible by ¾-size doors. Mother knew exactly where everything was. I hated to crawl in that dark space. Mother didn't. The difficulty came when the house was to be sold. I remember sitting on the top step sorting through what was important for me to save. It was difficult, especially when my Uncle Arvid accused me of stealing, saying that I had no right to take anything since I was adopted. But, I pursued. And now I have a large amount of material to add to the book I hope to publish. Thanks, Mom, for being a saver, and leaving me with many memories of our attic and the special items I saved that I see and treasure in my apartment.

Just today I learned a surprising fact. In talking with my friends I was surprised to hear that most California homes do not have attics or basements. That even goes for mansions! I guess that high vaulted ceilings fill that space. I wonder if the weather has anything to do with it. I remember that a couple times during the winter, the snow had to be raked off the roof to prevent collapse.

So this is it? Have I covered the subject well enough? Actually, the answer is no. There is one more attic space! It's the attic space of the mind. In our brain, everything we have heard or said is stored there. There are times when the answer appears days later or something may appear you haven't thought about for years. This says something about how important it is to store good memories, and not carry hurt or anger through the years. Those of us who are advanced in age have a wealth of stories. It is important to share them or begin to write about it. That's what I am doing. But I wish I could remember more.

September 16, 2014

OLD FASHIONED PICTURE TAKING

Our son, David, stayed with my parents while my husband and I worked. David was about one and a half years old. My job was a part-time position three days a week. He enjoyed all the attention from my parents and thrived on all the love and caring. I knew my parents were happy to have their first grandchild for an extended time.

One day Mother told Dad that she'd like a camera. Dad had one but it was too complicated for her, she said. So he began the search and bought an expensive one (that's so like him) with many gadgets and settings. The problem for Mother was how to use it. She had no time to read the manual or even ask questions. When Dad became aware that she was not using it, he questioned her. All she wanted was to look into the little glass on the top, see the image, and snap the picture. Dad complied and bought an Eastman Kodak Brownie. Mother was pleased. This camera, she could handle.

One sunny day when David was playing in their backyard, Mother got her new toy and took one picture after another. I believe there were twelve photos on the film. On Friday afternoon when I came to pick up David, she told me that the pictures were ready at the corner drug store. I agreed to go and get them. As I walked back to the house I opened the envelope. What I saw on all twelve pictures was a gray background with a dark band across the middle. Some of the dark bands were at slightly different angles. As I pondered these unusual photos, I suddenly knew what had happened. My dear mother had held the camera backwards and had twelve pictures of her belt buckle.

April 21, 2012

MONEY

1. If you save all your earnings you are a miser
2. If you spend all you earn you are a fool
3. If you lose it you are out
4. If you find it you are in
5. If you owe it, they are always after you
6. If you lend it, you are always after them
7. It is the cause of evil
8. It is the cause of grief
9. It is the cause of happiness
10. It is the cause of sorrow
11. If the government makes it, it is alright
12. If you make it, it is all wrong
13. As a rule it is hard to get
14. But it's pretty soft when you get it
15. It talks
16. To some it says "I've come to stay"
17. To others it whispers, "Goodbye"
18. Some people get it at the bank
19. Others go to jail for it
20. The mint makes it first
21. It's up to you to make it last
22. They call it legal tender
23. That green and lovely stuff
24. It's tender when you have it
25. But when you don't it's tough

(I found this among my Mother's writings. Was she the author? I have my doubts.)

March 11, 2014

MY DAD

As I think about it, my Dad stands out as a perfect example of what a dad should be. He was caring, nurturing, and helpful, a quiet man, with a wry sense of humor. I have read several of his letters written to my mother before they married. It was obvious he loved her dearly. They married June 28, 1919 in Minneapolis at the home of their minister. There was no honeymoon since they moved directly into their newly mortgaged house. The next day the relatives were invited to come for dinner. Mother cooked the dinner and then served breakfast to everyone the next morning.

Speaking of cooking—as long as I can remember, after each evening meal, my father always stood, pushed his chair to the table, and said, "Thank you, Dee, for a delicious dinner." Mother privately said to me, "I could serve Dad sawdust and he would put milk and sugar on it and say it was delicious."

As Dad rose higher in the ranks of his job I observed several things. Once a month he would sit in his favorite chair in the living room to sign a stack of checks for the employees. I noticed that he had an unusual way of signing his name: Edwin L. Hoffm_____an. When I asked why he drew the long line he explained, "So no one can copy my signature". Another characteristic of my father was his humility. We lived in a middle class or maybe a somewhat lower class neighborhood. At one time, he and my mother talked about moving to a larger house in a "better" neighborhood. His comment was that this is our home, and we are comfortable here. I didn't want to move either. In fact, I said if they sold the house and moved I would stay with the house. My reason was obvious. I'd lose touch with all my friends so we remained where we were.

As General Superintendent of Minneapolis Moline, a rather large company, it was common for him to receive gifts from clients at Christmastime. Every year one certain client would drive up in front of our house in a large chauffeured automobile. Each year my mother dreaded this because she never knew when it would happen, and was usually caught improperly dressed (according to her). On one occasion, she saw a car pull up to the front curb so she quickly hurried to the kitchen to hide. After several knocks at the front door, she heard a soft knock on the back door. The door opened and a well-dressed gentleman stepped into the kitchen and handed my mortified mother a beautifully wrapped gift and said, "Will you please give this to Mr. & Mrs. Hoffman with my best wishes." He thought my mother was the maid. She often laughed when she told the story.

It is obvious to me now that one of my mother's main jobs was to see that my dad was always properly dressed. Dad wore tailor-made suits, beautiful ties along with white shirts that were properly starched, and shiny polished shoes. As they kissed at the back door before my dad left for work, she would often check the white pointed handkerchief in his pocket and then smile probably saying to herself as he walked to the garage "My, he is a handsome man."

My dad never spanked me. His form of discipline was a firm word or two followed by a logical reason for saying so. He taught me to drive, fish, shoot a riffle, and pistol, and play darts in our basement. When I was sick in bed he would stick his head in my bedroom door after arriving home from work and say "keep your feet warm". His endearing nickname for me was "Patsa". I never knew what that meant except it was said with a loving smile.

During World War II, Minneapolis Moline converted to producing equipment for the war effort. Dad was very busy, often traveling to different cities and working late hours. Due to secrecy requirements, he never talked about what they were building. But one evening at the dinner table he told us about a problem they were having with the construction of a fighter plane. It seems that every time the test pilot would put the plane in a steep dive the wings would tear off. They checked and double checked the engineering calculations and the manufacturing process but had not found the problem. They tried different wing materials, different bracing, and different angles but nothing worked. At a moment of deep despair and frustration, the plant janitor said he spotted the problem. He said that they should drill a line of small holes along the wing near where it attached to body and that would prevent the wing from breaking off. In desperation, they tried it and it worked! Success! When they asked the janitor how he knew this would work, he calmly replied that toilet paper never ripped at the perforated line so he figured the same principle would apply here. What? This was a joke? Dad never told jokes at the dining room table, so we were completely caught off guard. For the rest of the meal he just smiled.

Dad took me to several concerts that still vividly remain in my mind. We heard the famous concert pianist, Ignacy Jan Paderewski, perform in an auditorium in Minneapolis. A concert grand piano was placed in front of the stage curtain. The audience roared with applause when he walked on stage and sat at the piano. He looked old and walked slightly bent over. His entire program was played by memory—one thing I was struggling to do. I also remember he returned to the stage and played several encores. Each time the crowd stood to applaud. They didn't want him to stop. My father whispered to me that the people really wanted him to play his famous Minuet in G, Opus 14, which he totally ignored. I read many years later that he was the least proud of this piece.

It was well known that Paderewski detested any talking in the audience when he played. If this happened he'd turn to the audience and say, "I established a certain standard of behavior: no talking during a performance." And then turning to the guilty parties he again would explain, "I am sorry to interrupt your conversation. I deeply regret that I am obligated to disturb you, so I am going to stop to allow you to continue talking!" I can imagine this was extremely embarrassing for the guilty ones.

In my recent research I learned of his renowned wit. One story told about him being introduced to a polo player. The speaker continued, "You are both leaders in your spheres, though the spheres are different." "Not so different," Paderewski replied. "You are a dear soul who plays polo, and I am a poor soul who plays solo." I'm sure I would have loved to have known this great man, but realize today more than ever how grateful I am to my dad that I got to hear this great pianist. An additional quote regarding practicing, he said, "If I miss one day of practice, I know it. If it is two days, the critics know it. And if I miss three days the audience knows it."

I also remember hearing Sergey Rachmaninoff, a very famous and popular Russian concert pianist. He was an imposing figure, very tall with very large hands. Many of his compositions involved huge handfuls of notes—not easy for pianists with small hands or short fingers. Because of Dad's love for music we also attended several Minneapolis Symphony concerts at the University of Minnesota.

One event that he and I did was listen on the radio to Fred Waring and The Pennsylvanians. The chorus, orchestra and the choral/orchestral choices were truly inspirational.

Dad was never really very affectionate. He occasionally would allow me to sit on his lap when I was young, and/or at times would pat me on the back congratulating me about something I had done. He was a model what a father should be. Even though his overt love was lacking, I never doubted for one moment that he loved me. I just knew.

Picture 5: My Dad - Edwin L. Hoffman

September 17, 2013

GOOD ADVICE FROM DAD

My dad was very different from my mother. Mother was mostly on edge and quick to give advice. She never was still. When she read the newspaper her one crossed leg would be twisting side to side. Also, Dad said that when they went to bed at night mother would begin writing in the air with her index finger. She explained to me that it was a list of what to do the next day. My father wanted her to settle down for he was ready to sleep. I say this in order to explain the constant calmness of my father. Here are three examples of his good parenting:

(1) Breakfast was over and I was ready to leave for junior high school. The day before the girls in my class had come up with the idea to wear a piece of tape over our left eyebrow. The tape represented absolutely nothing other than to just get noticed. The next morning as I got to the door to leave for school my father asked about the tape. He questioned whether I had hurt myself. I told him no and about the plan. Immediately he spoke in a firm but calm voice. "Remove the tape. It smacks of mob psychology." The tape was removed. A lesson learned.

(2) At age fifteen I began learning to drive. Brake, clutch, shifting, gas pedal, and hand signals were all taught with calmness by my father. My mother was a nervous wreck in the back seat. There was no driver's test for my license, so at age sixteen I was allowed to use the car alone. My father would give me the keys with this advice: "Now, Helen, if anyone should call on the phone asking for you, what time should I tell them you will be home?" With that kind of sincere trust in me I never once went against the will of my father. Another lesson learned.

(3) My dad played the violin—mostly self-taught. During the day when he was at work, I would pick up the violin and try to copy what I had heard. An opportunity came in the sixth grade to have violin lessons at school. My mother allowed me to take Dad's violin without his knowledge. About four months later parents were invited to a concert. As the orchestra filed into the gymnasium I walked in with Dad's violin tucked under my arm. When my father saw me he said to Mother, "What's she going to do with that violin?" He was surprised to learn that it was his violin and afterwards he became my calm violin teacher at home ... but not for long.

March 20, 2012

MY FIRST ADVENTURE AWAY FROM HOME

My father approached things differently than my mother. He always gave much thought before acting. So when he decided that it would be a good thing for me to experience traveling on my own, he told me about a trip that he had planned for me. I was sixteen years old. He said I would leave from the Grand Union Depot in Minneapolis and arrive in Chicago the next morning. This meant I would sleep in a Pullman car. My aunt and uncle would meet me. My mind raced as I pictured myself having to get undressed—and questioned would it be a top or lower bunk. When I asked how I would know when it was time to get up, my father calmly said that the porter would awaken me. Then he gave me the next surprise. I would return home on an airplane. I remember my heart racing when I tried wrapping my mind around all of this adventure.

My suitcase was packed, Mother loaded me with do's and don'ts, and I left home to take the streetcar to my downtown church where I played piano for choir rehearsals. After the rehearsal I boarded another streetcar for the Railway Station. With a bit of anxiety and lots of excitement, I finally found the information about the proper train track to Chicago. I boarded and settled in a seat as the train slowly began to pick up speed. It was about 9:30 p.m.

Soon the porter began setting up the sleeping quarters. He put my suitcase on the lower bed. After using the tiny bathroom I began the struggle of changing my clothes and settling down. The clickity-clack of the rails and gentle swaying of the car felt strange. I was sure I wouldn't be able to sleep. Sometime later the train began slowing down. I raised the curtain a bit and saw we were at another station. I think it was around 2:00 a.m. I hadn't slept a wink.

Once again we were on our way. Sometime later we were at another station. Again I lifted the curtain and saw a train directly across from me with a girl looking out her window. We smiled at each other and gave a quick wave. I wondered if this was her first train ride.

I looked at my watch and realized it was close to 5:00 a.m. and my worries began—how would I be awakened? Would the porter reach through the curtain and touch me? I moved closer to the wall. I heard movement up and down the aisle; he was coming closer. My heart began racing. Finally the moment came and

I heard the words as he pushed on my mattress, "Miss Hoffman, it is 6:00 a.m." So that was it? It was such a simple gesture, just a push on the mattress.

I had a great time in and around Chicago seeing the sights on Friday, Saturday and Sunday morning. On Sunday afternoon my family took me to O'Hare airport for my trip home. They pinned a corsage on my lapel. This was to be another first: my first commercial airplane ride.

I boarded the Northwest Airlines 2 engine plane and had a seat next to the window. A businessman to my left was reading a newspaper. He sensed my excitement, leaned over, and said, "…First time flying?" I answered with a giggle, "Yes." I desperately wanted to tell him about my adventure but he had already gone back to his newspaper. The flight was thrilling, clear and bright sun with fluffy clouds. Soon the Minneapolis airport came into view, and I watched as the wings had a job to do and the airspeed decidedly changed. We landed with a thud and taxied up to the gate. Through the window I saw my parents and two of my girlfriends welcoming me home. I felt like a celebrity. After all, I had had a three-day fairytale trip that I can talk about today that happened many years ago.

March 26, 2012

MINNEHAHA SINGERS

The choir at my high school was known as The Minnehaha Singers. Since I came to the Minnehaha Academy at the beginning of my senior year, I was a real newbie! Fortunately, several students were from my home church and one formerly lived in my neighborhood. He and I went to the same grade school. Everyone seemed quite accepting of this new kid in the class.

My first period class was Government. As I walked into the room feeling a bit apprehensive, I found a seat and then turned to the student on my right to say hello. I immediately recognized him from my neighborhood, and without thinking I rather loudly said, "Sonny". He acknowledged my greeting and his cheeks began to turn bright red as the class responded loudly in unison - "S-o-n-n-y." Sonny obviously was what his family and neighbors called him, but in school he was called Wayne. Over the years we often talked about this event. I think he forgave me for letting the cat out of the bag.

Later in the day there was a rehearsal of the Minnehaha Singers. As I walked into the room I was greeted by Professor Pearson, the well-loved and respected director. (He and I had met a week before when he tested my voice, declared me an alto, and learned I played the piano.) He shook my hand and told me where to sit. It was a large group of SATB singers—probably close to 50 voices. I could tell that I would love this class. A couple of weeks later I was asked to be the piano accompanist. We sang for special programs at school and also when we traveled by bus to a variety of venues.

One program I will never forget was going to a prison. The school bus dropped us off at a prison—it was a state prison. When we arrived, the inmates were seated in the audience and applauded as we filed onto risers on the stage. The concert went well. Most musical numbers were without piano accompaniment. For these I gave the pitch by quietly humming the key. The singing was going well. Finally, the last selection on the program was "The Battle Hymn of the Republic," which included the choir, three trumpets, and two of us seated at the piano.

I remember it being very warm even though the stage doors were open. My piano partner, Laverne, sat at the lower keyboard range and I at the upper. All was going well until I realized that some of the notes were missing and they were not mine. I gave a quick glance to my left and saw that she was slightly leaning over. To me, it looked like she was having a fainting spell. I gave her a jab with my left elbow and she responded with a few more notes.

Within the next minute she was experiencing the same problem. Again I used my elbow but this time the jab was more pronounced. She played on for a couple more measures and then slumped once again. The music at this point was rising to a climax with three trumpets and singers blaring away at full voice. The piano needed to be supportive. It really needed all four hands.

My next jab was a lot more forceful hoping to keep her awake until the music ended. This time it did not work. My jab was too strong and she fell off the piano bench. The only thing to do was to take over both piano parts in order to support the last two pages of the climatic ending. When the applause had ended I searched for my seatmate and found her lying on the grass beyond the open door. She was lucid and apologized for letting me down. My comment? "Thank goodness it didn't happen to both of us."

April 15, 2014

MY FIRST UNFINISHED PIANO PIECE

During eleventh grade in high school, there was a citywide music composition contest. Each school held its own event, and I entered at my school. The musical composition had to be an original and performed by the entrant. Another directive was to provide a hand-copied score of the music to be performed. I had worked on most of it up to the ending but couldn't decide how to end it.

The day came for the contest. I was very nervous. The stage was set, the contestants were seated in the front rows, and the announcer called on the students one by one in no particular order. Finally my name was called. I ascended the stage stairs and sat down at the grand piano. As I began I knew what I was doing but in the back of my mind I also knew that the ending of the piece was still unwritten. As I approached the finale, my sense of "playing by ear" took over. With several ascending and descending flashy runs and big chords that grew louder and louder, I ended with a flourish. I was amazed and thought it sounded pretty good.

At the conclusion of the contest, the results were announced. To my utter amazement I had won first place and would be representing my school in the citywide contest. But then it hit me. What did I actually play as the ending of my composition? For the life of me I couldn't remember it or duplicate it. My only hope was to write something that perhaps sounded like what I played and add it to the unfinished score. As I worked on it I wondered if anyone would recognize what I had originally played. The winner was announced. It was not me. Oh well, Joseph Haydn's *Unfinished* Symphony No. 8 has been a famous composition for over 200 years.

Do you think this story should go down in history? My answer? You bet! You then may ask why. My answer? Because you will be able to read it in my book!!!

May 27, 2013

THE MAN BEHIND THE MUSIC—Dmitri Shostakovich

A symphony concert held at the Green Music Center last Saturday night featured three Russian Composers: Mussorgsky, Rachmaninoff, and Shostakovich, all heavyweights. Together with a packed house and outstanding acoustics, the music totally took my breath away as I listened to each man, whose history was reflected in his music. But the one that grabbed my attention after reading the notes in the program booklet was Shostakovich's Symphony No. 10 in E minor.

Toward the end of his life, Shostakovich is reported to have said: "The Revolution, I am convinced, is what made me a composer. I was very young in 1917, and my first childish compositions were dedicated to the Revolution, and inspired by it." Shostakovich belonged to the first generation of musicians educated under the Soviet system, which rewarded talent only when it conformed. Eventually his works became too forward looking and the dictatorship criticized every piece to the point that he stopped composing. He actually went into a depression.

In July 1953, four months after Stalin's death, Shostakovich once again began writing and produced his 10th Symphony. He finished it in September. This was a herculean task since the composition had four lengthy movements with a full orchestra. It is now regarded as his finest, but also resulted in a heated debate among Soviet musicians at the time. Was he promoting himself or as one of a collective group? Many now feel that it was a reaction to the Stalinist period.

His volume of work is legendary. Besides many foreign honors and degrees, he wrote fifteen symphonies, an opera, and smaller works for various instruments, he was a concert pianist and a professor of composition in a number of schools of music. During his down time he began writing music for the cinema that allowed him to express the emotions that he observed on the screen.

Shostakovich was born in St. Petersburg in 1906 and died in August 1975.

May 14, 2013

AIRPLANE ATTRACTION

Ever since I was a little girl in Minneapolis I have had an interest in air flight. It probably started as a result of a family of two brothers and a sister living next door. Joe was a pilot for Northwest Airlines. His sister, Evelyn, was a flight attendant, and a younger brother, Gene, was a mechanic. Gene took care of my father's car when it needed attention. Quite often I would crawl under the belly of a car alongside Gene and would ask lots of questions. I wonder if he ever got tired of my being so inquisitive. Joe, the pilot, was not as accessible since he was gone a great deal of the time, but he got the same treatment with all my questions when he was home.

One day Joe announced he was going to take my father and me for a ride in his plane. It was a piper cub. I loved it as we circled the airport and surrounding areas, finding my house, and then making a smooth landing back at the airport. I was hooked. My father also was interested in airplanes. Often after dinner he and I would get into the car and drive to Wold-Chamberlain airport close to our house to watch planes as they landed. My father knew the schedule. He would check his watch to see if they were on time. We parked in a great place since the planes would come over our heads to land. I also remember seeing the Ford Tri-Motor Plane fly over our house on its descent and being able to see people in the windows. All this added to my love of flying. (I sometimes wonder did this really happen or was it a dream?)

By the way, the Ford Tri-Motor was also called the "Tin Goose" because it was made of corrugated metal construction with a new alloy call ALCLAD that combined the corrosion resistance of aluminum with the strength of DURALUMIN. The Tri-Motor first flew on June 11, 1926 and was the first successful US passenger airline.

Now fast forward to my married life with children. Each of them can tell you how often I would say, "If I had had the chance, I would have become a pilot." That was enough evidence one year for a special Christmas gift for me from my family. We were gathered in San Francisco together with relatives. After all of the gifts had been opened, David handed me a small biplane that had been an ornament on their tree. I looked at it and said thank you. He urged me to look closer and when I did there was a small rolled-up note attached. When I opened it I read, "We want you to put our money where your mouth is." It was for a Glider Ride! At first I was really surprised, and then a bit of apprehension flooded over me. Everyone was laughing. I faked laughter. During the next few days the weather conditions were unsuitable, so it was necessary to postpone the event. No need for me to worry.

A couple of years later I came to California in the summer for a visit. It was a beautiful day. Out of the blue David, said, "Mom, how about taking that glider ride today? I couldn't think of a reason to avoid the trip so off we went. My thoughts were to tough it out and act nonchalant.

When we arrived in the town of Calistoga it was close to noon so we decided to have lunch. I carefully chose from the menu what I thought would not affect my stomach while flying. Once at the airport I watched how it was done and set my mind to do it. I walked with the pilot out on the field, climbed in the back seat, put on my seatbelt (no helmet), and the pilot jumped in the front. The glass cover slowly shut us inside. We were attached and pulled by a single engine plane. The glider pilot explained while we were still on the bumpy tarmac that these were the most bumps I would feel during the entire ride. I sort of relaxed.

Up, up we went, towed by a plane that soon made a wide curve to the left and began gaining altitude. Suddenly I heard a loud click, and we were separated from the plane. We were on our own, and I braced myself. I soon began to relax. It was an exhilarating experience and very quiet. During the ride I asked a lot of questions, and observed the beautiful scenery, especially the many wine fields.

One thing I learned was that the pilot watched the soaring of the birds as they floated on air currents. This way he knew where to steer the glider to keep it aloft. Once on the crest of an air current, he would stay with it until it was time to descend. The landing was smooth as glass. The trip lasted approximately forty minutes. My family met me with smiles and pats on the back as I prattled on and on about my experience. I offered to pay for my two teenaged grandsons to experience this great ride. They firmly declined. Were they timid? I'll never know.

July 17, 2012

MY FAVORITE COLOR—AND WHY

It took no longer than a blink of my eye for me to know the answer to this question. No, it was not the color my mother always told me that would suit me best. She would often say, "You should wear the color RED." Since she sewed all my clothes, perhaps she had serious thoughts about the subject. And then she would add her reason—that it was because my hair was black.

As I grew older I definitely preferred another color. To me this color was cool (not in today's usage) but in my definition "to look classy." I saw it in Navy uniforms, Airline Stewardess', and doormen standing erect welcoming shoppers as they opened the door. Their navy or powder blue jackets with gold buttons and white pants or skirt, plus a gold pin identifying their profession always caught my eye. Now add those fashionable blue and white spectator pumps that I wore. Oh boy. I really felt "classy."

The color blue also caught my eye in other areas. My first time visiting San Francisco I was fascinated by the Pacific Ocean as it roared to shore— plus the accompanying dazzling blue sky and lily white clouds. Each time I was again scheduled to return to Ohio I would gaze with intent as the waves and sky met and were in constant motion. I wanted to keep this scene in my memory so I could shut my eyes and relive this beautiful picture.

MY TEENAGE YEARS

Once I entered junior high school the only subject that girls talked about was boys. The boys in my class were carefully scrutinized and rated. It became a game. This one was cute, another was too pimply, and still another was too quiet, too short or too tall. Most of the seating in class was designated by the teacher. As a result I sat in full view of Harland—a tall blond fellow who was well dressed. The problem was that he paid no attention to me. I was not allowed to date, so there had to be another strategy.

Several of my friends and I decided to have a dinner and invite boys to attend. Betty convinced her mother to have it at her house. We also decided to make it a dress-up affair wearing long dresses and try a special hairdo. We thought this would automatically make the boys see how great and pretty we were. So plans were made and invitations given.

My mother and Betty's mother agreed to make spaghetti, and we girls would decide on a salad, dessert, and drink. Betty's ping pong table in her basement would be our dining table decorated with streamers and balloons. This was a "talked about affair" for days on end. Every detail was gone over many, many times.

The day of the party I came home from school and was running on high. My dress was hanging in the dining room ready for the evening. That day my Mother was canning tomato juice in the kitchen. There was a large pot of tomatoes cooking on the stove. Sterilized bottles filled with juice were standing ready to be capped. As I came in the kitchen door to make my way into the dining room I passed by an array of capped bottles of juice on the kitchen sink. Just as I walked past—one of the bottles unexpectedly exploded. Boom!!! Fortunately I shielded my face with one arm but the glass and the hot juice sprayed liberally over both arms and part of my face. Mother rushed me into the bathroom. I was crying loudly. She first began to pick the glass shards from my face and arms, and then with cold cloths wipe off the tomato juice. When I was clear of glass and juice, she applied a soothing burn ointment. The worst part was what she did next. She made a sling out of some white material. It was to hold my arm away from my body. Then it suddenly hit me. How was this going to look in a couple of hours at the evening's dress-up party—me in my red and white polka-dot long dress partially covered with a sling.

Well, I gathered my courage, put on the dress, adjusted the sling and off I went. The best part was that the sling was the center of attention when the guests arrived which was good for me. Of course, I told the story dramatically. The dinner went well and the boys were well dressed and courteous. Games were played with lots of giggles and gentle touching—and soon the evening was over.

What did I learn about what happened that day? I guess it was anything can happen unexpectedly—so deal with it and go on. Not bad advice if you can follow through with a laugh realizing there now was a story to tell.

November 6, 2012

MY VERY FIRST JOB

"Now is the time for all good men to come to the aid of their party." I believe this phrase was a speed test to indicate one's typing ability and proficiency. It was a weekly test in my typing class in junior high. The results were recorded by the teacher. I always scored well. I loved the challenge. Because of my high scores, I was presented with another challenge. My teacher was asked to find someone to work for the local Five & Dime store for about four-to-five hours on Saturday morning typing "who knows what." I would be paid two dollars for the day.

Of course my mother was pleased that I had been chosen, but along with her pride, most likely her thoughts were whether I could handle the job. So she gave me many, many, instructions: how to behave, how to get along with people, and to always be polite. Also there would be a time for lunch. Mom packed my lunch—with far more than I could eat.

The time came for me to leave. I was nervous—but at the same time honored to have been chosen to fulfill a need at the Five & Dime. As I headed down the sidewalk, I turned to wave and mom's face represented both anxiety and pride, as her little girl was soon approaching young adulthood.

From this experience it would appear that I was now destined to be an office worker. Stay tuned: It ain't over till it's over.

By the way, the sentence used in typing classes was invented by James W. Weller, a teacher. It is also used as "Now is the time for all good men to come to the aid of their country."

Feb. 6, 2017

GOOD KID/BAD KID

As an adopted, three-month-old child, my parents began treating me as a gift from Heaven. As I grew, I had everything I needed and more. Looking at pictures of those early years, my mother dressed me like a princess: white coat and leggings, frilly dresses, polished shoes, and a closet full of more wearing apparel. Was I thrilled with all of this? I don't think so, since at times I was a spoiled brat. My mother would spank me but often I would run, sometimes around the dining room table. It was a game to see if she could catch me and we'd end up laughing. She also would make me sit at the table until those horrid vegetables were eaten. My father only used spoken words, accompanied with a look that said he meant what he said.

I remember leaving the house many times without telling my mother where I was going. She gave me warnings, but the next time she handled discipline in a different way. She got a long rope from the garage, tied it around my waist, and then fastened it to a steading on the front porch. The porch had no windows. My extreme embarrassment made me crouch in a corner. I cried no tears because I didn't want to be discovered. Was this a sure cure?

I was given many kinds of lessons to improve my behavior and to make me more sophisticated as I grew older. I attended Sunday School and church. I memorized Bible verses and the Ten Commandments and was taught how to pray. A lady who taught elocution came to the house once a week to teach me poise. It was my duty to memorize poetry and selected stories and be ready to stand facing my mother and teacher, and recite "Casey at the Bat," and similar works.

Piano lessons were begun at age five and continued through high school. Once when we were shopping downtown, mother took me to a restaurant to teach me the proper way to hold a fork and how to put my napkin on my lap and my gloves on the table. Elbows were always kept off the table. I remember one incident when a lady gave me a dollar and commented how lady-like I was. Mother made my clothes, which were different from my friends and classmates. I longed for ones from Dayton's Department Store in downtown Minneapolis.

I wore Dr. Scholl's shoes because of a defect in both feet and went to a chiropodist every Saturday. At age sixteen I refused to wear those shoes anymore and hobbled in the popular blue and white spectator pumps in order to look fashionable.

Interestingly, my father thought it important for me to learn to drive, to shoot a rifle and a revolver, and how to fish. He bought my first bicycle, one of the best. It had a horn, headlight, tail light, basket, all with a shiny chrome finish. This made it very heavy to pedal and difficult for me to keep up with my friends on their bicycles. I really wanted a less expensive one.

Looking back, I indeed was a spoiled brat at times, and then I married. My husband dearly loved me and helped me slowly grow out of some of my bad behavioral traits. Now concerning my leftover flaws I just live with them, and thank my mother and father for raising a pretty good kid.

July 16, 2013

A PROVERB: TRUE OR FALSE?

A proverb I often heard my mother quote from the Bible during my growing years was "Train up a child in the way he should go, and when he is old, he will not depart from it." (Proverbs 22:6) My mother believed this verse whole-heartedly. I think she quoted it to justify her direct and sometimes severe instructions meant for my ears. Both she and my dad were brought up in the faith of the church, and they endeavored to raise me in the same way.

For me there were strict rules for daily living. No lipstick or fingernail polish, no movies, dancing, or playing cards. No bad language such as "gee" or "darn," any kind of liquor was forbidden, and my dresses had to be the right length. Mother made most of my clothes. This all sounds very restrictive now, but then it was the behavior most of my friends followed.

There was Church every Sunday including Sunday School, and a youth group every Sunday night that included games, a Bible devotion and prayer. Early in my youth I was taught to give an offering to the Church. On Saturday before bedtime my Sunday clothes were laid out on our dining room table together with my offering envelope. When I was young, Mother gave me money for the offering but when I began to receive an allowance, I had to save a portion for Sunday School. The discipline of giving to the Church remains with me even to this day. It's a good thing.

There was a small phonograph in our living room. I bought "popular" records and sheet music at a downtown Woolworths store in Minneapolis. There I could listen to a pianist play your requests. As I listened, I remember thinking someday this would be a great job for me. I loved the rhythms and tunes of the popular songs of the 1940's. I would listen intently to the melody and chord structure and then when I got home attempt to play it on my piano. Having "perfect pitch" was a great asset. I remember one of my favorites was Glen Miller's "In the Mood." At my junior high school, the students would gather in the gym to dance during the lunch hour, and, guess what? I was the pianist, playing "In the Mood." I was never allowed to dance, a decision I rue to this day. (More on that subject in the chapter "I Can't Dance.")

My very first movie at a theater was Disney's "Snow White and the Seven Dwarfs." Mother and Dad took me to see it. Even though it was being shown in our neighborhood, we drove some distance to another location in order not to be seen. I was ten years old.

I was allowed to date when I was fifteen. My first beau was a young man who had graduated from high school and was working in the city. We attended the same Lutheran Church. I remember the thrill of cautiously holding hands in the church pew trying not to be observed. We both sang in the choir. When he walked me home after an evening meeting, we would stand in front of my house and talk. Mother admonished me that it did not look right—and what would the neighbors say? Soon another beau swept my heart and lasted for nearly three years. Actually he "dumped" me. I was heartbroken, but then I began college.

The Church had a campground in Menagah, Minnesota. It was 160 miles north of Minneapolis, and I went for several summers for a week with 30-40 kids plus counselors. A school bus stowed our sleeping bags, bedding, and suitcases tied down securely on the top. The boys' cabins were across the lake. All the cabins were sparse each with ten double bunk beds. There was a crude small wooden table but no chair, screens with flaps that could be lowered in case of rain, and one light bulb in the center of the cabin. We washed and brushed our teeth in the lake. Outhouses were tucked back in the woods. After breakfast there were periods of Bible studies and singing. The Pastor stressed memorizing Bible verses and some verses are still in my memory. After lunch was a quiet rest time for an hour followed by swimming, a favorite activity. There was a dock, lifeguard, and water games.

As I grew older I began to rebel. I wanted to be more like my friends who wore lipstick and went to movies. One day I bought natural colored fingernail polish. When my father saw it he questioned me in his usual quiet tone of voice. When I pointed out it was a natural color he said no more.

Quite often I was sick with bronchitis or pneumonia and had to remain in bed for sometimes up to three weeks. On one occasion, Mother had a nurse come to tell me about the "Birds and the Bees" since I was a captive audience. All I remember was looking as she turned the pages in a book of colored pictures and not understanding a word she said. I believe I was eight or nine years old. Later in life, Mother would cite parts of the "Birds and Bees" story and end with saying, "You remember what the nurse told you, don't you?" I still didn't know what it was all about.

In looking back at the whole process of being raised, I am truly thankful for my caring and nurturing parents. Because of them I never desired to smoke, do drugs, or run away from home. However, I now occasionally wear fingernail polish, go to movies, have a glass of wine, and regularly attend church. Also when something goes wrong you might even hear me quietly say "shit"—but I can justify it since someone told me that it was a legitimate word in Sweden (that is, if you pronounced it right). To be emphatic, at 88 years of age, it doesn't get any better than this. And for all these many years I have not departed from the faith.

October 21, 2014

SOULMATE

What do I mean when I say, soulmate? Let me explain. Bert and I met at Bethel College in St. Paul, Minnesota. The year was 1946. Did I fall for him immediately? I would absolutely have to say no. In fact I thought he was a show-off, especially when he played the piano. He was very thin, seemed to wear a purple sweater almost every day that made me wonder what he had with the color purple. It never crossed my mind that it may have been his only sweater.

I realized he noticed me occasionally but I did not respond. I thought he was not my type—except he played the piano expertly when I heard him and saw his fingers travel up and down the keyboard. I remember stopping at the doorway one day when he was practicing and realized he was playing Chopin's Revolutionary Etude. Now he had my attention! I was impressed.

I knew he had been in the service. Someone told me that he was in the Navy Medical Corp and had been overseas. New Guinea, I believe they said. In college he lived in the men's dorm. I was a half a block on the same street in the girl's dorm. There were apartments for married couples on the same street.

Early in the fall of 1946, the school agreed to allow the students to hold an Armed Services Day. Those who had been in the service put on their uniforms and paraded in step with flags, while music was playing the Air Force, Navy, Marine, and Army themes. I must admit he did look handsome in his Navy blues. All the students applauded and joined in the festivities. For many of the marchers it had not been long since their discharge. A short recognition program was held in the Chapel and closed with a homily and prayer by the president of the college, Dr. Wingblade.

The next time we were together was as a result of a directive by Dr. Wingblade. Bert and I played for alternating chapel services: he on Tuesday and I on Thursday. One day Dr. Wingblade spoke to the two of us to let us know that a second piano could be brought in to the chapel. In fact he emphatically said that it would be done. We agreed to give it a try. This meant we would have to prepare a prelude when the students entered and also accompany the hymn singing. We agreed that there would have to be practice time. A time was selected when we would meet. We agreed that he'd come to the girl's dorm and we'd walk together to the Chapel. I was a bit anxious but at the set time I began walking down the stairs of the dorm to meet him. He looked up and saw me approaching. I was wearing a pair of loud plaid slacks that must have struck him as a comedic scene for he burst into loud laughter. I was horrified. I stopped midway on the stairs, glared at him, turned on my heels, and raced up the rest of the way to my room. I was both mad and humiliated.

What happened next? I wish I could remember, but we did get together and the duo-piano practices and performances continued. It soon became apparent that Bert was a bit interested in me. The one thing that bothered me was that he made all the decisions about what we should play and how it should be played. It took me awhile before I began to assert myself, and at this point I began realizing we were quite a pair.

One Sunday he came to my home in Minneapolis for dinner. It was the first time he met my parents. When he arrived mother met him at the kitchen door. I had not forewarned him that she had just had one of many plastic surgeries on her nose and had several bandages covering part of her face and neck. This was all a result of earlier radium treatments that had caused her nose to deteriorate, and she slowly developed lupus, a progressive skin disease. She had the discoid variety. She welcomed him royally and with a flip of her apron proceeded to check the pots on the stove. She had prepared a wonderful dinner and in her usual style served it elegantly. Bert often commented on her tenacity in the face of her medical problems. Over the years she had told me about being left too long under a radium lamp. Actually the nurse forgot her, she said, and begged her not to tell the doctor. Unfortunately she complied and was now dealing with the nurse's mistake.

Bethel College was only a two-year school. During this time we both studied piano with Professor Theodore Bergman. He was very interested in our careers and frequently asked what the next step after college would be. Bert had been in the Navy as an Operating Room Tech., so logically, his first choice was to enter medical school. He applied to the University of Minnesota only to be told that Minnesota applicants had already filled the quota. This was a big disappointment, to be sure. Nursing was my choice. I honestly do not know why. I applied to Midway Hospital School of Nursing in St. Paul. All the paper work was acceptable until I had the required physical. After my exam the doctor was very blunt and said, "Are you sure you want to be a nurse? With feet like yours I'm not certain you'll be able to do the required amount of walking." My foot disorder was congenital and no surgical procedures had ever been suggested. So there we were. Both of us felt lost. This is when Professor Bergman came up with the solution: finish your college education at the McPhail College of Music in Minneapolis, and you both can be assured of teaching positions at the college to help fund the cost. Mr. Bergman was a Board Member of the school, and also taught piano and organ there. This seemed like a logical solution and so plans were made to transfer our Bethel College credits that applied, and we began classes in September of 1948. By this time we were engaged to be married.

Helen Hoffman Becomes Bride

The marriage of Helen Rowene Hoffman to Bertil E. Anderson took place Friday evening at First Covenant church.

Parents of the bride are Mr. and Mrs. Edwin L. Hoffman, 5300 Forty-fourth avenue S. The groom's parents are Mr. and Mrs. David Anderson of Chicago.

Gladys Osterberg, maid of honor, Alice Hoffman, Mrs. Marwin Lindstedt and Mrs. Richard Lundgren attended the bride. Arne Anderson, Chicago, was his brother's best man. Ushers included Robert Hamlet, Chicago; Roy Dalton, Earl Habberstad and Allen Larin. Judy Shetler and Craig Satterberg were flower girl and ringbearer.

The bride and groom are graduates of Bethel Baptist college, St. Paul. Both are students at MacPhail School of Music. She is a graduate of Minnehaha Academy, Minneapolis.

The newlyweds will make their home in St. Louis Park after Oct. 10.

Picture 6: Wedding. September 2, 1949

May 19, 2014

BERT'S CHILDHOOD

Everything I know about my husband's early life was told to me by a family member or by Bert himself. He did write a book entitled, *Crazy Swedes and Other Wonderful Loons*, in which he related a number of stories about his family and added some personal comments. He was brutally honest about himself, never boasting or enlarging the truth. Then there were additional conversations I remember—especially when we had company when he would tell a childhood experience in order to get a laugh.

His mother, Eva, openly told me about his antics as a child—how one time he dressed up in his sister's new dress when she refused to model it. He then paraded up and down the street much to his sister Ruth's dismay. Also when his mother would ask him to play the piano for company, he would purposefully choose a classical piece. Her response would be, "Don't play that, play a good old hymn we all know." I know that comment made him angry because he often told me so.

His piano lessons began at an early age with a neighborhood teacher. I think he was six years old. With his perfect pitch, and his obvious love for music, he progressed quickly. Fortunately his teacher saw his raw talent and made it possible for him to continue lessons at the Chicago Music Academy. He often told me about taking the streetcar to the Chicago Loop for his lessons and then afterward visiting the Museum of Art, The Field Museum, or the Museum of Science and Industry before heading home. It was a ritual he followed for several years. I believe his lessons were partially paid by his teacher.

The family, excluding his father, attended the Swedish Baptist Church on the south side of Chicago. His father would occasionally attend the Episcopal Church on Christmas or Easter, and Bert would join him. Several times in our conversations he would tell me how the festive music of the Liturgy, the candles, the mighty sounds of the enormous organ, and the smells and bells made a huge impression on him. Little did he know that many years later all of this would be his life's chosen profession.

I have four pictures actually torn from his mother's scrapbook and given to me before we were married. One picture shows Bert at the age of four seated on a new red tricycle. The caption on the back, written in her handwriting, says "stolen after one week." This must have been a heart breaker for such a young child. Two additional photos of Bert, ages three and six, show how skinny he was. I remember meeting friends of the family through the years who often commented on Bert's thinness as a child. In essence they told me they wanted to take him home and fatten him up. What they didn't say was, "Was he getting enough good food?"

One last picture in Eva's scrapbook was Bert in New Guinea at the age of nineteen. He was dressed in his fatigues, had a mustache and still looked very, very thin. His thinness was certainly the result of the onset of dengue fever and malaria while serving two-plus years for the Navy in New Guinea. It is my understanding that he was close to death.

When we met in college in 1947, he was tall, dark, and handsome, and very, very thin. Gradually his figure changed after we married in 1949, but his story telling never stopped.

December 1, 2014

BERT'S WAR YEARS—1942-1945

Tom Brokaw's best-selling book *The Greatest Generation* has prompted me to think about and highlight my husband's years in the service. He, like so many servicemen and service women, did not talk about his service time very often. There were short snippets now and then that have remained in my memory so I want those to be remembered.

When Bert was still a student at Fenger High School in Chicago, Illinois, he worked part time for a funeral director in two capacities. He played the organ for memorial services when he was available, and helped with preparations and presentations of the deceased. The Owner must have liked him since he offered to send him to college to be trained as a funeral director. World War II and the draft changed this opportunity when he enlisted in the US Navy.

At this time, his father was not living. His father died when Bert was sixteen years old. His family unit was his mother, his sister Ruth, and brother, Arne. He told his mother about his decision to enlist in the Navy. When his papers came he told her that he would be leaving for duty the following Friday but actually he was scheduled to leave on Thursday. Bert told me he did this on purpose in order to keep his Mother from coming to the train station to see him leave. He wanted no tears.

His first tour of rigorous duty was Boot Camp in Farragut, Idaho. The year was 1943. After the training was over he was shipped out not knowing where he was going. The final destination was New Guinea to work as an Operating Room Technician in a field hospital. The hospital was several Quonset Huts hooked together with living quarters at the far end. He often said it was a great adventure, and that the experience was very similar to the TV show "MASH" with Alan Alda, the lead actor.

Since he was a classically trained pianist, the base chaplains used his talents immediately. He played a small (I mean tiny) pump organ for both Catholic and Protestant worship services. In doing so he became well acquainted with the chaplains. In the operating room the scenes changed abruptly. An alert would sound to let the corpsmen know to get ready for an incoming flight of wounded sailors—some needing immediate surgery, and others to be treated by staff.

A tragedy Bert often mentioned had nothing to do with the war. On the base were two young men, twins—each one was scheduled to have a tonsillectomy. One made it; the other did not. (He died as a result of a short in the electrical equipment.) This event made Bert seriously ask the question, "Where was God?"

Another sad event was when Bert's best friend was accidentally shot through the stomach. The damage was so severe that nothing could be done to save the young man. All Bert could do was hold him while he died. Again, he asked "Where was God?"

Several months into his tour of duty he contracted dengue fever and malaria. His condition worsened. One evening one of the chaplains came to pray with him and in his closing words he said, "Bert, you will soon be seeing the pearly gates." At this point Bert said he gave up. It was no use to try to survive. The die was cast. Later the Catholic priest came to his bedside, leaned down and said, "Hey Bert, you have no right to leave this world—your job here is not over, and furthermore who will play the organ for Mass on Sunday." This made Bert mad, but as a result his fighting spirit took over and his condition began to improve. In a couple of weeks he was back on duty. Residual effects of the malaria, however, plagued him for many years.

It was now 1945 and the war with Japan was over, and the sailors were being sent home, except for the hospital crew. This left a fully staffed hospital with little or nothing to do. At this point their efforts turned toward taking care of the natives. First came a woman rubbing her belly stating in pigeon English, "Makea some more." The word traveled fast and what followed were more births, and treating many children with a variety of injuries.

Bert often told the story about a young native boy who was a patient. He had serious leg sores. The corpsmen had figured out how to make ice cream with their ice machine, and when it was served to a young lad he immediately spit it out. He had never ever tasted anything cold. But when the sweet taste of the ice cream lingered on his lips, he asked for more.

One day a directive came from Headquarters that the hospital was to be dismantled and all the equipment should be carted out to sea and dumped in the ocean. The hospital was well equipped with x-ray machines, surgical instruments, beds, and you name it. Fortunately someone in authority on the base made the decision that a missionary on the next island would benefit greatly with all the doomed equipment. The commanding officer gave these instructions. He said, "On your way be sure and stop by to greet Father so-and-so." And so the "goods" were delivered to a grateful priest and not dumped.

When all the loose ends were finished, the natives stood waving goodbye to the men and women who had been a part of their island home for several years. The Sommelsdijk, a Dutch cargo ship, would now take the troops across the Pacific Ocean to San Francisco. He remembered sailing under the Golden Gate Bridge, having dinner at a hotel, and knowing that soon he would be home. Once back in Chicago, Bert got a job working for Edison reading electric meters in homes and buildings. His next big move would be to Minnesota to attend Bethel College in St. Paul, and that's where I entered the picture in 1946.

Figure 1: The Sommelsdijk

October 28, 2014

GOOD NEIGHBORS

To live next to a good neighbor is a commodity desired by most people. More often one hears horror stories of tragic happenings, even murders in certain neighborhoods. Fortunately I can tell about a family that lived across the street from us in St. Louis Park, Minnesota—a suburb of Minneapolis. Their names were Will and Vista Lamb. They had three children—two girls and a boy. Will was an artist and was employed by the Minneapolis Art Institute as a teacher and exhibitor. As you might expect their walls were covered with many of his paintings. His workspace was in the garage so it was easy to see what he was working on since the garage door was often open.

I believe he also dabbled in sculpturing—and had a few examples here and there in his house. One heavy snowstorm gave an opportunity for the children to make snowmen in their front yard. There was another sculpture fashioned by Will of a snow woman that left no questions about the female anatomy. What was interesting was to see the neighboring children observing every aspect of this hefty snow lady as they circled the object several times. Another visitor was their dog who circled the sculpture and left a bit of yellow coloring.

On many evenings after our son, David, had been put to bed, Bert and I would go to the Lambs' home for coffee and conversation. Hanging on their wall was a painting that literally drew me into it. Repeatedly, I would comment about this painting and how much I loved it. It was called "Behind the Show". In watercolor, Will presented a scene where your eye immediately focused on an amusement park in the distance. There was a windmill, a roller coaster, a Ferris wheel, and some buildings. The sky looked dark with a potential brewing storm. In the foreground stood four shoddy buildings, each painted a different color. Lying on the ground were garbage cans, old tires, scattered lumber, and two electrical poles with wires stretching between them. I could easily see why Will named it "Behind the Show".

One day Will appeared at our back door and handed me the "Behind the Show" painting, saying he wanted me to have it since I had often commented how much I liked it. My jaw dropped, tears came to my eyes, and with a feeble thank you, I gladly accepted this wonderful gift. He then told me that he and his family would be moving to Indianapolis IN, how very sorry we were to see them leave.

One evening we treated them for dinner at a restaurant in Minneapolis. My mother came to babysit our son. When we returned we asked Will and Vista to come in to meet my mom and found her lying on the sofa. Will's painting was hung directly above her. I was anxious to know how she liked it so I said, "Well, Mom, how do you like our new painting?" Her response was "Well, I've been lying here trying to figure how I could clean up that mess in the front." I then told her that the man she just met was the artist. I guess it was the wrong thing to say—but Will laughed, and then we all laughed. I often think of Will and family, even more so when I look and still admire the "Behind the Show" painting that now hangs in my apartment above the sofa.

April 29, 2014

ONE MORE STUPID THING I'VE DONE

During my growing up years my mother always had something brewing on the stove or in the oven. This included canning season. Sterilizing the glass jars and lids, followed by preparing the fruits and/or vegetables always seemed to me to be a lot of work. What made it worse was when the outside temperature was over 100 degrees. But this was a yearly routine, mostly in the summer, and I must admit it was nice to go to the cellar during those long winter months and bring up something tasty for dinner that Mother had canned.

I helped a few times, but really knew very little about the canning process. However, when my husband and I bought our first small house it seemed to me that I should imitate my mother and can something. My uncle had built a fruit cellar in the basement. It had empty shelves for a few months until I had an idea. I would start canning in order to fill the shelves.

I went to the grocery store, bought twelve ears of corn and canning jars and lids. The cookbook told me exactly what to do: shuck the corn, and with a sharp knife remove the kernels, heat water to boiling, sterilize the jars and lids, fill the jars, add salt and water, seal jars, and place in the water bath. With pride I placed three small jars of corn on one of the shelves in the fruit cellar.

Several months later as I was preparing dinner I realized that I had no vegetable to add to the menu. Ah, ha, I said—now's the time to use one of the jars of corn. I brought it up from the cellar, heated it on the stove and served it. Several minutes later my husband asked me the question. "What kind of corn is this?" "Why do you ask?" I said. "Well," he said, "be sure you read the label so you never buy this kind again". I left the table in tears and to be honest it took me a couple of years to tell the story and enjoy laughing about it with my friends. Did I ever can anything again? What's your guess?

March 26, 2013

DAVID

Nearly every new mother to some degree is possessed about the growth and nurturing of her first child. Of course this child is the cutest baby in the whole world. Girls are dressed in frilly outfits, and one dresses a boy to look "manly." Baby showers provide colorful linens, filling dresser drawers with multiple sizes of changes of clothes, and fancy equipment for us to use. We wait to hear the ooh's and ah's as adoring family, friends, and neighbors peer into the bassinet or the parent's arms. I was no different. I was one of those mothers.

In my generation I did not take any anti-pregnancy pills. There were none. So if it happened it came as a complete surprise. I remember the look on my husband's face when I told him that maybe we were going to be parents. I remember his broad smile and firm hug. The doctor said in order to be sure, I should bring in a urine sample that would be tested on a rabbit! In one week the answer came. It was positive. As a result everything changed in our lives. Our conversation was totally about the baby. Telling our parents and friends was *so* much fun. My mother made two maternity outfits for me to cover the "bump".

So our first child was born on December 13, 1951 in Minneapolis, Minnesota. Driving to Deaconess Hospital in a snowstorm was no easy matter. We left the house 7:15 a.m. and got to the hospital in half an hour; a nurse whisked me to a labor room, and in a few minutes asked me to walk a short few steps to the delivery room. The baby, a boy, made his appearance at 9:15 a.m. It was a close call. Bert told me later after he parked the car, signed some papers, and found the delivery room, a nurse came through the delivery room door holding a baby. Bert told me later that the seven-pound little boy with skinny legs looked directly at him, and he felt as though the little one was saying, "Are you my father?"

Here are two things I will never forget about that day. First was seeing my parents walking down the hall shortly after I was back to my assigned room. They were holding hands and looked like two little kids on their way to discover something special. When the nurse brought the baby into the room, it was the first time I saw him, and I said with surprise, "Red hair!" The nurses' response was "What's the matter with red hair?" I turned to look. She was a bright redhead.

The second thing I remember was student nurses walking down the hall singing Christmas carols. After all, it would be Christmas Eve in two weeks. As they sang "O Little Town of Bethlehem" I thought about the Biblical story in the Gospel of Luke—"and Joseph also went up from Galilee, from the city of Nazareth, to Judea, to the city of David, which is called Bethlehem." Our son was given the name David. David was also Bert's father's name.

Jumping ahead another generation, our first grandchild was born to our David and wife, Trish, in Bethlehem, Pennsylvania, on December 13, 1978, and was given the name David. He just had to be named David.

March 11, 2014

A BIG MOVE—TO ROCK ISLAND

One of the most traumatic decisions my husband and I ever made was for Bert to enter the Seminary. I use the word "we" because we prayed and talked about it together. He dropped his nearly completed course work for a Doctorate of Music at the University of Minnesota, and started to prepare for the Ministry at Augustana Lutheran Seminary, Rock Island, Illinois. It was l956, and he was 31. Perhaps at this point you are wondering how this all came about. It did seem strange to us also for we were happily engaged in what we loved to do—music in its many forms.

Dr. C. Vernon Swenson was the pastor of Augustana Lutheran Church in Minneapolis, and Bert and I were on the staff as choir directors and organist. One Sunday evening visiting at their home, Bert and the pastor began a rather lengthy theological discussion. At one point the pastor said to Bert, "Have you ever thought about going into the ministry?" I heard the question but not Bert's answer. It was not until driving home that Bert spoke after a rather long period of silence and said, "Well, what do you think?" I knew at this point the die was cast, and I started to cry. I knew we'd soon be moving to Illinois.

The first thing we had to do was tell our parents. Bert's mother could not understand his becoming a Lutheran minister. "After all," she said, "he was raised a Baptist." To her the difference was monumental. My parents lamented the fact that we would be taking their precious grandchild away from them. As we sat talking on their front porch I could see that it would take some assurances from us that we were doing the right thing. We tried but even today I am not certain we convinced them at the time.

We had a house so we talked to a realtor. We bought the house in St. Louis Park for $9,500 with a generous down payment of $1,000 from my parents. Our agreed selling price was $10,500, and it sold rather quickly to friends of ours. Next we made a hurried trip to Rock Island to find housing and David stayed with my parents. Bert registered for his first semester. Also, Bert had agreed to play for a wedding at the Seminary Chapel for our friends Donald and June. Fortunately we were able to stay in their apartment while they were on their honeymoon.

June was kind enough to introduce us to her friends, Bill and his wife, who in turn listened to our plight of needing housing. Bill told us his older sister owned a house, and wanted to evict the current older couple because of their lack of care of the property. He told us he would see to their eviction and that we could rent it after they moved out. Bill took Bert to see it. When they returned all Bert did was roll his eyes and that told me that the house would certainly not be found in a *House Beautiful* magazine. We would manage, he said.

That same week we made an appointment to see the Dean of Augustana College located on the same property as the Seminary. After a rather lengthy conversation the dean offered us part-time teaching positions, and we could begin in October. This was an answer to prayer—a house to live in and jobs for both of us. We were off to a new adventure.

May 5, 2014

CHANGE HAPPENS

Yogi Berra, an old super star with the New York Yankees, was famous for his quotes. One of my favorites—"If you see a fork in the road, take it." What he most likely meant was be ready for change; it's bound to happen. For most people life seems to be full of forks in the road. Your choice can bring joy or fear. Often one has control of which road to take, and then there are times when life dictates a new road.

Case in point: My husband and I had a baby in 1951! For the next three years everything changed. I stayed home and Bert continued teaching, working on his Doctorate at the University of Minnesota, and serving as Music Director at Zion Lutheran Church in Hopkins, Minnesota. In the middle of his third year at the church, the pastor at Zion Lutheran informed him that the Church council had arranged for a second pastor to be called who was also qualified to serve as Music Director. Whoa—this meant a loss of income, which we could not afford. However, Bert didn't panic and it wasn't long before he learned of a position at First Augustana Lutheran Church, downtown Minneapolis. He was interviewed and was hired. About two weeks later the Pastor of Zion happily informed Bert that he would not have to leave because the person they had called was unable to come. At this point Bert had already signed a contract for the new position. He would begin in a month.

We found a true home at First Augustana Lutheran Church, and became members on January 22, 1956. David was soon baptized. The baptism was conducted following a morning worship service. When the church was nearly empty, the pastor knelt down in front of David who was seated in the front pew. The pastor explained what was to happen and then asked if he had any questions. Of course we had already informed him what it was all about. David then spoke up and said he had a question. His question was "Will you make the water a little cool and a little warm?" The pastor assured him it would be done.

David was old enough to attend Sunday School in our new church, and I began directing the children's choir. Bert was kept busy with three additional choirs plus playing for all the worship services. We were happy. The pastor and Bert had an ideal relationship. Both of them enjoyed discussing the Faith of the Church.

One day during our fourth year while visiting with the pastor, I heard him say to Bert, "Have you ever thought about entering the Seminary?" I really don't remember Bert's exact response. However, on the way home he was not his chatty self. We rode in silence. Finally he said "what do you think?" I knew immediately we would be moving to the Seminary in Rock Island, Illinois. How would we tell my parents and Bert's mother? That was our concern. I'm sure they would feel an immediate loss knowing their grandson would be living so far away.

We sold our little house on Colorado Avenue in St. Louis Park, moved to Rock Island, Illinois without a place to live and no job. Within two days a house for rent became available, and we both got part-time teaching jobs at the adjoining Augustana College. Bert began classes in September at the Seminary and David entered kindergarten. Was it a challenge? Was it a huge change? You bet.

Five years later following graduation and ordination, Bert was assigned to his first parish in Jersey City, New Jersey. This time, the fork in the road was dictated by the Seminary. We were sent there. It was still a big challenge.

Before retirement in 1989 we had served four churches; two in New Jersey, one in Michigan, and the last in Ohio. The interesting thing was that my husband did not pursue these churches, the churches pursued him. Each time we had a choice. It still was a fork in the road every time we moved, but again our prayers for God's guidance aided us in our decisions.

The reason for our retirement was my husband's illness. In 1985, Bert's cardiologist at Ohio's famous Cleveland Clinic told him he had cardiomyopathy and that he would have at best five more years of life. In 1989, we both reluctantly retired after much prayer and thought. During his retirement he wrote three books. I'm certain this activity lengthened his life by several additional years. He died in 1993. For me the change to living alone was a huge fork in the road, but I continued to teach piano at home and was on call as a substitute organist for worship services, weddings and funerals at a variety of churches.

The Christmas of 2010 was spent with family in San Francisco. Heading to the airport for my return to Ohio my daughter-in-law asked me, "Mom, have you ever thought about moving?" I said "Yes". Her second question—"Would you consider moving to California?" I paused and agreed. That started the ball rolling, and by the next August, I moved to Merrill Gardens in Sonoma, California.

With each of the changes in our life, we felt and knew it was the right thing to do. However, if we had made different choices we also knew that God would be with us equally as well. As an organist I played the old hymn "Abide with Me" many, many times. I am once again reminded of the words in the third stanza—"change and decay all around I see, Thou who changest not, ABIDE WITH ME". To this I say, Amen.

January 8, 2013

LET'S HAVE COFFEE

Being Swedish predisposes you to be a coffee drinker. When I was very young coffee was always available at our house. It was served at all meals, plus there was an additional coffee hour in the middle of the afternoon. I remember when I was on the farm during the summer it was my job to take a basket of goodies and coffee in the afternoon to my uncles who were bailing hay or plowing the fields. The temperature could be in the high 90's but coffee was still their drink of choice. I never touched the "stuff" and wondered how they could drink this smelly liquid.

As a pre-teen, my drink of choice was milk, orange juice, or Ovaltine. Under the Ovaltine lid there was a silver round piece that could get you items related to the Little Orphan Annie's radio program. I remember mailing several of them to the station for a decoder that would give me clues to an upcoming story line. My mother would not buy another can of Ovaltine until the first can was empty. Even though I really didn't like the taste, I drank it in order to be loyal to Little Orphan Annie.

All through high school and college I never drank coffee. I still didn't drink it when I got married, but my husband made up for it. My coffee-free life continued until my twenty-ninth birthday.

Our son, David, was in kindergarten, and one day he gave me a note announcing a picnic for his class that included the parents. We were to meet at a nearby park at noon. When I arrived, I observed that all the parents had brought their lunch. I must have missed the information about lunch so I felt uncomfortable. A lady holding a tray of filled coffee cups approached and asked the question, "Do you use cream or sugar?" I said no and took the filled cup in order to have something in my hand. It tasted awful, but I nursed it like an alcoholic beverage.

That evening at dinner I told my husband about the event. He said, "Try it with some cream and sugar." To be honest it wasn't that bad. While we were still at the table the telephone rang. It was my mother wishing me a happy birthday. I said "Mom, you will never believe what I did today. I drank my first cup of coffee." Her answer was a loud "Oh, no!" She sounded as if I said I had just smoked my first cigarette. As a result, I began drinking coffee with cream and sugar. But soon it began showing up in my waistline. Pants were getting too tight so I decided to drink it black. Since then it has been my drink of choice especially with dessert.

An interesting insight is the coffee routine in Sweden compared to the US. In a restaurant in the US a waitress comes with the coffee pot and fills your cup soon as you are seated. Your cup is kept full throughout the meal including dessert. In Sweden, coffee does not appear until after the dessert is served. Then the guests adjourn to a coffee table in another room and coffee is served in small cups together with a sweet bun or cake. The coffee is very strong but delicious.

Today my favorite choice in coffee is that it is decaf, black, and served piping hot with a piece of apple pie and ice cream. It doesn't get any better than that for me.

October 23, 2012

AN UNEXPECTED TRIP

My son David and I had spent a week with my parents in Minneapolis and it was time to return to our home in Rock Island, Illinois. We would be traveling by train from Minneapolis to Davenport, Iowa, one of the Quad Cities, which was about fifteen miles from our house. My husband would meet us there.

Our bags were packed and my dad loaded them into the trunk of his car. I was concerned about him driving since he had broken his leg and was on crutches. He assured me he was fine. There were five in the car—my mother, my mother-in-law, David, my dad, and me. Finally we were on our way to the Union Station near downtown Minneapolis. David was excited to be riding on a train. He was six.

It was obvious that the two mothers were there primarily to see that David and I were properly settled on the train. They fussed with luggage, made sure we were seated in the right place, and each of them gave me instructions to follow. I could see my father standing on the platform watching us. All of a sudden, to our surprise, the train began to slowly move forward. It startled us. As I looked out the window I saw my dad smiling and waving goodbye. The two mothers immediately began blaming each other for not hearing the conductor's announcement to get off the train. This was followed by additional "you should haves" from each of them. I remember being very disgusted. Finally there was nothing to do but sit down and enjoy the ride. Our conversation was obviously overheard by the other passengers, and I could see many people smiling and talking about our problem. When the conductor came by for our tickets, he listened to the two mothers' stories and then agreed to let the two old stowaways ride free.

I knew the next stop was going to be St. Paul, a short distance from Minneapolis. As we approached, the train began to slow to a stop in order to back into the station. As it gradually slowed David was watching the maneuver. When the train made a complete stop David excitedly said in a loud voice, "Now you can jump, Grandma." The whole car filled with laughter.

How did the two stowaways get home? My mother told me later that she called my dad to come pick them up at the St. Paul Station. His answer? "You got yourself into this, now it's up to you to figure out how to get home." With that advice, Mom called a taxi.

September 8, 2014

TRAVELING WEST

The year was 1958. My husband's assignment was to serve a year of internship as a Lutheran minister at a church in Portland, Oregon. Our plans were to leave Rock Island, Illinois in mid-August, and include a vacation before arriving in Portland on Labor Day weekend. We were fortunate to find a seminary family to sublet our rented house. I remember sitting with my husband and David, our six-year-old son, mapping out the routes to travel plus a discussion of what to take with us. We had no idea where we would live for it was up to us to find our own housing upon arrival.

We headed west in our trusty 1950 Ford that was fully loaded including a zippered car top bag. David sat on his little sturdy suitcase in the front sit between my husband and me. Our intent was to save money by eating breakfast and lunch from a cooler and dinner at a restaurant near a motel. Our first stop was Omaha, Nebraska. The next morning, we found a picnic table along the highway suitable for our breakfast. A tablecloth, light aluminum bowls, disposable glasses, and a thermos looked inviting. We were hungry, and it was windy. As I poured the puffed rice, the wind scattered it and the bowls flew. David happily rescued them. Lunch was easier with peanut butter and jelly sandwiches. My husband told me that in a couple of days we would be entering the Rocky Mountains. Sure enough it happened. In the distance I saw the outline of the mountains, and as we got closer we finally entered this magical land. I was speechless.

A couple of days later we were nearing the Grand Canyon. When we came to Flagstaff in the late afternoon, my husband insisted that we continue to the center of the park for the hotel. This was against my wishes. I wanted to find a resting place near Flagstaff, get up early and travel in the morning light. I was out-voted so we drove on. Soon there it was—"You are now entering the Grand Canyon". A bit later was a sign that said, "Scenic View, 1,000 feet." By now it was totally dark. I began to laugh. We drove on. Another sign, same words, and I laughed harder. Not long after, same message. I was doubled over. Finally, we came to the hotel. My husband left the car while David and I waited anxiously only to learn that there was "no room in the inn". However, it was not completely lost. We now had a motel reservation at the other end of the park so we drove on. You guessed it. At each sign reminding us of a scenic view I laughed, and then the sign appeared, "You are now leaving The Grand Canyon". I wondered if any tourist had ever driven through the canyon at night. In the morning, we did go back and reveled at the remarkable views.

From the canyon we continued west crossing the Mojave Desert. It was hot. A so-called air conditioner attached to my window provided moist hot air. My dad had given us a bag to hold water and we were to hang it in front of radiator to cool the engine, he said. At one point we stopped to assist an elderly couple change a flat tire. They were extremely grateful and gave my husband a bottle of after shave. Close to Bakersfield, California, our car stalled. The radiator was out of water. We then learned, from a repairman, that the bag was really for replacing water in the radiator. As a result, we had to spend a day and a half in Bakersfield while repairs were made. A nice cool movie and an air-conditioned motel saved the day.

It was Thursday, August 21, as we continued our journey north from Bakersfield, California. We spent part of a day at Knott's Berry Farm, drove through a short section of Los Angeles, and continued on Route 1 hugging the cliffs overlooking the Pacific Ocean. It was my first view of the rolling sea. We were all eyes and ears. At one point, I began to feel sick. Car sick, that is. I couldn't take the winding narrow road at dizzying heights, up and down, in and out, so we headed for the main highway. Lots of traffic but signs assured us we were heading for San Francisco.

When we arrived we found a motel, changed clothes and rode a cable car into Chinatown. There we walked the crowded streets and chose a restaurant for dinner. It was on second floor with a great view and different from any Chinese restaurant I had ever seen. Food carts were wheeled up and down the aisle for us to select our preference. It was fun trying to eat with chopsticks. Our bill was according to how many plates we chose.

In the morning while David slept Bert and I attended an 8:00 a.m. Episcopal Church service half a block from our motel. David was still asleep when we returned. I doubt we would do that today. We had breakfast, checked out of the motel for some sightseeing. First stop was Telegraph Hill, then Fisherman's Wharf, followed by a great boat ride around the Bay. Seal Rock was our next stop. We marveled at the large seals, some clinging to a large rock and others cruising through the huge waves. Of course we couldn't leave without traveling down the crookedest street in San Francisco, Lombard Street. We finished by driving through Golden Gate Park. By 5:30 p.m. we were crossing the amazingly beautiful

Golden Gate Bridge heading north. It was a sunny day. I remember turning around to take a last look at the San Francisco skyline and marveling at the picture postcard scene.

The next tourist stop was the redwood Forest. Of course we had to drive through the center of a huge redwood tree. We marveled at the surrounding beauty, and the luscious aroma of the redwoods. Crossing the border into Oregon, beauty was everywhere. I imagined living there. Later that afternoon we arrived in Portland.

Our first duty was to find First Immanuel Lutheran Church which was Bert's assignment for the next year. There we met Olga, the church secretary, who told us to go next door to meet the Pastor, The Reverend Carl Sodergren, who had recently been hospitalized. He was very charming. He explained to Bert that it would be necessary for him to take over until he was well enough to assume his duties. I knew Bert could do it.

Our next job was to find housing. We checked the ads in the local newspaper and found a listing for an apartment. It was an impressive three-story house on a hill with white siding, blue shutters, and huge pillars guarding the front door. It looked appealing. We walked the many steps to the front door. It was un-locked. We stepped inside. No one was in sight. Bert called out, "Hello, hello." No answer. Down the hall there was a slightly open door showing some light. He called hello again. A faint voice answered and we heard someone ascending the stairs. It was the owner.

He showed us the apartment, we liked what we saw, paid our first month's rent and moved in. Our furnished apartment on second floor consisted of living room, bedroom, and kitchen. We agreed that it would be suitable for one year. The meager furnishings were early 1940's. The bath was down the hall and was used by two other apartment dwellers. This was to be our home for one year, and we were eager and ready to begin our new life.

LIFE IN PORTLAND, OREGON   1958-1959

Once we got somewhat settled we did some sightseeing, grocery shopping, and became better acquainted with our church family. The owners of the house we lived in were very amiable. The weather was beautiful with cool breezes at night and comfortable during the day. Bert began his job at the church with gusto. He visited people in the hospital and at their home, and got his "marching orders" from the pastor who was required to stay home while recovering from a heart problem. We worked at getting settled in our apartment. There was not too much to do since the apartment was furnished. School for David would be starting in a month. He was six and would be in second grade.

Bert's salary was meager. As we discussed our finances we thought it would be good for me to find part-time work. Fortunately, it didn't take long, and I began working for Montgomery Wards in their Personnel Department. A concern for me was that David would come home from school an hour before me. The owner's wife agreed to always check on his arrival. One day as I approached the house, I was met by David who said, "Hi, Mom, how was your job?" As we walked to the door and up the stairway to our apartment he seemed excited. He led me into the kitchen. I noticed that the table was set. He then explained, "I thought you would be tired and hungry on your first day of work so I made you some oatmeal." He took the coffee pot off the stove and poured it into my cup. It was quite thick but I drank it all with gratitude and tears. I then warned him not to use the burners when I was not at home since it needed a match to light it.

The memories of that year are many: Skiing at Mount Hood, swimming at Cannon Beach, visiting the beautiful Lambert Rose Gardens, singing in the choir, invitations for meals at many homes of the parishioners, and attending women's functions at the church and the best of all enjoying fresh Coho salmon.

A family who owned a restaurant and also ran a catering service, invited us to their home for dinner along with two other couples. When we were seated at the beautifully set table, the telephone rang and the host left to answer the call. He soon came back and exclaimed, "I forgot that I had a catered dinner scheduled tonight." He promised the clients that he'd be there shortly. He then took the large beautifully arranged salad bowl from our table, plus the rolls, plus the vegetable dish and condiments, and called a restaurant to buy a turkey and ham. We watched as it all disappeared. His wife, like magic, went to the kitchen, changed the menu and served it. I was impressed.

The State of Oregon was celebrating the 150th anniversary (sesquicentennial) with a huge Rose Festival Parade on June 8, 1959. As an employee of Montgomery Ward, I was chosen to represent the company on a beautiful float. My parents, visiting from Minneapolis, and my husband and David sat in the stadium where the parade began. David ran down a few steps in order to get closer. We waved at each other as I passed by. A lady seated next to my mother said, "Look at that little boy waving at that lady." David heard it and turned to inform her and said, "That's no lady, that's my momma." It was a long day—but a pleasure.

Here is me on the Montgomery Ward float:

Picture 7: I'm the one in the carriage; not the one holding up the fountain

Some other memories of our year in Portland: 1) Roller-skating with the youth group and Bert falling and breaking his wrist. 2) Skiing at Mount Hood. 3) Bert suffering with sun poisoning after a cloudy day at the beach and having to go to the emergency room. 4) Acquiring a canary to care for while the owner had surgery. 5) Dressed for a rainy day in raincoat, hat, boots, and umbrella, and finding I was the only one dressed like that. 6) The most unforgettable scene has to be when I was seated at a dining table as a guest in a lovely home. I was facing a very large picture window revealing a view of Mt. Hood colored pink by the setting sun and shadows, and then being served Coho salmon all pink with all the trimmings. It just didn't get any better than that.

As a family, we all benefitted during a year's stay in Portland. We were treated well. We were happy people and hated to leave to return to Rock Island, Illinois—Bert to his ministerial studies, David to third grade, and me to resume teaching. I'll get to the rest of the story in the chapter "THE JOURNEY BACK."

May 2013

A BIRD TALE

Our family lived in Portland, Oregon during the year 1958-1959, where Bert served First Immanuel Lutheran Church as an intern. One day a young man, a member of the church, asked if we would take care of his parakeet while he was in the hospital and during the time it took to recuperate from surgery. We accepted and soon we had the equipment and food supplies in place. The bird was named Petie.

At first it was easy. He had a swing, food cups, and room to flap his wings inside the cage and take a bath if he so desired. Watching him for the first two days I saw that Petie never took a bath. When I opened the cage door to determine the situation, he immediately flew out the open door and into the kitchen and landed on the sink. I began running some water. He appeared excited. I made a bowl with my two hands and filled it with water. He jumped in and took a bath! This was a complete surprise. When he finished I put a small hand towel on the radiator, and he flew and settled on it, fluffing his feathers until he was dry. This became a frequent ritual.

Petie didn't like when I talked on the telephone. He would land on my head, walk toward my face and pull on an eyebrow. Nothing would stop him until I stopped talking and put the phone down. He also would sit on the top edge of a newspaper, sway back and forth while one of us was trying to read. One day our son, David, set up his electric train on the living room floor. The train had an engine, box car, a couple of gondolas, and a caboose. Petie would watch and then fly down to check it out. David put some seeds in the gondola and while the engine ran slowly around the track, Petie jumped in and ate the seeds. Weird bird, we thought.

One night when we were in bed we heard the fluttering of wings. It couldn't be Petie, or could it? After all, the cage door was shut. In the morning he was in his cage on the swing with his head tucked under his wing, but the cage cover was on the floor, and the cage door was open. He had somehow learned to open the door, but not how to shut it. Later we discovered his trick. He would attach his talons to the door, rev up his wings and give a hearty push, and the door would pop open.

In June of 1959 my parents came from Minnesota for a visit. Of course we enjoyed showing them around Portland. Mother was especially thrilled with the beautiful gardens, and Dad the Ocean. In the evening they loved to play Chinese checkers. Petie also joined in. He would fly to the board, assess the situation and then begin pecking the marbles out of their holes, one by one. My Mom and Dad loved it. Also at dinnertime Petie would leave his cage, land on the table and look to see what we were eating. If it was lettuce, he would go for it. Again my mom thought this endearing. My dad was not so sure.

Downstairs in our building a mother and daughter rented one of the apartments. They were from Alaska. The ten-year-old child was being treated for brain cancer at a nearby clinic. When she wasn't too sick, she loved to come and play with David and watch Petie's antics. The mother was grateful for the diversion for both herself and her daughter, and Petie loved the attention.

After Bert's year of service was over, and it was time for us to return to Illinois, the owner of Petie did not want him back. Fortunately, an elderly bed-ridden lady who Bert had visited on numerous occasions accepted Petie. We learned later this weird bird became a tremendous blessing to her, giving her much joy and comfort in her waning years. According to reports Petie was now a normal parakeet. Perhaps it was because of all the practice he had of being weird with us.

April 1, 2013

THE JOURNEY BACK

We were finally on our way after packing our few belongings, saying good-bye to our lovely church family, and mapping our trip from Portland to our home in Rock Island, Illinois. Heading northeast toward Spokane we encountered a very different view of Oregon—miles and miles of wheat fields. It was so different from the lush green landscape that we had just experienced.

In addition, David, our son, began to feel sick. This continued for several hours and finally when reaching Spokane, we headed for the nearest hospital emergency room. The report came back after chest x-rays and blood work that he had pneumonia. In consultation with the doctor it was determined that he should stay overnight in order to be monitored. My heart sank. Bert with his comforting words and common sense convinced me that it was the right thing to do. As I kissed David I told him we'd be back early in the morning. That night we didn't sleep very well in our motel, and arose early and headed for the hospital. Thankfully his condition had improved. We were given explicit instructions by the doctor for our trip east. Bert made a comfortable place for David in the back seat. He slept off and on until we drove through part of Glacier National Park where we observed one beautiful scene after another.

From there we entered Canada heading toward Medicine Hat, then Moose Jaw, Regina, and Winnipeg. It was a few years before the Transcontinental Canadian Highway was built in 1962, so the present highway was two lanes each way and without much traffic. Distances between towns were lengthy, and when we thought we could see an outline of buildings on the horizon, it turned out to be grain silos. We were mighty hungry by the time we found a restaurant. After another long day of driving we turned south and entered the state of Minnesota. My parents were at their summer residence in Emily, Minnesota and were anxiously awaiting our arrival. By this time David felt much better, had no fever, but was still taking the prescription ordered by the doctor. When we arrived and my mother and dad learned of David's condition, mother treated him with all the special care she could give. She also cautioned me that I should be more concerned about his condition than I exhibited.

We stayed almost a week. Good food, good fishing, good conversation, and beautiful scenes gave us the rest we needed. My parent's summer home on Lake Ruth was an ideal place. But soon it was time to leave. So we began the next part of our journey heading for Rock Island, Illinois, our home for the next two years.

December 3, 2013

ON NEEDLES AND PINS

It was the last year of Seminary training for my husband (and for me), and soon he would find out where he would be sent for his first call. He had spent four years at Augustana Seminary in Rock Island, Illinois and one year of internship at a church in Portland, Oregon. During those Seminary years he and I taught music at the adjoining Augustana College. The salary was meager. To help pay the rent for an old house, we rented rooms to college students that helped pay our rent. Bert also had a church job playing the organ and directing the choirs. I sang in the choir and David sat in the front row. David was five when we first arrived and now was nine years old.

The time had come to learn where he would be sent. A select group of Bishops had met to determine where the Seminarians were best suited to serve. I remember Bert pulling into our driveway and seeing him walk in front of the living room window before opening the front door. I tried to read his face before he entered. The minute he opened the door I knew he was pleased with the choice. We were to move to Jersey City, New Jersey where he would be the Pastor at Bethany Lutheran Church. My first question was "Where is Jersey City?" We looked at a map that showed it directly across the Hudson River from Manhattan. Wow, I thought. This was to be a new adventure for sure.

The Ordination Service for his class was scheduled for Seattle, Washington. This meant another cross-country trip. We left Rock Island, traveled a bit south through Colorado, New Mexico, Arizona, up the California coast, into Oregon, and on to Seattle.

Seated in the balcony in a large Lutheran Church, David and I witnessed a very impressive service as each ordinand was commissioned to a life of "preaching and teaching the Gospel of Jesus Christ".

After three days we left for the East Coast using the northern route and spent part of the time traveling into Canada. We stopped a few days in Northern Minnesota at my parent's summer home before continuing to our final destination in New Jersey.

I will never forget leaving Pennsylvania and traveling north on the New Jersey Turnpike—six lanes each way with fast moving vehicles. Soon there it was—the Statue of Liberty and the skyline of New York. I was impressed. We left the turnpike at the sign for Jersey City, and drove on to Communipaw Avenue. It was a hot day in July, the streets were lined with old Brownstone houses with children playing in the street, and others sitting on the stoop or hanging out the windows. It was a multi-racial mix of faces. My husband read my face and said "Different, huh?" We found the church and the parsonage, and breathed a sigh of relief for we had arrived. Our furniture came two days later. I was now ready to fulfill my duties as a pastor's wife. After all, I and the other wives had been given specific directions on how to fulfill this new role.

June 5, 2012

A PASTOR'S WIFE

It must be difficult to be a pastor's wife, right? This is a phrase I've heard over and over during the many years I served as a pastor's wife. Each time I was asked the question my truthful answer was a firm no, not really! I then would elaborate on the privileges and/or provide a silly response such as "I am now able to sleep with my Minister."

During Bert's four years at the Seminary, the wives of the Seminary professors had meetings to prepare us for our new life. I was now primed and ready to do what I had learned: keep smiling; help everywhere and everyone I could; dress demurely; keep my child clean and teach him to be polite; and most of all, be ready for unexpected company with freshly made coffee cake or whatever. Of course, one must dust the furniture every day.

I remember to this day thinking "I can do that." By the time of Bert's ordination as a pastor I thought to myself that "My work has now begun." I was anxious to prove that I could measure up as the perfect minister's wife! For the first four months I gave it a valiant try, but I was miserable. My four months on the job was a bust.

One day Bert came home for lunch and found me on the bed crying my eyes out. "What's the matter?" he said. When I explained that I was a failure as a pastor's wife, and didn't measure up to all I had been taught, he hugged me and responded with "My goodness, Helen, just be yourself." My husband added, "You know, if the congregation accepts you as a result of who you really are, that will be gravy." He was so right.

From that day, I changed my life (actually, my thinking about myself), and I became a real person who just happened to be a pastor's wife.

June 5, 2012

LEARNING FROM THE BEST

When I was a young girl living in Minneapolis, I never imagined that one day I would live in New Jersey and be able to travel across the Hudson River to visit the magical city of New York. Looking back I don't think I knew much about the East Coast at all. In school I could put the names of states in their proper place, but I don't remember ever hearing about Jersey City. After Bert graduated from the Seminary, he was assigned to his first parish at Bethany Lutheran Church, Jersey City, New Jersey. At the time New Jersey to me was a far off country. I never heard much about it except when there was a sensational murder or the Mafia was in the news. I guess I had some anxiety about our move but at the same time I tried to look at it as just another adventure.

It was the middle of July 1961. We were on our way to the East Coast. As we entered New Jersey from Pennsylvania soon there it was—the Statue of Liberty! I gazed at it as long as it was in view. To me it appeared much smaller, but the New York skyline was as I had seen in photos. We exited the turnpike on to Communipaw Avenue, a major thorough-fare in Jersey City. There I saw row upon row of brownstones with children running forth and back from sidewalk to street, and women leaning out of windows and sitting on the steps watching their kids. The temperature must have been in the high 90's. All this was nothing like I had imagined. My husband turned to me and with a smile said, "Welcome to Jersey City." He knew I was anxious. He had been here before so he saw it differently than I did.

Even though it was challenging at the beginning, the congregation made us feel very welcome. But for me, I was like a fish out of water. Perhaps this is what became apparent to Ingrid Regnell, one of the church members. I began to see that she befriended me in order to help me adjust to my new surroundings. I had heard that she was a clinical psychologist. How did she do this?

For one thing, she asked if I would be her guest at an opera at the Metropolitan Opera House in New York City. She would drive. Of course I had read and seen pictures of the Met, and listened to the radio and records of the many well know opera singers who performed there. But when we walked toward the building and then opened the magnificent doors, the interior beauty of the building took my breath away. It was far more than I had imagined and more than I had ever seen. The usher led us to our balcony seats. The seats were plush, the chandeliers dazzled above, and the orchestra was ready to begin.

The opera was "Marat de Sade," narrated by the Marquis de Sade. The story was entirely unfamiliar. In the program booklet I read that it took place in an Insane Asylum. Throughout the story the main character, Marat, spent most of his time on stage sitting in a bathtub. The story line was hard for me to follow. With differing degrees of insanity, characters would appear intermittently and then leave the stage. Also there was nudity. I mostly listened to the music and watched the action. I also wondered why Ingrid took me to see *this* opera. At the end I remember her looking at me closely as I struggled to express my thanks. I did learn, however, that the words *sadism* and *sadistic* derived their meaning from Marat.

Following the performance we drove south to LüChow's, a famous restaurant in lower Manhattan. She told me she did not have a reservation but we'd take our chances. As we entered the parking lot, there was a long line of people waiting to enter. Ingrid turned to me and said "Follow me." She headed straight for the doorman and politely asked how long before we could be seated. "At least 1½ to 2 hours," he said. She told him she had a guest from out of town (that was me from just across the Hudson River) and would he allow her to take me in to see the decorations. LüChow's was famous for its changeable seasonal décor. He opened the door, motioned for us to go in, and as we walked down the aisle we were met by a waiter who asked "How many?" "Two, sir," she answered, and with that the waiter seated us at a table for two. Wow, I thought, this woman is a winner. And besides that the dinner was a winner, and so were the decorations.

As I began to eat, I thought to myself New York and New Jersey weren't all that intimidating especially if I was with Ingrid. By the way, she assured me that she never used her psychological skills outside her office. That was good to know, and so I began to relax.

As I sit here today I realize even more how much I learned from Ingrid, and how it has affected my life through these many years. She was the best.

August 21, 2012

WHO ARE TODAY'S HEROES?

What makes someone a hero? It seems comic strips or Disney characters are easy to spot as heroes. Dick Tracy, Superman, and Batman are easily identified. They are usually pictured carrying a gun, wearing a cape, or a disguise. They are always classified as the good guys. One is always assured that the outcome will be positive, and most often they appear "just in time."

Real life heroes are different. There is usually no costume unless it is work related. Also an ordinary citizen can be heroic and receive honors during his or her lifetime. There may be a plaque, a key to the city, or a front page spread in the newspaper. Others are given posthumous awards. It is gratifying in either case as good deeds are recognized like with Nelson Mandela, who was incarcerated for eighteen years to end the policies of racial apartheid and oppression in South Africa. It is amazing that he endured. He was a true hero!

I often wonder while reading obituaries if the description of the deceased is, in my words, overdone. Can anyone accomplish so much? Of course, I recognize an obituary is no time to broadcast "the dirt" about the deceased.

Today is November 11, Veterans Day. On this day it is important to honor all those who have served in the military for the purpose of securing our freedom in our beloved United States of America. There are thousands and thousands of books and movies relating gripping stories of heroic deeds, loss of life, and permanent injuries while wearing the uniform of the USA. Today our flag, with its red and white stripes and 50 stars, flies proudly all across our nation reminding us of what it took to secure our freedom.

So, what about those who are never publicly recognized? They're often called "unsung heroes." For example, a mother caring for a severely disabled child on a limited budget, or a grandmother raising not only her own children but also her grandchildren. All this on a small pension. I think of my grandmother who left her family behind in Sweden and made a life as a bride on a federally donated plot of land in America. It certainly must not have been easy to leave the homeland knowing that she would most likely never see her parents again. These particular stories and others over the ages have been duplicated thousands and thousands of times.

Do you consider yourself a hero? Probably not, but consider this: Think back over your lifespan. How many times have you denied yourself so someone, maybe a family member, would benefit? It may have been easier to have spent your time or money on a bigger house or bigger car or a bigger something. I see heroes as kind people doing kind deeds. Even though they will not receive a shiny medal, they, too, deserve at least a standing ovation as true heroes in my book.

November 11, 2014

I CAN'T DANCE—JUST ASK ME

One of my regrets in life is that I never learned to dance. Oh, I tried to copy Shirley Temple and even went to the neighborhood Shoe Repair shop and had taps added to my shoes much to the dismay of my mother. It was fun to display my mediocre tap dancing ability on my front sidewalk while singing "East Side, West Side." My closest friend, Gladys, also had taps on her shoes, which made it even more exciting as we tapped and sang together.

In junior high school one of the favorite activities following the lunch hour was to go to the gymnasium where the students danced. I did not dance because I didn't know how but volunteered to play the piano. Actually the truth of the matter is that during this era the conservative church that I attended frowned on dancing along with movies, playing cards, and alcohol, and my parents insisted that I follow these rules. Being musically inclined, however, my body wanted to follow the rhythm of the dance but my moral teaching said no. As a result I never learned to dance.

Many years later while living in New Jersey my husband and I were scheduled to attend a dinner/dance sponsored by the school where I was teaching and my husband was on the board. In my new black dress and my husband in his clerical garb we strode on to the dance floor and swayed back and forth in time to the music. At one point I became aware that he had a handful of the back of my dress. It was though he was hanging on so we wouldn't trip and fall. We swayed back and forth and when the music stopped we sat down and returned to our table. We were not very impressive, but we got through it.

On our next move to a new city in New Jersey, we along with over a hundred people from various Lutheran churches gathered for a large dinner/dance. I was nervous and had to do something before the event. I went to the local library and came home with two books by Arthur Murray that displayed the footprints for several dances including explicit directions. Each of us holding a book, tried to hang on to each other while listening to the music. We learned two dance moves: the Box Step and the Waltz. We were ready.

However, a month before the big event we had dinner guests and told them about the dinner dance, and the effort we had made to be prepared. One lady fairly shouted that we must learn the Swedish Polka. With a Swedish Polka record on the phonograph, she taught us the steps. Seemed easy—four steps forward, turn and four steps back followed by the twirls. We practiced this new dance and felt we were prepared.

Dressed and ready we entered the huge ballroom with tables for ten scattered throughout surrounding a large dance floor. When the dinner was over the music began. Bert looked at me, stood up, and he and I joined the crowd doing the appropriate box step or waltz to any tune that was played. We smiled at one another with satisfaction.

Not used to this much exercise we agreed to sit down. All of a sudden we heard the rhythm of a Polka! Bert grabbed my hand, and we made a turn back to the dance floor. Wow, here's our chance and we entered in enthusiastically. Four steps forward, turn, four steps back—when all of a sudden a huge crowd came barreling toward us dancing the GERMAN Polka. There was no chance to make any correction, and in the process I was knocked to the floor. I began laughing hysterically while my husband was shouting for me to get up. I couldn't move. My laughter made me immobile. With dancers trying to avoid my crumbled body, Bert grabbed my arm, guided me back to the table, and we agreed that we really needed not only a rest but also some good professional dance lessons. Did we do it? No, but we continued to happily dance the Box Step and Waltz with vigor.

September 3, 2013

A FOOLISH MOVE

During the years my husband was pastor at Bethany Lutheran Church in Jersey City, New Jersey, I would occasionally visit people in the hospital who were members of the church. It was a sunny clear day, I had time, and so I headed for the hospital. I parked the car along a street one block from the hospital's front entrance. As I got out of the car, I stepped up on the curb and looked back to check whether I had locked the car. In so doing I noticed that the front tire appeared to be a bit low. "Oh, well", I said to myself. I'll check it when I come back."

Sometime later I left the hospital, unlocked the car, got into the front seat, and suddenly remembered that I needed to check on the tire. Just then I saw a man walking toward me on the sidewalk. Certainly he would be able to easily see the tire. Our eyes met—and on the spur of the moment I responded by pointing my finger downward towards the tire and mouthing, "Is it flat?" He obviously misunderstood my gesture, opened the passenger side door, got in, and sat down. He then closed the door. My heart stopped. Why did I do such a stupid thing, I thought? Didn't I remember all the advice I'd heard and read in the news about bad things happening to good people?

I needed to say something so I blurted out "Oh, I'm sorry, I wanted you to tell me if my tire was flat. Will you look for me?" Fortunately he opened the door to get out, and the moment he did I shut the door, slammed the lock button, and sped off. I never gave any thought as to what he thought about my action, but was thankful that perhaps I was leaving a dangerous situation.

It took quite a while before I shared this story with my husband. I wasn't afraid of being scolded, but more likely admonished about being more careful. Now as I look back and once again relive this story, I realize again how naïve I was, and then again "how lucky"—or was it that my prayer in the morning of being safe for the day actually was answered?

May 6, 2014

CAUGHT IN THE ACT

Early one Saturday morning my husband and I left Jersey City, New Jersey heading for Minneapolis, Minnesota to join our nine-year-old son, who had been visiting his grandparents for two weeks. Somewhere in Pennsylvania our trusty Volvo car died but Bert was able to safely pull off to the side of the road.

We sat for a few minutes thinking what to do, when suddenly we were pleasantly surprised by the appearance of a tow truck. We breathed a sigh of relief. Upon examination the driver discovered a hose connection had broken. He said he'd be willing to take us a short distance to an auto repair shop in the town of Carlisle. We climbed into his truck, took off with our Volvo bumping along in back.

When we arrived the manager met us with kind words and said he'd get us on the road as soon as possible. His mechanic looked under the hood and indeed the hose connection was in need of repair. By now it was nearing closing time. The manager left to make a phone call and came back and told us that he had ordered the necessary part. The downside was that it would not arrive until Monday. He suggested we stay at the Molly Pitcher Hotel down the street. We left with luggage in hand and checked in.

The hotel was "quaint"—old furniture, lace curtains, and a bathroom down the hall. Oh, well, we'd tough it out. During our evening walk we discovered a Lutheran Church. Bert tried the door. It was unlocked. As we were viewing the stained glass windows and paintings, a gentleman approached. It was the pastor. We told him our story. He invited us to come to services the next morning, which we did. As we left the Sunday service the pastor remembered us and invited us to meet him at the church at 3:00 p.m. He was to pick up his daughter at a camp about one hour away, and he thought we might like to ride along. We accepted his invitation and when we returned we spent a lovely Sunday evening visiting in his home.

The next morning was Monday. We went to the car dealer who told us to meet a certain bus at the bus station at 10:00 a.m. for the delivery of the part for our car. We were there at 10:00 a.m. The bus came. No part. We were told that the next bus would be at 2:00 p.m. The bus came. We were there. No part. The last bus for the day was at 5:00 p.m. The bus came, we were there, and still no part.

As we left the bus station walking dejectedly toward the auto repair shop, I spied a Volvo coming toward us. Since Volvos were not a popular car at the time, it was rare to see one that looked exactly like ours—a 1962 model #PV544. I quickly stepped out in front of the oncoming car and motioned him to stop. When the car stopped, I walked up to his window and blurted out, "Where do you get your car fixed? We also have a Volvo."

He could tell that I was stressed and asked for an explanation. When I told him of our plight, he motioned for the two of us to get in his car. He drove us to his home, poured us a drink and offered a few snacks, and told us an interesting story. It turned out he was a lawyer who was collecting evidence about this particular car dealer. He was attempting to run him out of town because of his shady dealings, which included the tow truck business and the Molly Pitcher Hotel that he owned. He wrote down all our information in his notebook about this charlatan car dealer. The three of us got back in his car and left for the auto shop.

The lawyer drove around behind the auto garage. As the three of us entered the back door, he cautioned us to let him do the talking. When the manager saw the lawyer, he immediately recognized him and literally turned ashen white. The lawyer told him (more like commanded him) to have the hose repaired immediately. Actually it only needed a piece of garden hose and a couple of clamps. With profound thanks to our Good Samaritan lawyer, we were on our way to Minneapolis in fifteen minutes. I made a phone call to my parents with a brief explanation of our interesting three-day delay. Even though we'd be arriving late, I said we'd have a fantastic story to tell.

May 8, 2012

A NEW WORD

How many words do you know in the English language? Can you carry on a normal conversation without sounding stupid? My guess is that most of us have enough words to enter into a normal conversation. And then have you ever been aware of a person who uses four- or five-syllable words and it makes you wonder if they understand their meaning?

Well, today I learned a new word to add to my vocabulary. It came in an e-mail entitled "Early Word." This title is not what you may think—i.e., that "Early Word" is giving you a new word to learn each day. No, it was actually written by a Christian minister who writes something to think about each day. His messages often have a valid point that give me pause; something that makes me more aware of how to live as a Christian in today's world.

The message today was a new word that means the following:

> *"Those who render opinions that are beyond their expertise."*

Goodness, that's me more often than I like to admit! Unless I have a lofty degree in a certain discipline and the conversation is about that subject, I probably should be listening and asking questions instead of making statements that prove I *really* do not know anything about the subject being discussed.

Okay—here's the word. "ULTRACREPIDARIAN."

It means "a person who doesn't really know what is being talked about". When I think about this, I am certain I have added brilliantly clever comments now and then to deep conversations. I may have even dared to think that I have given my listener the impression that I was full of knowledge. After running this thought around in my brain I'm embarrassed to think how many times I may have done this, and what kind of impression I may have made. Oh dear!

Well, there are a couple of subjects I do know something about—music is one. It was my career, and I have a framed degree on the wall that says so. I can usually answer common music questions. For example, how music is written, or how many sharps and flats in major and minor scales, and questions about rhythm. But here again I admit freely my knowledge is limited. My lifesaver is that I have a number of music textbooks, and I usually can find the answers. Or better yet, I can ask Siri on my smart phone.

As I grow older my answers do not come as quickly as I would like. When I try to remember the titles of orchestral pieces and their respective composers, or piano compositions that I have played, it often takes a continual humming of the tunes hoping that this will jog my memory. Sometimes it works and sometimes not.

I remember hearing the story of two gentlemen who were seated side-by-side on an airplane. As the plane began its ascent one turned to the other and asked, "What sort of business are you in?" "I'm a clergyman," he replied. The first gentleman asking the question responded with, "Well, my philosophy on that subject has always been Live and Let Live. Yes, that works for me. It's that simple." After a moment the second gentleman asked, "And what sort of business are you in?" "Oh, I'm an Astronomer. I study the stars and all the planets". "Well," said the other, "my philosophy on this subject is very simple. It's best described as Twinkle, Twinkle, Little Star. How I Wonder What You Are. Yes, indeed. This philosophy has always worked for me." Maybe this story depicts how one appears when trying to be learned. Instead maybe one should smile and perhaps say, "Oh, that's interesting. I have a question for you that I have often wondered about."

Here's some advice: Next time you would really like to impress someone, feel free to use the word, "ultracrepidarian." Ultracrepidarian doesn't sound as offensive as saying, "You know what, you don't know what you're talking about!"

January 19, 2015

LOOK BEFORE YOU LEAP

Every church musician I know has stories of unplanned events: things that just happened. I am no different. When these unplanned events occurred, it reflected either a growth in character, or a job change. But I loved what I did. I was a musician. There was no turning back. Did these embarrassing events change who I eventually became? You bet. I learned to accept my mistakes and gradually learned how to laugh at them and myself.

Case in point: In the lovely rather small Lutheran church in Jersey City, New Jersey, I decided to start a junior choir, children ages 8-12. My husband, the pastor, gave me encouragement. The choir of both boys and girls met on Saturday morning for an hour, and the goal was to sing at Sunday morning worship services. Being a member of the Chorister's Guild, I purchased suitable music, and used easy to sing hymn tunes, and warm-up exercises. The children were given credit for attendance at rehearsals, Sunday worship, memorizing music, deportment and being on time. These points were accumulated throughout the year with the major prize being a one week prepaid trip to a summer church camp. It was a highly desired prize.

When the season was almost over, I sent a letter to the parents to come to a closing program where the choir awards would be presented. In order to round out the evening I made an attempt to find a film that would be something about music and entertaining. I went to the library located in Jersey City's Journal Square. It was a good sized library. Since I had no title in mind, I asked the librarian if she had a film—one having to do with music. She scanned a prepared list and made a suggestion. She found it and I was happy. That afternoon I set up the projector to preview it (remember this was in the 60's) and as soon as it began to run the film broke. The church secretary and I tried vainly to make repairs but time ran out since the program was that evening. The film would have to run from the point where it broke.

The program was set. The children were excited. After a few opening remarks by my husband, I began to explain about the reason for the evenings program. I thanked the parents for being cooperative, and thanked the children for their hard work.

It was now time for the film. I remember telling the crowd that I had not been able to preview the film but hoped everyone would enjoy it. The lights were lowered, a switch made the large projector reel spin and the first images appeared. I was devastated!!! It was an art film all about Adam and Eve in the Garden before they covered themselves with leaves. The children's giggles and the congregation's wide-eyed looks made my heart sink.

There was no stopping now and it ran for another ten minutes. When it was coming to the end I sidled up to my husband and whispered, "Please say something appropriate to get me out of this." The projector was shut off, the lights came up, and my husband approached the front of the church. He smiled broadly and then turned to the children sitting in the first two rows, and said "Well, kids, how'd you like that?" I certainly didn't have that comment in mind. Fortunately for me, the congregation thought it was amusing.

The next day I met a father of one of the choir members who said "Well, next time you are going to have another 'peep show' let me know. I'll be there." Thank goodness for an understanding congregation. Did I learn something that evening? You bet. Take time to be better prepared.

July 29, 2014

A CAMPING TRIP TO REMEMBER

During our stay at Bethany Lutheran Church in Jersey City, New Jersey, we found the congregation very friendly. On one occasion we were invited by Dottie and Hez Gardner to stay at their cabin on Saranac Lake over Labor Day weekend. It was a seven-mile boat trip from the Saranac Lake dock to their Island hideaway. Our combined gear plus food for a three-day stay was securely stowed. It was a picturesque scene of beautiful weather, calm water, and blue skies, as Hez skillfully motored the rapids and avoided all the large rocks, some of which were slightly below the water level.

During the weekend it was our 15th wedding anniversary. Dottie set up a table on the front porch; we dined on fresh fish, and enjoyed the gorgeous view. Following the meal Dottie presented us with a decorated cake and Champagne. I remember exclaiming how clever she was to have concealed this surprise in the boat without us noticing. As Hez popped the cork on the Champagne it flew off and struck a dinner bell hanging from the ceiling. We laughed as it was a perfect ending to a great celebration. This trip prompted thoughts about returning someday to go camping on our own. The Gardners freely offered their tent and equipment so we decided to make plans for the following summer. We had never been camping before but the Gardners made it appear fun and exciting.

In August of the next year we met the Gardners in Saranac Lake in two boats that got us to our destination—a campsite on another small island. The men set up the 9x9 tent, hung a tarp over the picnic table, set up a five gallon tank of fresh water from across the lake, and we were all set. As they got into their boat leaving us behind, Dottie shouted, "What else do you need?" "Everything," I shouted.

As they left I tried to be happy, but as the sun began to set, my heart experienced some fear. What was lurking in these woods? Would my husband go with me if I had to use the outhouse? It was a steep walk uphill. We had flashlights but it still seemed scary. We bedded down for the night in our sleeping bags. It seemed very cramped. In one corner was our gear. In the other corned was our dog, Mickey, and our three sleeping bags lined the other wall. A multitude of zippers closed us in. During the night I awakened to Mickey's growling. I was certain a dangerous animal was lurking nearby. I poked my husband to give me assurance. He assured me all was well.

I finally began to see a wisp of light and felt better. Bert got up, made a fire in the pit, and the propane stove was lighted for a breakfast of eggs and bacon. I must admit it was good. In the afternoon we got in our boat and found a great place to swim. A natural pool made by surrounding rocks became a small bathtub. The sun had warmed the water. It was delightful but as the sun began to set my fears again crept in.

The second night our sleeping arrangements seemed more uncomfortable. Our supplies included only two inflated mattresses. Bert graciously offered the two to David and me. During the night it began to rain. I mean rain! And there was wind. It beat down on the tent with vengeance. Would we blow away and never be found? We also made a mistake and accidently found out that just a slight touch on the surface of the tent would cause a leak. Considering how cramped we were it was difficult to avoid causing little streams of water invading our sleeping quarters.

As daylight slowly approached we decided to get up. The rain had subsided enough to start a fire and have breakfast. However, the tarp only covered two of us seated at the table, so we took turns to endure a steady stream of water trickle down our back. To be fair we kept changing seats. Since it was Sunday we found a church service on our portable radio. At one point we heard the sound of an airplane overhead flying fairly low. With a snicker in his voice David, exclaimed, "Do you think they'll find us?" We laughed, but I was secretly hoping that someone would come to our rescue.

The next day more rain. We soon ran out of drinking water, and the steady diet of hot dogs and baked potatoes became annoying. Finally we made a mutual agreement that we should break camp. Bert took the water container back across the lake while David and I began packing and taking down the tent. Remembering that it took two boats to get us set up we had a logistical problem to see how to leave in only one boat. Bert masterfully arranged the gear to fit. As we got in the boat it appeared that the boat could sink. One healthy wave could do us in, and it was still raining. Bert started the motor and we slowly put-put putted our way back to shore. Mickey stood on top of the gear at the prow with his tail wagging and ears flattened to his head as if to show us where to go. The small boat motor was pushed to the max as we traveled ever so slowly. At one point I started to laugh hysterically as I thought about Katherine Hepburn in the movie "The African Queen," with her messy hair and rumbled clothes. There was a resemblance of this scene as I envisioned it. We all were wet and I know we smelled. We finally made it to the dock where a couple of men took pity on us and helped us unload. They tried to hide their knowing smiles, but I didn't care. I thanked them profusely. The next stop was a nearby Motel. While Bert took a long nap David and I swam in the nice clear cool water of the pool. What did this experience teach us? For me it was to never go camping again. That rule has held to this day.

August 28, 2012

JESSE

It was an ordinary day. I was at home doing housework, Bert was in his office at the church, a stone's throw away, and David was at Upsala College, an easy ride on his motorcycle to Tenafly. The telephone rang and it was Bert telling me that he had gotten an interesting call from a social worker who was looking to place a young boy, and at this point had been unsuccessful. She was desperate thinking perhaps by calling the local churches she might be more successful. Her question to Bert was would he be interested in talking to the young man, and/or making a plea to our members. This is when Bert called me about the situation.

We agreed to see him and the date and time were set. When they arrived, a nicely dressed fifteen-year-old Cuban boy stepped forward and introductions were made. His name was Jesse. As we sat facing one another in our living room, I was very uncomfortable. I thought to myself, "How demeaning for him to have to beg for a place to live hoping this one would be successful." Several homes had been tried—the last one was with a family who were having company for Christmas so he would have to leave since they needed the bedroom. In another his bed was in the basement and his duties were to take care of the other children.

Bert took him upstairs to show him the bedroom. They talked about the color of the walls—they were PINK! It was made clear they would be changed. As they walked back Bert explained that if he decided to come and live with us, we would never ask him to leave, but if he wanted to leave the door was open.

So ... the die was cast and he moved in on the last of November, 1970. And then something wonderful happened. He immediately became a part of the family—he fit like a glove. We knew so little about him except that he had had a difficult upbringing, starting his life in Cuba. After a couple of weeks, it was so easy to give him a hug, assuring him the he was now safe. My theme song? "Hug him in the morning and hug him in the night." He accepted it so easily.

There are so many memories about Jesse. Where do I begin?

Ah! Here is one of our favorites:

Jesse attended Tenafly High School, a short walking distance from our house. One day we received an announcement in the mail that an open house was to be held, and of course we eagerly wanted to attend. As we wandered the halls, our first room to visit was with his Spanish teacher. After an initial intro she assured us that Jesse had made tremendous progress in the class; his grammar needed a little work but his conversational Spanish was excellent—the best in the class. That's when Bert said, "Did you know that Jesse is Cuban?" With a laugh she told us that she had once asked Jesse if he was Spanish and his response was "Oh no, ma'am. I'm Italian." Well, there was no fooling her now.

Today, Jesse is married to a wonderful woman, Virginia. He manages several HVAC stores. And he is a wonderful father and a very proud grandfather. I could not be prouder of him.

June 12, 2012

MY THREE UNUSUAL SONS

The title infers that my sons are like no others. In some respect this is true. Some families have twin boys or triplets. I did not. Some have boys of differing ages from the same father, or different mothers. I did not. There are those who intentionally adopt a trio of boys from a foreign country. I didn't do that either, so this is my story.

Son #1 was born in Minneapolis, Minnesota on December 13, 1951 and we named him David Brian Anderson. December 13th was a significant day in Sweden called St. Lucia's Day. This day heralded the coming of the Christ Child to be born in Bethlehem, the city of David. In addition, David was Bert's father's first name. David was our only child until the year 1969, when another son joined our family.

Number #2 son was Jesse Antonio Delgado born in Havana, Cuba. When he was seven, during the Cuban uprising, he came to the States together with his father and younger brother. He arrived at our house at the age of fifteen. The year was 1970. He had been in four foster homes after graduating from ninth grade at a Catholic boarding school. He was placed with us through the New Jersey Social Services Agency. From the very first day he fit like a glove. He was a joy to have him in our home. Even though he had relatives in Florida he made the choice to stay with us and has remained a wonderful addition to the family.

Number #3 son, Lars Hollander, came to the United States in 1970 as a foreign exchange student from Sweden on a sports scholarship. He was 16 years old and lived with us. English was a bit difficult for him at first but he learned quickly. One day I asked him what food he missed the most. He said, Swedish meatballs. The next evening I served my version. I am not sure they measured up to his standards, but he was polite and said they were good. He stayed with us until the sports program was over. However, there was a spark of family togetherness—and we were sad to see him leave.

Then, in 1974, for our 25th wedding anniversary, we made our first trip to Sweden, and were able to meet Lars' father and sister in their home. Later, on another trip, we were able to stay with Lars and Mia, his wife, in their lovely home. Mia unfortunately died of cancer a few years later. Then he met Maud, a delightful young lady that was a good mate for him. In 2007 he and Maud surprised me for my 80th birthday in Mansfield, and they came again for my 85th in Sonoma, California. He said to me many times that he just had to be at his mom's birthday celebrations.

So there you have it—my three universal sons—one we raised in the USA, one we got through pure luck from Cuba, and another great addition from Sweden. A picture was taken of the four of us at my birthday celebration. When I look at the picture, as I often do, I treasure the photo almost as much as I treasure my three sons that call me MOM. My only regret is that Bert had a much shorter time to be called DAD.

June 12, 2012

p.s. I recently celebrated my 90th birthday and Lars & Maud were again part of the festivities, as were David & Trish and their extended family, and Jesse & Virginia and their family. Here's a picture from the party.

Picture 8: Jesse, David (Bean), Lars, and Me

ADDING ONE MORE—CINDY

Not long after Jesse became our first foster child, a call came from a New Jersey case worker asking if we'd accept another foster child. A ten-year-old girl named Cindy was one of eight children being relocated because of parental neglect. We agreed and Cindy arrived. As one would suspect she was quiet, nervous, and cautious about her new family. She immediately connected with our dogs, and poured her love on them and for a time tolerated the rest of the family. At dinner times she would push her food around her plate, did not make eye contact, and had a habit of constantly scratching her head. We thought the scratching was a bad habit.

She came on a Thursday in February, seemed pleased with her new bedroom, and we registered her for school the next day. The New Jersey Children's Services gave us $100 per month, so on Saturday we went shopping for new clothes. (She came basically with very few items). When we got home she hung up the clothes in the closet and placed her underwear and socks in a dresser drawer. Each evening when she was tucked into bed I tried to kiss her goodnight but contact was never allowed. That changed later.

She loved school and came home for lunch every day. Chicken noodle soup and crackers were her favorite entre. At lunch she began to talk a bit about her family and about school. She was an excellent student and loved to do homework. One of her hobbies was collecting recipes from the newspaper and magazines for her mother and telling me that her mother was a far better cook than I was. That certainly could have been true. She attended our church and Sunday school.

One Sunday morning I was scheduled to play the organ for the early service. Before I left I put a pot roast in the oven, set the timer, and instructed Cindy before she left for church to check if the oven was on. After the 11:00 a.m. service we all walked back to the house. When we opened the door, there was no usual pleasing aroma of Sunday dinner. Hurriedly I rushed to the oven only to learn that it was cold. I immediately turned to Cindy and said, "I thought I told you to look into the oven to see if it was on?" She innocently answered, "I did, and it wasn't." Dinner was served at 3:00 p.m.

In late February a call came from the school nurse to say that Cindy had head lice. Poor child! That's why she did all the head scratching! I applied the prescribed treatment as her tears flowed. This meant no school for a week. This was a huge disappointment since she had been chosen to be in a school play. All the bedding had to be washed and there were daily combings and washings. After a week she was clean.

Cindy was permitted to meet her mother and her siblings in the Child Protection Services office once a month in another city. We gave her a weekly allowance, which she saved in order to buy her mother a gift. Her choice was a box of chocolate covered cherries, which we gift-wrapped. During each visit I sat in the car. After an hour she was back, sat down, looked sad, and I drove off. There was very little conversation on her part. That afternoon a call came from her case worker who told me when Cindy gave her mother the candy, she opened it and said, "Cindy, you know I don't like chocolate covered cherries." I wanted to lash out at her mother and ask, "How can you be so cruel to your own child?"

Little by little Cindy began to blossom, entered into family events, and gained weight and grew taller. She was allowed the privilege of telephoning her sisters, and her brother. They lived nearby and came to visit now and then. Also her father would drive by the house periodically to see if Cindy was outside. She would tell us when she'd seen him and that she waved. The monthly visits with her mother also continued over the next one-and-a-half years. Cindy's father was a pleasant man but not strong enough physically and emotionally to take care of the whole family. Periodically her mother was given a test to see if she was able to resume family responsibilities.

Finally she passed the test and the wheels of progress spun into action. The case worker told me that people who are continually given a test finally learn how to successfully pass the test. As a result Cindy was slated to return to her home along with her siblings after being with us for nearly one and one-half years. The day came. She was excited. We were sad. Our son, David, who was in college, Jesse, and a neighboring friend, purchased a bicycle for Cindy for her birthday.

The gift-giving scene was electric. Cindy was thrilled. Not only was she going home but she was going home with a bicycle. As the van drove up our driveway, emotions were mixed. There were hugs and tears (mostly on our side), and with a wave they were gone. I went inside, felt drained, cried, and prayed for the safety of this, our sweet Cindy.

Picture 9: Cindy with her children Caroline and Robert

Many years later we made contact and met Cindy and her two children at a restaurant in Tenafly, New Jersey. At this time she was divorced and living with her father and her two children. Here is a picture with me and Bert, Jesse and Virginia with their daughter Lauren, and Cindy, Robert, and Caroline.

Picture 10: It was wonderful to see Cindy and her children again.

Over the years there were several meetings. I was pleased that she came to Mansfield for my husband's funeral in 1993. As far as I know she lives in Pennsylvania with her second husband. I wonder if I will ever see her again.

January 21, 2014

CINDY'S STORY CONTINUES

In August of 2015 while gathering material for my book, I happened to run across a small slip of paper listing Cindy's cell phone number. I set it aside. It must no longer be in use by now, I thought. Still again and again it would show up. Finally after a few days I decided to call Jesse. I told him about finding this information and that I was hesitant to make the call. Without hesitation he firmly said, "Yes, Mom, absolutely, you should call her." Finally I picked up the phone and dialed.

A young sounding voice answered softly, "Hello." I asked if she was Cindy. The moment I said my name she quickly answered, "Oh, I'm so glad you called. I've been looking for you for the past two weeks." She said she searched on Facebook and even checked the obituaries.

Our conversation was mainly filling in the blanks, that she still lived in Pennsylvania, worked for Xerox, mainly at home, and her husband just reached 70. Her daughter Caroline is a doctor working toward certification as an anesthesiologist, and son, Robert, has an Engineering degree. I thought how could this be? The last time I saw Caroline she was a rather shy thin little girl with curly blond hair. And Robert? He was the direct opposite, a typical teenager, with an over-abundance of bravado. As I remember he did not like school. They lived with their father in Tenafly, New Jersey.

We exchanged more stories of our lives plus cell phone numbers and e-mails. I told her about my writing a book and the "My Story, Your Story" group that keeps spurring me on. Also, David urged me to find out what happened after the last time I had any contact with Cindy. So this is it. The contact has been made. I am sure the Cindy story will continue and hopefully we will meet face to face at some point. I thank God for the result of finding that little piece of paper that kept reappearing time after time.

And indeed, the story does go on!

An e-mail came from Cindy asking if she could come for a visit the weekend of December 29, 30, 31, 2016. I answered with a definite yes. Thursday afternoon I heard a knock on my apartment door. She was HERE. With great anticipation I opened the door and immediately happy hugs followed. It had been over 20 years since we had seen one another. It didn't take long to begin conversing about what had happened since last we saw one another.

It pleased me when I heard her say, "You and Dad taught me parenting skills." Also, when looking at a family picture she made the comment that she looked happy—and then added she had never experienced that emotion before.

Later I received an e-mail from Cindy informing me that she and her husband David would not be able to come to my party on June 10. However, instead, they would arrive in time for my real birthday on June 4. It was my first introduction to her husband David—a delightfully engaging gentleman. How wonderful that after all these years we are still in touch.

June 6, 2017

A LETTER—GRANDMA TO GRANDSON

Grandma Hoffman (my mother) lived in Minneapolis, Minnesota and her Grandson, David, lived in Jersey City, New Jersey. This distance called for two types of communication - by telephone and/or the postal service. For Grandma it was difficult to be separated from her only grandchild so she often sent him notes (often with money). David received the following letter to thank him for a pincushion he had sent her as a Christmas gift:

Dear David,

Once upon a time a little girl lived on a farm with her parents and three brothers. The children were given the responsibility of caring for many pets and some of the animals, and performing many odd chores too numerous to mention. Many short cuts were invented and one among them was a large "family pin cushion". Because of it the children were taught to sew and darn.

The cushion was made from scraps of silk and velvet material and featherstitched with colored embroidery thread. It was stuffed with sawdust and a tassel was attached in each corner as a finishing touch, which made it very attractive and useful as well.

The children were each given a section for his and her own possession where needles and darning needles stood proudly threaded ready for immediate use for mending a rip, sewing on a button or darning a sock or mitten. The children were taught how to use them and that a stitch in time saves nine.

One section was owned by the parents and was private property indeed. Fine needles and embroidery needles were inserted there and a thimble rested in the center. The children wondered why the elders used such a hindrance.

Strict rules were set for this useful household article. The older children were familiar with these rules when it was introduced to the younger. Occasionally the little fellow whose name was Arvid pulled the thread out of the needles and pushed them into the cushion to disappear. It had to be ripped open on one side and the contents removed and then sewn together.

Also occasionally the needles were misplaced and got into the wrong territory which caused friction in the family, and grandma settled many a quarrel amongst the children when she sat in the little rocking chair (now standing in your room) reassigning the needles and placing them in their respective order.

This little girl who herself now is a grandmother, has a pin cushion all her own thanks to a fine grandson in New Jersey.

Goodbye

This letter is a treasure not only for David but also for me. It indeed shows that my mother was a good writer, had a good imagination, and had a way of telling a story. I saved several notebooks of her writings and will pass them on to the family.

Note: The little rocking chair referred to is now residing in my great grandson's bedroom in San Francisco, California, and was previously rocked by his grandfather, David (Bean), and me, his great grandmother, Helen.

April 3, 2012

SWEDEN, HERE WE COME

It was the year of our 25th wedding anniversary, 1974. We talked about taking a trip, and finally made plans to go to Sweden. Both of us had relatives there, and we understood the language and could speak it at about a third grade level.

It was a thrill to finally be on an overnight SAS Airline flight out of New York. I stayed awake to watch for the rising sun and everything below. We landed in London and then on to Arlanda airport in Sweden. A bus transported us to Stockholm to a prearranged hotel. There we learned there was no reservation for us. Somehow our communication with the hotel was lost. With luggage in hand we were directed to a building that would make a reservation for us. A taxi took us to a small old hotel. I loved it with its windows opening to the street.

The next two days we walked and walked, ate Swedish meatballs and tasty pastries, saw beautiful historic churches, and visited Gamla Stan (Old Town), the King's Palace, and the Vasa Ship. This historic ship built during 1626-1628 sank after one nautical mile on its maiden voyage with a loss of fifty-three lives. It was recovered in 1961, after 333 years, and was now in the process of being restored by the spraying of seawater. It was a truly remarkable exhibit.

The next day we boarded a train south to Västerås, for a visit with Bert's cousin, Ann-Marie. When we arrived we had another big surprise. Lars Hollander met us together with Ann-Marie. Lars had lived with us in New Jersey a few years earlier and eventually we came to think of him as our third son. We had a great visit seeing the sights of this rather large city and catching up on news of our relatives. Ann-Marie had done research on a plan for us to see more of Sweden. We rented a car (a VW) and headed north to visit Bert's cousin in Kvissleby. There we heard more stories and saw pictures of more relatives.

Finally we headed west toward Norway crossing the border near Storlien, a famous ski resort. Once in Norway even though we spoke Swedish we realized that the language was quite different. If we listened carefully catching a few familiar words in each sentence we were ok. We stopped for gas and asked a kind gentleman how to get to "Trollstegen" (steps of the Troll). He told us that this road was built by the Germans during World War II.

After leaving Trondheim, a beautiful city, the climb began. We soon learned if a bus was going down the mountain, it was our duty to pull off on to the nearest stopping point before continuing. We finally made it to the top where we saw grazing sheep busy noshing. There were no trees, but small colorful flowers were scattered over the area. We stopped to take it all in. The view was incredible.

On our descent we came to a small village that had a ferryboat landing. Assuming we were going in that direction we got in line. A man soon came to our window and said (we thought), "The ferry will arrive in a few minutes, but the road ahead is closed because of a landslide." "Now what?" we mused. Hoping we had heard right, we turned around to go back down the Trollstegen. It was beginning to get dark, and a light rain started to fall, and the road was more treacherous. Would the brakes hold? With no guardrails could we navigate to avoid going over the edge? As I held my breath, my husband drove carefully until we were back to a highway heading south. At this point we were more than hungry. Finally we came to Lillehammer, the town now famous for the Olympics of 1994.

Lillehammer felt like an oasis—a motel, a hamburger dinner, and a good night's sleep prepared us to continue to see the sights the next day in Oslo, Norway. Finally we returned to Ann-Marie's home and two days later left for the USA.

There have been many untold stories in this presentation. They will come later in more detail. I promise.

Life is interesting, to say the least. Today, Monday, November 26, 2012, I received a letter from cousin Ann-Marie's son, Lars. In the letter he told of his mother's death on October 27 and that the funeral was November 26. It saddened me greatly since I have been with her on many occasions – once when she came to the United States, and the five times I have been in her home in Västerås. We have also talked on the phone and written many letters over the years. May God give the family strength and peace. I will miss her. But—life goes on, so I must proceed with my story.

November 26, 2012

LEARNING A NEW SKILL

Many times I have heard the old adage that one is never too old to learn something new. In this story I wasn't that old – but it certainly was a new skill and one that I have continued to use for the past 40+ years. It has become very handy in the following circumstances:

1. Calling a meeting to order
2. Calling the dog
3. Signaling family members
4. Hailing a taxi
5. Cheering a team score
6. Using this skill instead of applause at a concert
7. And not the least—just showing off.

So what is this tremendously fascinating feat? Let me first tell you how I acquired it.

Our son, David, who was seventeen years old, had just begun college in East Orange, New Jersey and lived on campus. He had a motorcycle and would pop into our home fairly regularly since the college was about forty-five minutes away. On his first visit I heard the roar of the motorcycle and met him at the back door. As he burst through the door he greeted me with the following, "Mom, I've learned something new that's fantastic". Of course I assumed it was related to one of his courses perhaps Mathematics or Chemistry. But no, it was not—he had learned to whistle with his fingers! He proudly showed his skill as we stood in the kitchen. "Okay," I said, and then added, "David, you are not allowed to leave this house until you show me how to do it."

We then stepped out the front door onto the cement walk. Again he showed his whistling skill and it reverberated throughout the neighborhood. I was filled with excitement. When we got down to the particulars it took me several tries but then I had it. This began a signature skill for which I have been known over many years. Can I do it today? Oh yes.

June 18, 2012

KENNETH JEWELL CHORALE

Once we were settled in our new parish in 1973 in Farmington Hills, Michigan, I began hearing about the Kenneth Jewell Chorale. Mr. Jewell was a nationally known choral conductor and instructor. The singers were all professional musicians, and gave several concerts during the year. The first time my husband and I attended a concert it became a dream to one day be a part of the organization.

Two years later I went for an audition. To say that I was nervous was an understatement. My husband went with me, trying to calm my nerves while waiting outside the rehearsal room. We could hear the singing. Finally we were asked to come into the room. Bert was my piano accompanist. The four section leaders and Mr. Jewell asked me a series of questions, and then asked me to sing. When I finished they thanked me and said I should wait in the hall.

Finally the door opened, and I was asked to come in. There were a few comments but what I wanted to hear was—am I in or out? They welcomed me with applause, and I was asked to join the second half of the rehearsal. I was seated in the alto section next to Barbara Windham, one of their famous soloists. She gave me assurance by sharing her score with me. I saw it was filled with pencil markings as reminders of tricky rhythms or added sharps or flats. I thought to myself if she who is a professional has to do this I certainly should do the same. My score from then on was filled with reminders.

For the next five years I was privileged to be a part of many performances. We toured with the Detroit Symphony Orchestra, Antal Dorati, conductor, to New York City and Washington, D.C. in 1979. We sang Strauss' Opera, "The Egyptian Helen" at New York's Carnegie Hall, and the Kennedy Center in Washington, D.C. London Records recorded the performance. The Chorale also recorded Christmas albums in 1976 and 1978. In addition we joined the Detroit Symphony in a Ravel opera, plus works of Bernstein and Stravinsky, Handel's Messiah, The Verdi Requiem, and Bach's St. John Passion. Our concerts were usually a mix of traditional and contemporary works. The women wore long dresses, and the men tuxedos. We were paid for each concert. We also sang in Detroit's Cobo Hall for their yearly automobile show.

In 1980 my husband had an opportunity to accept a new parish in Mansfield, Ohio. It was a large congregation with three pastors. He would be the Senior Pastor. Bert asked me how I felt about moving since I would have to give up the Kenneth Jewell Chorale. He knew how much I loved it. I was impressed that this potential move was not only for him. It included me. After I thought and prayed about it and decided that this was an opportunity for him, I agreed that he should accept the call. During my final concert with this wonderful choral my eyes welled up with tears. I found it difficult to sing. We moved shortly afterwards to Mansfield, Ohio.

January 28, 2014

DID WE MAKE A MISTAKE?

Making a decision sometimes has unexpected results. Case in point was an agreement my husband and I made to have a paroled prisoner come to live with us. His name was Barry. He was in prison in Michigan for robbery and drugs. He had nowhere to go upon release since his sister would not have him and his brother was too young. His mother and father were former members of our church. Both had committed suicide separately early in Barry's life. We did not know them. My husband visited Barry in prison several times. I went once. He seemed like a nice young man, tall, and well spoken. We decided to have him come. I was apprehensive knowing that I would have to deal with Barry during the day when my husband was working.

He arrived at the end of March 1977. At first he blended in with our plans, attended church, sang in the choir, went with us to a concert, church affairs and was cordial to our guests and neighbors. After a month or two it was time to help him find a job. After several inquiries a job offer came from one of our parishioners. Barry accepted. The problem was he did not have a car. Another parishioner countersigned for a suitable car. The job did not last—too much hard work, he said. He did not look for another job. With time on his hands he joined with unknown friends and was gone from home quite often.

In July of the same year we took a vacation and drove to see family in New Jersey. We left instructions with Barry to watch the house and our two dogs. He also had our telephone numbers in order to get in touch. We called home a couple times and learned that everything was okay. On our drive back home we had no idea of what lay ahead. We arrived about 7:00 p.m. When we opened the door, we were shocked at what we saw. The piano was in the middle of the living room, pictures that once hung on the walls were missing, and as we walked through the house it was obvious a significant robbery had taken place. We called the police, made a report, and then decided to go to a motel for the night. It was too unsettling to stay in the house. Our house had been violated.

The next morning when we came back it was worse than what we had first observed. I started to make a list of the missing items. My heart sank as the list grew longer and longer. Also my anger began to boil as I thought about all we had done for Barry. How could he betray us in this manner was my question I asked my husband, "Where did we go wrong that he could do this to us?" He answered, "We didn't do anything wrong. *He* did." Looking back it took a long time for me to accept this.

While making a list for insurance purposes I realized that I was discovering more and more stolen items. Missing was my grandmother's old treadle sewing machine, a silver butter dish that dated back to my grandparents wedding, and *all* our glassware, linens, bedding, and sterling silverware. He even found a bag of Indianhead pennies hidden in my closet. It became clear why the piano was left: it was too heavy to drag through the house to a truck parked in our garage. (Barry had an accomplice.) I was angry and mourned the loss of these precious items. I couldn't sleep.

A couple of weeks later the police called to ask if we had owned a stereo. They gave me the numbers listed on the unit and it matched numbers I had on file. Interestingly enough the stereo had been sold to a cousin of Barry's robbery partner. This cousin became suspicious when she found a tape in the tape deck that was a recording of an Easter service at our church. The stereo was returned to us.

Another clue came in our telephone bill. There were lots and lots of telephone calls made that became useful information to the police and resulted in the arrest of Barry's partner. He was charged and a court case proved him guilty. Bert had to testify. This was very stressful for both of us. The partner was jailed.

All during this time Barry was on the run. He called my husband many times. He vacillated between crying and apologizing for his actions, and then changed his story threatening to malign my husband's name with false accusations. This went on until the first Saturday in December when he called the police to turn himself in. He said he was tired of running. The weather was below freezing.

A trial was set for December 23. The day before Christmas Eve was no time for a pastor to have to go to trial. While we sat nervously waiting in the court house hallway, we were informed that the bus bringing Barry from the prison broke down. The trial was dismissed when he copped a plea and was returned to prison.

Did this end our trauma? Not for me. Whenever the doorbell rang I immediately wondered if Barry had escaped from prison and was standing at the door. Also I had a difficult time consuming job of listing all the stolen items for our insurance company. The total was over $10,000.

As to the trauma for my husband? Of course he suffered stress and remorse over the actions of Barry who should have made a better life choice. But, again I was reminded that we did not make a mistake—Barry did.

July 31, 2012

PARTNERSHIPS

On my bedside table the clock-radio is set to automatically turn on at 7:00 a.m.. It provides me with the latest news, weather, traffic report, and commercials. I listen to everything except the commercials until one day when the following commercial caught my attention. The announcer said, "Where would Barnum be without Bailey?" and then followed by, "Come to the most mediocre circus in town." and followed by still a third, "Where would Orville be without Wright?" All this concluded with the sound of a motor, a crash, and the comment, "Well, I guess that isn't going to work." The subject was about partnerships, and something about Kaiser Permanente, a health organization. I didn't get the point. That's when I clicked off and got up to start the day.

But then I thought about a couple more examples. If it wasn't for Abbott and Costello, we would never have known "who was on first?" Or, how would Fred Astaire dance cheek to cheek without Ginger Rogers? Partnerships are an important element in our lives. Oh, maybe not as "partners in crime," but there are good partners. In my case it was my parents. They demonstrated love for one another: a kiss at the door when Dad left for work, and always thanking Mother for each meal, and her care of the household affairs. These were daily actions.

When I began seriously dating Bert, he also commented on my parents' behavior with one another. I firmly believe one of the reasons our marriage lasted for forty-four years was because of what we experienced day after day in our childhood homes. Bert's father died when Bert was sixteen years old. He wrote and published a book in 1991 titled *Crazy Swedes and Other Wonderful Loons*. It related many stories about his parents that also attested to the fact of their love for one another.

Marriage, if we are lucky, can last for years. If it is a good partnership with a lot of give and take and love, it can be ideal. If one member of the partnership dies, a new partner may appear on the scene bringing new life for a few more years. In my case no one ever measured up to what I had with Bert. When we first met in college, we soon learned of our similar backgrounds: our parents were Swedish, both of us had studied piano since early childhood, and our religious backgrounds were compatible. And—he was tall, dark, and handsome. I was tall.

I would be remiss if I didn't mention the great partnership my husband and I had. We often discussed our problems but sometimes we disagreed, albeit a few decibels louder. It usually turned out that Bert "had a better idea." I say this because it is true. He often amazed me with his intellect and good judgement even though I couldn't see it at the time. One thing he asked of me was to totally take care of our budget and paying the bills. He trusted me to make good judgements. If Bert needed cash I would give it to him. One thing we occasionally disagreed about was the amount to give to our church. He always wanted to give more. Every year in January the amount was always increased.

Another area he insisted that I take care of was when we decided to invite friends to our house for dinner. I don't know why but in this situation I was a procrastinator. All sorts of reasons to delay making the calls crossed my mind. For instance, I wondered if the date be suitable. Also, is it a good mix of personalities, and who should I call first, and what if they cannot come, and on and on. Finally after several times of Bert asking if I had made the calls, I then, but not before, was forced to begin the task. To this day I often put off making specific calls with reasons that seem logical to me. Why? I have no idea.

March 4, 2013

PS: I do not believe in horoscopes but this one caught my attention.

Horoscope for March 4:–

"Defer to others, and know full well what must be done. Understand that Lady Luck is riding on your shoulder. You will gain a greater understanding of the interpersonal dynamics of an important partnership. Opportunities come through this person. Tonight: Say "yes." (Gemini)

BOGIE, A DOG TO REMEMBER

Bogie, short for Bogart, was David's dog. He was an English Setter who was never still except when sleeping. Bogie was a puppy, cute, not cuddly, but who couldn't love this little furry animal. He tolerated our number one dog, a mutt named Mickey.

Bogie and David left our home in Tenafly, New Jersey in his car filled with his belonging heading for graduate school at Lehigh University in Bethlehem, Pennsylvania. After he arrived it wasn't long before trouble began. Bogie was closed up in David's one-room off-campus apartment. While David was in class, Bogie had lots of fun finding things to keep him busy during this time such as tearing papers, chewing on shoes, and making messes. It soon became obvious it was not going to work to have a dog living with him. What to do. On his first visit back home a deal was made to leave Bogie with us until the end of his first year. That's when trouble began.

Bogie hated to be chained in the yard and would often escape. Trying to catch him was difficult. He would run through the neighborhood with me after him to no avail until one of us gave in. Bogie also was a terror in the house unless he was sleeping. I needed to watch him closely. One day he stole a half pound of butter off the counter, plus parts of a raw chicken. He also ate most of a Christmas wreath made of pinecones, plus—would you believe—one of my bronzed baby shoes. The evidence was the tiny bronzed button I found on the floor. Whenever the doorbell rang, he was the first one to the door barking and jumping up and down followed by racing through the house and returning to terrorize young and old.

As he grew in size his stature was quite intimidating. When awake he was never still so it was even difficult to pet him. A couple of years later we moved to Michigan and took both dogs with us. Bogie had to be tranquilized (out cold) and was safely placed in the backseat of our VW along with Mickey who was used to riding in the car with Jesse, the driver.

One of the first things we did after our move was to find a vet that had an office close to our home. One day it was necessary to take Bogie to the vet. I left the house in my little VW with Bogie situated in the back seat. There were no seat belts. There had been a significant snowstorm two days earlier so the roads were still a bit icy and the plows had pushed a significant amount of snow to each side of the road.

While I was driving, Bogie decided to jump over the front seat landing directly into my lap. My vision was completely obscured. The only thing I could think to do was steer the car onto the right shoulder. As a result my car sank in about a foot of snow. I was stuck. I was going nowhere. Almost immediately a car pulled alongside, rolled down their window and asked if they could be of some help. I answered yes, and asked if I could take the dog with me. They agreed. I grabbed a hold of his leash, opened my door, and with that Bogie darted out the door and soon disappeared into a wooded area. What to do? I told the generous couple that I wouldn't be able to leave without my dog. They drove on.

Not long after another car came from the opposite direction, stopped and asked if she could make a phone call for me. I said yes and in order to not stop traffic on this two lane road, she drove her car to the opposite shoulder and—you guessed it—she, too, sank in about a foot of snow. She opened her window and yelled angrily for me to go to the nearest house to call a tow truck. Before I could get out of the car another car came. This driver recognized her friend's car and the two of them left for parts unknown.

While I sat trying to make sense of what had just happened, a nice young man in a pickup truck stopped and said he would be glad to pull me out of the snow. As I got out of my car I heard a voice at the top of the road saying "IS THIS YOUR DOG?" Would you believe that I hesitated and almost shouted, "NO WAY." But instead I retrieved Bogie, put him back in the car, made a U-turn and headed for home. I called the vet with an explanation of why we were not keeping our appointment. Later we learned that English Setters are basically hunters and love to run. This explained his running whenever he got loose.

There are many more stories about this animal—but let me tell you one more. Our American flag was propped up in a corner of our back hall. Bogie ate it.

June 26, 2012

FAMILY TRADITIONS

In the famous Broadway Show "Fiddler on the Roof," Tevye, the father, sings the joyous song "Tradition" with great conviction. This song highlights some of the family traditions that for centuries have been a part of this Jewish family and literally for all Jews. He sings it with pride while the family dances. As I thought about it I began remembering some traditions that have been a part of my family.

The first one that came to mind was regarding birthdays. For over 100 years a pedestal cake plate was always used to carry a birthday cake. My maternal grandmother originally owned it. Her cakes were baked in a wood stove and were proudly set on this shiny glass plate. When Grandma came to live with us the plate was given to my mother. The fact that the cake was elevated made it indeed appear very special. When mother came into the dining room carrying the pedestaled cake with candles flickering, she would carry it with pomp as the birthday song was lustily sung. With a silver handled cake knife, even slices were cut for each of us.

Many years later when I married, the plate was passed to me and used for years in the same manner. When I was preparing to move and selecting items to bring to California, I knew I would not be baking cakes anymore so I gave the plate to my daughter-in-law. And guess what? On one of my recent birthdays at their home in Glen Ellen, California, the plate continued its function and tradition. It was such a joy to realize that the old tradition was still being used. Thanks, Mom.

The second tradition that I remember also had to do with birthdays. I honestly do not remember when or how it started. All I know it was started after I was married. Whenever someone had a birthday, a candle would appear in something edible. It could be in the center of a grapefruit half or a large pastry for breakfast, and it always was a surprise to the birthday person. One time I made a hole in a hot dog bun and stuck a large candle in the center. The funniest was a candle in the middle of a bowl of oatmeal.

One summer my husband was forced to spend two months in bed after a heart attack. He had to cut out sweets and his birthday came during this time. I knew exactly what to do. I found an empty round tin box that had held a fruit cake. I covered the tin with heavy shiny white paper, used frosting to write "Happy Birthday," and attached small candles and a large one in the center. When I walked into the bedroom with the faux cake singing Happy Birthday, Bert looked at me and said sadly, "You know I can't eat cake". I assured him that none of us would eat this one. He chuckled and seemed pleased and blew out the candles.

Our adopted son Jesse had been with us a little over one year and had observed this silly tradition of birthday candles in something. A few days before his seventeenth birthday I asked him if he would like a birthday party. "No," he said and then added with a smile, "just put a candle in something and that will be fine." He became a true member of the Anderson family on that day.

Most traditions continue for years. This was not the case with the tradition of getting "a candle in something." Maybe it needed a rest. After all it was not one of the popular traditions in Tevye's family, and probably not found in any family. Many years later, however, it showed up one more time at my 80th surprise birthday party with family and friends. When it was time to sing the birthday song, I alone was served one piece of cake with a lit candle in the center and told it was a reminder of the past. My, oh my, maybe the tradition is still alive. I guess time will tell.

October 16, 2012

MUSIC KIDS SAY AND DO THE DARNDEST THINGS

Here are three fun stories.

1. It was a Saturday morning and I was about to begin a rehearsal with the junior choir at the Augustana Lutheran Church in Minneapolis. There were 30 children seated in tiered seats in three rows in the choir room. We had music to rehearse for next Sunday, and anthems to learn for Sunday services. At this rehearsal I decided to teach the children some musical terms that appeared in all our music. I began by explaining "p" for *piano*, meaning soft, and "f" for *forte*, meaning loud, followed by the word "*ritard*," indicating to gradually grow slower.

During the lesson I became aware of Robert who was not paying attention, so, of course, I called on him and said, "Okay Robert, stand up and tell us the meaning of the word "ritard." It was obvious he had not been listening, for he paused a moment and then said—"I think it means when someone is 65 years old and quits work." I gave him credit for quick thinking. He obviously was describing the word "retired." This young lad became a physician and most likely is retired!

2. It was a Thursday afternoon in my piano studio. Nicholas was at the piano having a difficult time keeping the beat (rhythm) of the piece he was playing. I had him clap the rhythm, I sang the song several times with him as he played, and we counted aloud the rhythm and still it was incorrect. I then reached for my metronome, a small instrument that could be set to a particular beat, speed and volume. Nicholas continued with the same rhythm problem as the metronome kept going and I kept singing.

I'm sure Nicholas was happy when the lesson was over as he quickly bounded up the stairs to his awaiting father. By the time I climbed the stairs he had gone out to the car and his father was waiting for me. I could tell that he wanted to say something. With a big grin he said, "When Nicholas came up the stairs I told him he looked so sad so I asked him, Nicholas, what's the problem?" He said Nicholas paused and then said, "Well, if Mrs. Anderson would quit singing and using that *thermometer*, I could do a lot better." Needless to say I made a note to explain the difference between a thermometer and a metronome at the next lesson.

3. It was another children's choir session. It was popular for boys to have water pistols, and it appeared that most every boy had one at this rehearsal. At first I asked them kindly to put the pistols away but soon learned that my directive was not being obeyed. The pistols kept appearing first here and then there. My next move, I asked for the pistols to be deposited in a box with the assurance that they would receive them back after the rehearsal. Well, my eagle eye kept spotting additional fire arms. This called for drastic measures. I summoned all the boys to leave their seats, line up against the wall with their hands placed on the wall above their heads, and I began a body search for the elusive guns. Much to the enjoyment of the girls in the choir (and for the boys), two additional guns were added to the stash.

At this point I turned and realized that there were parents in the hall watching us through the window. They were obviously enjoying what they saw. I was not sure if my action would be considered "cruel and unusual punishment" but seeing them with big grins on their faces it made me also enjoy the moment. And admittedly it has been a great story to tell all these years.

April 10, 2012

MAKING A WORTHWHILE DISCOVERY

Before I moved to California, a family where I lived in Ohio gave me information about a monument that was unique. It was in New Jersey, and I was able to discover it while visiting my New Jersey family in 2009. On a sunny Sunday afternoon, Virginia, my daughter-in-law, and I set out with directions from her GPS to find what was called The Russian Teardrop Monument. It was located in Bayonne, New Jersey about twelve or so miles from our starting point of Elizabeth, New Jersey. We had great difficulty locating it since the directions took us only so far and no monument was in sight. After several attempts we decided to continue on the road and there in the distance we saw the top of what appeared to be the structure we were looking for.

We parked the car and walked to the fence that framed a beautiful structure that shone brightly in the afternoon sun. A sign at the entrance said that the monument was a gift from the Russian people after the destruction of the Twin Towers in Manhattan on September 11, 2001, and added the words, "To the Struggle against World Terrorism."

The monument was 100 feet tall. The jagged lines divided the monument into two tower-like pieces and a 40 foot steel teardrop gently hung in the open center like a bell. Around the base were names, carved in black granite, of all of the people who lost their lives on that fateful day. There were 3,024 names listed.

I learned that the original site for the monument was to have been in Jersey City, New Jersey, but the city turned it down because it obstructed their view of the New York skyline and the Statue of Liberty. After this the Bayonne citizens accepted the project and prepared the land for the monument to be erected.

The monument came in five parts—four to become the memorial, two on each side, plus the teardrop. It weighed 175 tons. The cost to install was $2.2 million. The artist was Jurab Tsereteli, a Russian, who was seventy-two years old at the time. He was present at the dedication on September 11, 2006. LeAnn Rimes sang "Amazing Grace" on the program.

The massive memorial points to the World Trade Center and the Twin Towers that once sat in full view across the Hudson River. Also, the Statue of Liberty is in full view. Colorful flowers and several trees graced the small patch of land, plus the flag of the United States.

One must be cognizant of this remarkable donation by the Russian people. No matter what one thinks of the politics of the country, I am so grateful that this memorial was accepted. My only regret is that it is difficult to find, and most likely unknown by the majority of US citizens.

August 13, 2013

FIRST ENGLISH LUTHERAN CHURCH, MANSFIELD OHIO 1980 -1989

In 1980 Bert accepted a call to serve as Senior Pastor at First English Lutheran Church, Mansfield, Ohio. He knew it was not going to be easy leaving Antioch Lutheran Church in Farmington Hills, Michigan for it had been our home for nearly seven years and things were going well. We had moved before but to leave this parish was a difficult choice. However, the decision was made and we moved in May 1980.

Anyone who has moved knows the tedious job of unpacking boxes. As I was pondering where and how to begin, the doorbell rang. When I opened the door a woman and her young daughter introduced themselves, said they lived down the street, and asked if they could help me unpack. Their request took me by surprise for I was not ready to have company or help, so I declined their offer with grateful thanks. It was obvious that they felt rejected and I felt guilty. Unfortunately we never met again.

The church building was an imposing figure in the city's downtown. With its prominently lighted bell tower, a façade of old granite sandstone and its many peaks and spires, it was easy to see on Park Avenue West. Inside the large sanctuary was a curved balcony (three sides), and two beautiful large stained glass windows on the east and west side of the balcony.

The attached four story education building was built several years before we arrived. On the first floor were three central offices, plus a chapel for 50-60 people. The chapel was used for Saturday evening worship. In addition it served for smaller funerals, weddings, and Lenten and Advent services. The chapel had a two manual organ and a piano. Continuing down the hall was "The Emmaus" room, a large meeting area that included a kitchen. The second floor had studies for each of the two pastors, many class rooms and a library. Additional class rooms occupied the third floor. A penthouse on the fourth floor was occupied by a couple hired for security duties. I was grateful there was an elevator. The lower level beneath the sanctuary had a well equipped kitchen, several Sunday School rooms plus a large meeting space that included a stage. The reason for giving you this information is to point out that there was a great deal of ministry going on before our arrival. The church was thriving under the ministry of Pastor Jerry Schmallenberger.

Picture 11: Installation Sunday at First English Lutheran Church, 1980

And so we began. I say we because even though I was not employed until one year later, I chose to attend many events and meetings in order to become better acquainted. A group of seniors who met once a month on Friday morning for a program and lunch was one of my favorites. "Friendly Fridays" was specifically for those who were 80+ years. Even though I was only fifty-three, I felt at home.

Bert was very busy on Saturdays. As a result I had the day for myself, so I decided to explore my new city. On the first Saturday I made a list of every Thrift store in town. On the next three Saturdays I went in, walk every aisle and you guessed it—I always found something I couldn't live without!

Mansfield was called the "City of Churches" so I made a list of the churches. The Roman Catholic Church, United Christian, Methodist, and Episcopal, were in the downtown area. I was pleased to see their old stately buildings still standing. While driving around the city I learned the layout of the city and was an aid to Bert when he was unsure how to find his way.

In 1981 I was appointed full time Music Director/Organist. Marty, a delightful woman and an excellent organist/Music Director, found it necessary to resign in order to take care of her mother who was gravely ill. I was truly sorry to see her leave. We had become good friends. During her final Sunday, I remember going downstairs to have a good cry.

One day a member of the congregation asked if Sweden had any special event that the congregation could celebrate. He said the previous pastor had introduced "Fastnacht," a German celebration held the night before Ash Wednesday. (The term Fastnacht means "fat night"—a time to get rid of all the fat before the Lenten season begins.) On that evening there was a dinner of pancakes, sausages, sauerkraut, applesauce, and ice cream followed by "in house entertainment." One of the many Sunday School classes would be responsible

In determining a Swedish event, I thought of Saint Lucia's Day, a Swedish tradition celebrated each year on or near December 13 in Sweden and also in many areas of the USA. The more I thought about it the more excited I became and began writing a script and got help making costumes. A member of the congregation constructed a battery powered wreath to be worn on the head of the chosen Lucia. It had six candles that could be turned off or on. (In Sweden Lucia wreathes use live candles. I didn't want to take a chance of fire.) In the ancient story Lucia was engaged to be married. She was wealthy and secretly was using her dowry to help the poor. She would travel by night carrying food for the hungry. Her hands were occupied so she positioned a candle on her head in order to find her way. Since she was to marry, her fiancée was angry that monies were being swallowed up that were designated for him. Lucia's fate? She was burned at the stake.

In the high school Sunday School class, five girls were chosen by secret ballot, and Lucia was one of the five. This was determined by the Sunday School teacher, and revealed during the program when my husband opened the envelope. I admonished him not to mention that it was similar to the Miss America pageant. Sure enough that's exactly what he did. We had words on the way home.

The first program was in the main sanctuary on a Sunday evening closest to December 13. Every year the outline of the service was the same: a choice of hymns, special music and the Lucia story told in a different way each year in order to keep the story fresh. That was a challenge. The program continued for eleven years.

Here is a picture of Lucia and her court:

Picture 12: Lucia and her court

One day I came across "Saints Alive," a musical specifically for retirees. The Sunday School class loved it and was eager to learn the music and put on the show. After weeks of practice we presented it during the church's "Fastnacht" celebration. It was so much fun that we took it on the road and presented it at other churches in the area. You can read all about it in the story called "Saints Alive— a Musical."

Soon after Bert died in 1993 I wanted to find a way to express his life using generous memorial monies that had been given. I reasoned that the church didn't need another plaque on the wall. I discussed it with Pastor Phil Carl who had been our Associate Pastor and was now serving at Good Shepherd, a senior center, in nearby Ashland, Ohio. He knew Bert well and Bert was very fond of him. When Phil suggested a lecture series, I knew it was the perfect answer!

A committee was formed, a constitution written and Dr. Walter Bouman, professor at Trinity Lutheran Seminary in Columbus, Ohio was the first presenter.

It was 1994. His subject was the life of Dr. Martin Luther. Each year a presenter was chosen. The series continued for sixteen years.

As one would expect there were many comical unexpected happenings in those first few years. I'll never forget what took place one Christmas Eve. Imagine the scene: A crowded church, hanging wreaths with white lights and white bows strung around the balcony, two gorgeous trees with tiny white lights, candles in every window, and an Advent Wreath with flickering candles made the sanctuary an impressive sight. The service was nearly over. It was past midnight, and we were about to sing "Silent Night," the closing hymn. Alongside the organ console was a panel of buttons and switches plus a telephone. The telephone allowed me to be in contact with the sound booth in the balcony where the service was broadcast. Also, I was able to raise and lower the sanctuary lights. I reached over, lowered the lights, and played the introduction for Silent Night. The congregation sang with intent. When the hymn was finished, the choir began to recess while I continued to play since the station did not want any "dead-air". At this point I was quietly improvising (playing my own choice) when suddenly I realized I was playing "Happy Birthday to you. . ." I heard a few snickers of controlled laughter. Quickly I tried to determine what to do. Should I abruptly stop or continue? After all, I reasoned, it is Jesus' birthday. I played on.

When the service was over, I raised the lights and began the Postlude. Not long afterwards I saw Bert coming down the aisle. As he walked behind the organ console toward the Sacristy I heard him say one word. In a deliberate tone of voice he said, "Tacky!" It was obvious that he thought what I did was inappropriate. Was he right? Well, needless to say, I never did it again.

The life of a pastor is always full of surprises. In the midst of many meetings, hospital visits, funerals, weddings, Bible Study groups, confirmation classes, and time for sermon preparations, there were times when he would leave his office and play the organ in the empty sanctuary. He had a vast repertoire from his years studying organ and serving as organist. He said many times when playing, he escaped interruptions and his mind could continue to work on a sermon or Bible study material. (Musicians will understand how this works.) Bert was very diligent in preparing his sermons and spent the entire week preparing.

The junior choir performed several biblical presentations on stage. "Daniel" and "Jonah" were favorites. The senior choir presented a program that was a big hit. Each member was asked to fashion their black cassock and white alb in a unique way for a program called, "Choir Member of the Year," much like Miss America. They were judged by three ten-year-old boys, each wearing a red bow tie—and coincidentally, all named Matt, Matt, and Matt. Each Matt had a scorecard to register his vote of 1 through 10, 10 being the highest. The totals were tallied to find First, Second, and Third place. One couple fastened Christmas lights on their robes and sang "Let the Lower Lights be Burning." The big winner was Dotty playing the lamps, turning them on and off to the tune of "The Blue Danube." She was crowned with a Burger King crown!!

Bert was very conscientious in his role as Pastor. One example I will never forget. We were at the home of one of the members. There was lots of conversation. I loved it. Long before I even thought about going home, Bert said, "get your coat, we have to leave." I must have questioned his request since he made it clear that it had to be now! When we got in the car he explained he needed to go to the hospital. But it is past visiting hours, I thought. Arriving we went directly to a patient's room. As we entered, the gentleman appeared to be sleeping. His wife and two daughters greeted us. Bert approached the bed, knelt down and took his hand. I observed he was taking his pulse. (Given Bert's time in the Navy as an Operating Room Technician, and working at a hospital in Chicago after his term of service, I knew what he was doing.) A few minutes later the family asked if Bert and I would mind staying so they could go to the cafeteria. "It has been a long day," they said. Bert stood up slowly turned to them and said, "I suggest you wait. He is dying right now." I was stunned. I thought how did he know? Did he actually receive a message from God? All I know the family was grateful for his presence and prayers.

Both of us were involved in several activities in the city. Bert joined the Kiwanis Club, attended their noon lunches, played the piano and served on committees. He rang Salvation Army bells one Saturday during the holidays. He also was a member of the local Ethics Committee at the Mansfield General Hospital. And then there were many times he was asked to speak. It always amazed me how eloquently he spoke, sometimes on the spur of the moment.

For me Church Women United, a national, ecumenical Christian women's movement representing Protestant, Roman Catholic, Orthodox, and other Christian women, soon became my priority. It was good to meet together and be actively involved in many causes. At one point I was the local president.

The time finally came when it was clear Bert needed to retire. He was living with a debilitating illness called cardiomyopathy that became increasingly more invasive. Several trips to the local hospital and the Cleveland Clinic, and with the advice of his doctors, he made the decision to retire. He announced to the Church Council the chosen date - Sunday, June 4, 1989. I also submitted my resignation. His physician, Dr. Donald Beddard, a member of the church, expressed his concern to both of us that he had recently seen Bert having problems during several worship services. He had observed him sitting on a stool in the pulpit. Another time he preached sitting on the top step in the chancel. Can you imagine what was going through my head and heart watching him from my seat at the organ?

During the remaining years the ambulance made several trips to our home. A few days of treatment and once again he'd be back home. However, there were times when I was not certain he was going to make it. I remember an evening when I was scheduled to play the piano for a high school presentation of the musical, "Guys and Dolls." On my way to the school I first stopped at the hospital to see Bert. I expressed my nervousness and asked if he had any advice for me? His answer: "Be sure to keep your 4th finger on B-flat". (Every pianist knows the fingering of right hand flat scales has the 4th finger on B-flat.) Even though he was not doing well he still had that twinkle in his eye and made a comical remark to calm my nerves. After the performance I raced back to the hospital not knowing if he'd still be alive. He was awake and I stayed answering his questions about the performance.

The church went all out for our last Sunday. But first let me tell you about Bert's plan for his final Sunday. It was clear that he wanted the service not to be about him, so he chose confirming 9 high school students. This was his focus. His sermon was directed to the confirmands, the hymns, and the positive feelings were obviously planned carefully. It wasn't until the closing hymn, "I Love to Tell the Story" (his favorite) had been sung, that the Church Council President, Bob McCready, made a gracious presentation on behalf of the congregation. We were overwhelmed with a bountiful check. A beautiful luncheon followed in the undercroft. Later we were treated to a hilarious comedy skit in the sanctuary. I remember laughing so hard that I almost lost my breath. The skit was written by former pastor, Phil Carl. Our sons David and Jesse came plus several friends from near and far.

During our retirement I continued to teach piano, had student recitals, prepared students for contests and attended musical workshops. In addition I was a substitute organist in many local churches. We also purchased a two manual electronic organ for our home. It was a help for me, and also for Bert to continue his love of music, playing from his vast organ repertoire. He also conducted services and preached in several neighboring churches.

Several years later, after Bert died, the subject of homosexuality was in the news media and in particular at First English Lutheran Church. There was a great deal of conflicting information making the subject complicated. Feelings soon intensified and the subject erupted in my church from pulpit and pew. At this point I realized that I was in opposition to what I heard on Sunday morning. *The Lutheran*, the church's monthly magazine, began to discuss the subject in each issue. Also, the national ELCA Church announced a sexuality in-depth study for congregations. When it arrived my two pastors led the study. It soon became obvious to me that there was a wide division. It was an incredibly emotional and an uncomfortable time.

In 2009 delegates and clergy of the ELCA met for meetings in Minneapolis, Minnesota. Previously a question to admit "active" gays into the clergy was in effect if they promised to remain celibate. In 2011 the subject front and center was to endorse gay marriage. After several days of heated debate the final vote was to accept gay men and women to not only serve as pastors but permitted to marry. This historic decision was only the beginning of further intense discussion. The ELCA churches were permitted to agree or disagree by holding two congregational meetings several months apart. At these meetings each name was carefully identified as a bone fide member. All members were allowed five minutes to speak.

I said the following:

In the first decade of my life my mother warned me about new neighbors that had moved into the neighborhood. She said we needed to be careful because they were Catholic. However my mother and Edith became friends and drank lots of coffee in our kitchen. Their daughter, Patty joined the rest of the kids in the neighborhood and there was no problem. I am pleased to say regarding Catholics, I have attended Mass, sung the familiar hymns, and prayed the prayers. Also, I served one Sunday as organist for Mass. Over the years I've had Catholic friends; we often shared our faith. THANK GOD FOR THE CHANGE!

In the second decade of my life I was on the way to First Covenant Church, downtown, Minneapolis with my father. As we passed through a black neighborhood I asked him why black people lived under such poor conditions. I pointed out their run down houses, discarded autos, and junk in the yard. His answer was, "They have always lived that way. We just don't bother them. They seem to be happy." Over the years I've had many black friends. Even though some progress has been made, bigotry still remains. THANK GOD FOR SIGNIFICANT CHANGE!

"In the third decade of my life the women's issue was front and center. Women were speaking forcefully about the inequalities in the job market and they were asking for equal pay. One slogan became front and center—"breaking the glass ceiling in board room and life." As of today women are presidents of famous companies, in colleges, and as senators, and representatives, and now there are even women pastors. More needs are waiting for resolution. I THANK GOD FOR THE CHANGE!

Now in the fourth decade of my life, the Evangelical Lutheran Church's acceptance of gay men and women has called for studies of homosexuality, including their role in the church. Unfortunately this is the reason we are meeting here today. So my question today, WHEN WILL THE CHANGE COME?

Within a few months some congregations broke off from the ELCA over the denomination's liberal stand. My church (First English, Mansfield) was one of them. I was devastated! This is the church where my husband and I had served for many years, and after his death I continued to be a part of the worshipping community. What to do? Ultimately I concluded that the inclusive Word of God was presented with greater abundance elsewhere. It was required for each congregation to vote either to agree or disagree to include gay pastors in the body of the Evangelical Lutheran Church. After two meetings it was a heart wrenching act when the votes were counted and my church announced they would be separating from the ELCA. I mourned deeply.

Those of us who embraced the vote of gay acceptance joined together. We called ourselves "The Remnants," and saw the need to continue regular worship. The pastor of St. Luke Lutheran agreed that we could meet there for worship on Sunday evenings. It was a very deep wound for all of us, and we needed to support one another for healing. We met in the sanctuary and St. Luke's pastor conducted the service and offered a sermon. After six weeks it was time for each of us to make our own choice so we agreed to disband. The final communion service ended with tears and hugs. Within several months most joined a church of their choice. I became a member at St. Luke, Mansfield, primarily since it had a significant mission in the community. I remained there until I moved to California the summer of 2011.

July 30, 2017

"SAINTS ALIVE"—A MUSICAL

The mailboxes for the staff at First English Lutheran Church were near the front entrance of the Education Building. One day I found a notice in my mailbox about a musical designated for senior citizens entitled, "SAINTS ALIVE." As I thumbed through the pages, I realized its possibilities. Since the church was an old downtown church, there were a large number of senior citizens. The members of the Homebuilders Sunday School class were ideal candidates. The class was named Homebuilders because it was formed during World War II, when most of them were buying their first homes. They had been together as a class for many years. Everyone was retired. I presented the idea, and immediately they decided - yes. We met the following Wednesday morning at 10:00 a.m. to hear what I had in mind.

At precisely 10:00 a.m. the entire class was waiting in the undercroft (the lower level of the Education Building). I passed out one song I had copied. They found it easy to sing and as the dialog was read I could see their enthusiasm growing. A vote was taken, they agreed to do it, and rehearsal schedules were arranged. Each person agreed to purchase their own copy of "Saints Alive" and to meet every Wednesday morning at 10.

The next Wednesday when I arrived a bit late everyone was waiting. "Where have you been? We've been waiting for you." From then on there were no absences and the rehearsals were full of energy. Everyone was in agreement to make it a good performance.

It didn't take long before I sensed that many of them had already memorized the music so it was time to fill the speaking and vocal solos. I was amazed who volunteered to read and/or sing solos. One woman spoke to me in private saying that she was dumbfounded that her husband agreed to sing a solo. "He has always refused to sing in the choir," she said, and then added, "You performed some kind of magic—I can't believe he is going to do this.". Now it was time to get on the stage and make "Saints Alive" come to life. To me it was a big challenge. I was young: they were worldly wise.

Everyone was like putty in my hands! Everything I suggested they were willing to try. I had them seated in two rows of chairs and I wanted them to stand at a certain point in the music. Because some had leg, hip, or knee problems, I challenged each of them to figure out how long it would take to stand up, and to then mark the spot in their music where they should *begin* to stand. They thought this was hilarious. When the music required singing a song as a round I explained the round as in "Row, Row, Row Your Boat." They did fairly well. I may have pushed the envelope to form three circles on the stage—and here's the difficulty—to sing the song while walking in circles. At first it was chaotic but they soon mastered it! Laughter sure helped. Oh, my, this was chaotic but they were determined and so was I.

The musical was scheduled for Tuesday night before Ash Wednesday. The church had been celebrating a tradition called "Fastnacht" for several years with a menu of pancakes, sauerkraut, sausages, and applesauce. There always was some form of entertainment, and this year we were it.

Picture 13: We are looking good!

We wore short-sleeved white t-shirts and each member chose words from the musical to display on the front of their shirts, e.g., Golden Years, New Saints, Priceless Antiques. My shirt was prepared by one of the members. On the back it said: "Director, Saint Helen." We were now ready to perform.

The night arrived and after a short pep talk the stage curtain opened. I sat at the piano on the main floor facing the stage. It all went well, and resounding applause came at the end as the group took their bows.

Needless to say their enthusiasm was not diminished. They did not want it to end. So arrangements were made to present "SAINTS ALIVE" at Trinity Lutheran Church, in Ashland, Ohio, and a couple weeks later at St. Mark Lutheran in Mansfield. We traveled in the church bus.

The final cherry on the cake was a party at the parsonage with everyone agreeing how great we were!

May 13, 2014

TWO STUPID THINGS I HAVE DONE

It was difficult to choose only two because during my life I have done many stupid things. However, one or more genes inside me always prompted me to laugh when I had been stupid.

Here are two examples:

(1) It was Tuesday—I had ironing to do. I plugged in the iron, picked it up and something rattled. I shook it, and it was very obvious that something was loose and it did not heat. So I set about to see what caused the problem. With a screwdriver in hand, I sat down on a living room chair. I loosened each screw and carefully placed it in order on my apron covering my lap. The doorbell rang. I gathered my apron with the remaining parts and went to the door. I dismissed the sales person, went back to the chair, laid out my apron, and realized I had messed up the order I had so carefully laid out. I put it back together. It didn't work, so I took it to an electrical repair shop on the avenue. He said he'd call when ready. "I don't know what happened but there seems to be some missing parts," he said. I bought a new iron, didn't tell him or my husband and laughed on the way home.

(2) The Blue Angels were coming to Mansfield. My husband and I went to the airport early to get a good position. My excitement was obvious. Finally they landed and the pilots stepped out of their individual planes. An announcement was made that family members were allowed to go out to greet the pilots. I swear I didn't hear the words "family members" and rushed out on the runway to greet my heroes. I was met by a police officer who said, "Do you have a family member here?" I sheepishly answered no, and had to walk back towards the crowd with a silly grin on my face—or was it egg?

March 19, 2013

OH NO, ANOTHER WORD HUNT

By this time you must realize my love for words. Finding amusing word similarities, and the many usages of a single word, and then actually writing a story about it is enjoyable. Why do I do this? It must have something to do with my brain activity and how the brain likes patterns. I like most things to be neat. I like things in a row to be straight and even, and I even fold newspapers and towels so their edges meet. Is this normal behavior?

This morning a word popped into my brain the moment I awakened and immediately I began to think about its many usages. The simple word: SCHOOL. Yes, it's a common word, and as I began to explore I went through my usual thinking process.

My first thought was a school house, and I wondered why school is coupled with the word "house"? In today's world most schools are in some kind of two- or three-story building. It usually is recognized immediately as a school by its appearance. There are lots of windows, an American flag, and a prominent name easy to see. Thinking a bit further I remembered seeing schools that looked like a house with white clapboard exteriors, and windows on all sides. Its foundation was shaped either square or slightly irregular. One addition to the school that made it unique was a raised area above the front door that held the school bell. Inside were student's desks and a schoolteacher who passed out schoolbooks and school papers, and the students wrote their lessons in school notebooks.

Okay. How about this? It's well known that colleges and universities never needed the addition of the word school to their names. But each university has a number of schools offered within such as a school of dentistry, and a law school. By this time one is smart enough to know it is an institution of higher learning with campus buildings of variable sizes and shapes. This is where one can become "well-schooled". After graduation some enter the school of hard knocks trying to find a job. Then I ask the question —why are fish spoken of as a school of fish? Is it because they are in a special class?

At one time or another many of us have probably sung a school song, a song that was written about the building, its surroundings, and happenings. One that comes to mind is Yale's Whiffenpoof song, "We're poor little sheep who've gone astray, Ba, Ba, Ba." Did your school have a song?

I can't leave this page without remembering a song that most people have sung at one time, or other. It's the classic song "School Days" written by Gus Edwards and Will D. Cobb (1907). Do you remember the words?

Chorus:
School days, School days, Good old golden rule days
Readin' and ritin and rithmatic, Taught to the tune of the hickory stick
I was your bashful barefoot beau, You were my queen in calico
And you wrote on my slate I love you so
When we were a couple of kids.

Verse:
Nothing to do you say, let's take a trip on memory's ship, Back to the bygone days
Sail to the old village schoolhouse, anchor outside the school door
Look in and see there's you and me, A couple of kids once more.
Member the hill, Natalie darling, and the oak tree that grew on its brow
They've built forty stories upon that hill, and the oak's an old chestnut now
'Member the meadows so green dear, so fragrant with clover and maize
Into preferred business plots they've cut them up, since those olden days.

January 27, 2015

A TRIP TO REMEMBER

It was Sunday morning and I was in church. At the end of the worship service I met Joe and Karyne Carey in the narthex. They had given a talk to the congregation about their upcoming trip to teach in Lithuania. I learned that Lithuania was one of the Baltic Countries located on the Baltic Sea. Across the Sea to the west was Sweden. Joe and Karyne were going to teach English in the month of July at the Lithuanian Christian College in the town of Klaipėda. An off-handed remark was made to me by Karyne. She said, "Why don't you come with us?" For the next few days her question haunted me and finally I decided to go.

I met with the school's Director of Education and was accepted as a qualified teacher. We left at the end of June, 2001. My flight plans were different from the Carey's but we agreed to meet in Copenhagen, Denmark. When I arrived they were nowhere to be found. As I waited and waited a slight bit of panic took hold until I told myself, "You are a rational adult—get a taxi and go to the hotel." Due to a plane delay they arrived four hours later. That evening we had dinner at the famous Tivoli Amusement Park. The next morning we left by plane for Vilnius, the capitol of Lithuania. There we met several other teachers. A bus took us to the town of Klaipėda. An old school facility was to be our dorm. The next morning I met my roommate, Ceralina from Canada.

The first week was orientation, and the second week classes began. I had eighteen high school students—most were from Lithuania, two from Latvia and one from Russia. Everyone had taken tests to determine their fluency in English. Some spoke either Lithuanian or Russian, and others Latvian or German. Classes were from 9:00 a.m. to 12:00 noon. We had workbooks, plus usable items from the resource room plus some games.

In the afternoon I met for an hour with eight girls for a Conversation Class. The purpose for this class was to immerse everyone in English. My evenings were spent on the next day's lesson plans.

Each Saturday the entire teaching staff visited an area of interest. Our first visit was to a Holocaust museum. It was very sobering. The next week we saw a unique site called The Hill of the Crosses. During the German occupation most churches were closed or struggling. As a result a dissident few began a counter measure on a nearby hill. This hill became a place to make a statement by erecting a cross and little by little hundreds of crosses appeared. The opposing forces destroyed the area many times by using bulldozers or setting the area on fire but miraculously more crosses would appear during the night. When I visited the area there were thousands and thousands of crosses of all sizes with little pathways weaving up and down the hill. It was truly an awesome sight. Off to the side was a platform especially built for a recent visit from the Pope.

Some things I will never forget:

1. Pocket Rockets: These were small city buses. Each bus had a number on their window designating their route. When it stopped you slid the door open, got on, shut the door, sat down while the bus was moving, and passed your money (fare) up the row ahead to the bus driver. If you needed change the money would come back in reverse.
2. Getting an infection in my foot and being "treated" in many and strange ways. For example, one "doctor" insisted that he should treat the other foot.
3. People (usually poor) selling flowers, vegetables and fruits on the street. I often bought flowers.
4. Maximas: a retail store that carried anything you wanted, including food and clothes; it was like a Wal-Mart. Problem: one needed a car to get there.
5. Introduction of peanut butter to my class. (I brought a jar with me.) Up to this point peanut butter was not yet available in Lithuania.
6. The Seaman's Festival held every year for one week in the summer. There were booths selling amber items, lots of food stalls, lots of beer, special programs, dancing, and fireworks each evening. The streets were jammed.
7. ATM machines. This life-saving machine was handy when I saw something I wanted to buy. It gave me quick money. I knew where they all were!!
8. Food. Restaurants had good food and were quite reasonable. Another other option was to buy and cook it ourselves.
9. The Lutheran Church. There was a Lithuanian service on Sunday morning, and an evening service in English. I played the piano several times.
10. Graduation ceremonies. Saying farewell to students. Gifts and photos.

My return trip included a stopover in Sweden to visit relatives, and then back to the USA. I was exhausted but pleased that I had the opportunity to see a good portion of the country and to meet so many people. Several students wrote to me for several months and I responded. It truly was a trip to remember.

July 2, 2012

LARS

His name was Lars Hollander. He became one of our sons when he stayed with us in Tenafly, New Jersey. He was sixteen years old. He and another young fellow were in the States on a sports scholarship. So it was not by birth, but by choice that Lars became a part of our family. (Anyone who calls me Mom like he did immediately becomes a son.) Lars was born in Sweden and still lives in Stockholm together with Maud, his fiancée.

On our first trip we celebrated our 25th wedding anniversary in Sweden. It was exciting to be on a huge plane (SAS, Scandinavian Airlines.). I was excited, didn't sleep, and the closer we got to Sweden my eyes were riveted on the landscape and the houses. Finally we landed at Arlanda airport, took a bus to Stockholm, and went directly to the Continental hotel that we had previously booked. The shock came when they told us that they had no evidence of our reservation. What to do? One of the registrars told us about a shop close by that would be helpful. It was just what we needed. Their recommendation was a small hotel. It was perfect. Instead of sleeping we went on a walk to see the sights. Following our three-day visit in Stockholm, we took a train to Västerås to visit Ann-Marie, Bert's cousin, and her son. When our son, Lars, heard that we were coming he surprised us by meeting the train with her. This was 1974. He made sure that we were invited to his childhood home where we met his father and sister.

At one time Lars served as a bodyguard for the King and Queen of Sweden. This afforded him many privileges. (At this point he now works for the Secret Service.) I remember in particular when he took us to view the historic Vasa museum situated on the island of Djurgården in Stockholm. Lars' status allowed Bert and me free entrance. As we entered and saw this massive vessel that King Gustav II Adolf contracted to have built in 1625 and learned that it sank on its maiden voyage, we were eager to learn the complete story. Why did it sink? Who was in charge? How was it rescued and brought back to life after 333 years? As we stood gazing at this magnificent structure, we read the following:

Her maiden voyage would be her last—she hardly left the harbor before sinking on August 10, 1628. The ship was well built but incorrectly proportioned with insufficient ballast to keep it upright.

It appears that the King was never completely satisfied. His ego insisted it be higher than any other war ship, have more canons, and have enormous gold carvings gracing the bow and stern. He never took into account the proportions of this massive ship and wouldn't listen to anyone who tried to convince him of the problem. As a result it dutifully sank.

Lars' duties as a member of the Royal Guard were to accompany the Royal family on trips, watch over the children, and sometimes drive when the Queen wanted to go shopping. (I thought it funny to learn that sometimes the Queen preferred to drive and Lars would sit in the passenger seat.) One day on our sightseeing tour with him we walked the steps to the Palace. With a wave of his hand we entered and did not have to stand in line or pay an entrance fee. We marveled at the architecture, the paintings, and the many items of blue and gold, the colors of Sweden. The Throne Room was impressive but seldom used, he said. We also toured the Town Hall, a beautifully constructed structure and world known for Nobel Prize events.

No matter where we went Lars seemed to be well known, especially when we walked down the main street in Old Town. Scattered here and there were foreigners displaying their wares on card tables, and encouraging people to stop and bargain. Lars told us this was illegal in Sweden. I noticed when the sellers saw Lars coming they hurriedly gathered their displays and disappeared somewhere until we passed. After we walked a few yards I turned to look and sure enough they were quickly setting up their displays again. We took a boat tour through the archipelagoes and boat locks that gave us an overview of the wealth and beauty of Sweden. During this visit, we were impressed once again by the friendliness of the people and their ability in speaking English.

It was a monumental surprise when Lars and Maud came to Mansfield, Ohio for my 80th birthday—June 4, 2007. I wonder if they will surprise me on my 90th in 2017?

November 21, 2014

P.S. Yes! They did surprise me on my 90th birthday!

PHEW! HOW DO SWEDES EAT THIS STUFF?

It was a trip of a lifetime for my husband and me. We really couldn't afford it but decided to scrimp and save in order to take a trip to Sweden for our 25th wedding anniversary. We had relatives on both sides of our family living there so plans were made to visit in late August, 1974.

Bert's cousin, Ann-Marie, had made arrangements for us to visit her in Västerås, a city west of Stockholm. A few days later we all traveled to visit her brother's family, Violet and Gunnar Kjellberg, in northern Sweden. Our meeting place was the Kjellbergs' summer home on one of Sweden's beautiful waterways. We stayed in a tiny cottage just a few steps from their house. The next day more family members came and the party was in full force.

Little did we know that there was a ritual for first time visitors to Sweden. As we gathered in the front yard a speech was made by Gunnar, Bert's cousin. He told a story about a long running event that had now become a tradition, and we were about to experience it. All the while he spoke the grin on his face foretold something really special was about to happen. Gunnar then gave an endearing welcoming speech that would befit royalty. As he spoke he asked Bert to step forward to where he stood. Behind his back he produced a rather large can, about the size of an extra large can of tuna. He had Bert hold the can and Gunnar proceeded to turn the key that began to release the pressure. All of a sudden the liquid contents of the can squirted directly at Bert and he shouted something and quickly backed away. Everyone laughed heartily and enjoyed seeing the reaction of the two American visitors. I remember the smell was nauseating. I wanted to leave the area.

Picture 14: Can you see the can of Surströmming on the table?

We learned that the can contained "Surströmming, " which is fermented Baltic herring. That evening Surströmming was served at the dinner meal. Everyone ate it heartily. Bert was brave as he ate the fish but then said, "If I can get it past my nose, it really tastes good." I didn't agree. While holding my breath, I cautiously tasted a tiny, tiny portion. It was awful. No one made any comments about my refusal, but smacked their lips as they downed this special delight. I had many times heard about "crazy swedes" but now I was convinced. Oh, well, I must remember I am a Swede, but maybe not so crazy that I would eat Surströmming.

June 3, 2014

TOO LATE, TOO BAD

Virginia has been a friend for nearly forty years. When my husband accepted a call to serve a church in Farmington Hills, Michigan in 1973, Virginia was one of the first people I met. It wasn't long before we found a commonality and even later when we moved to Ohio, the friendship continued. After the death of my husband, I would drive the 175 miles to Michigan, and she made several trips to Ohio to visit me.

Routinely on each trip I would pass a scene on Route 4 that fascinated me. It was an old house, run-down, weather-beaten, and obviously unoccupied for many years. Lack of care, and desperately needing paint, it had a charming cone shaped roof that hung over the front steps. It had once been covered with copper and now had turned green. The house always caught my attention, and I imagined Andrew Wyeth capturing it realistically on canvas. I must take a picture someday, I thought.

Once again I was on my way to Michigan. I looked forward seeing this picturesque scene and I slowed down to take another look. I'll stop on my way back and take a picture, I thought.

Following my visit, I was heading back to Ohio on Route 4 and saw the house in the distance that had caught my attention for so many years. I slowed down looking for a safe place to park. To my horror I shouted, "Oh, No!" During my three-day absence the lovely cone shaped roof had fallen to the ground. It no longer was the house that I admired. Sadly, I drove on thinking to myself – I blew it. An opportunity missed. However, this charming old house is etched in my mind, but unfortunately I cannot show it to anyone. If only I was able to capture it on canvas. Oh well. Too late, too bad.

February 26, 2013

A CANDLE HOUSE SURPRISE

During the summer of 2001 I taught English at a Christian college in Lithuania. The school was in the city of Klaipėda, a city well over 185,000. My students were mostly teenagers from Klaipėda, and a few from Russia, and Latvia. They were very eager to learn English. It was a great experience for me but very tiring. I was seventy-four. We met in the morning for a three hour class, and after lunch a two hour session. Preparation for the next day was done in the evening. Oh yes, another factor to be considered was that all the teachers made their own meals. We shared a small kitchen with a minimum of cooking utensils.

As teachers, we taught five days a week which meant Saturdays were available for special bus trips. On one Saturday we went to a private home in Klaipėda that had a cottage industry. Their product was making candle houses out of clay. Clay was readily available. The candle houses were an assortment of small buildings. Some were churches, some cleverly designed houses, and each had windows allowing a candle within to shine. An assembly line in their basement began with a lump of clay, and moved through many stages until the product was finished. We had an opportunity to make purchases. I bought three.

When it was time to leave Lithuania, we were given instructions how to pack the candle houses to avoid breakage. Into the holes fashioned for the candle we were advised to stuff paper or cloth inside. This gave me an idea. I took pairs of underpants that needed washing and carefully stuffed each house hoping this would prevent breakage. All three made it safely to Ohio.

In September of that same year, one of my friends, Phil Carl, had a birthday. Several of us from Mansfield drove to Solon, Ohio, north of Akron, to help him celebrate. I wrapped my candle house gift carefully and added a nice bow. After coffee and cake it was time to open gifts. As Phil untied the bow and tore off the wrapping, he reached in and took out a candle house church. I had purposely purchased a church since he is a minister. While examining the church he saw something inside and began to slowly pull it out. Out came a pair of my unwashed panties. Suddenly I realized that I had completely forgotten what was inside and I jumped up to retrieve them. Instead Phil waved them over his head with everyone enjoying the scene. Phil couldn't believe that I actually forgot about my dainties being inside. Oh, well, just one more stupid thing I have done, but it still makes me smile and is a time to reminisce.

June 18, 2013

IT'S ABOUT TIME

In the musical "My Fair Lady," Eliza Doolittle shouts in a loud voice, "WORDS, WORDS, WORDS!" as she struggled to learn proper English. For me, choosing the correct word in a word game or discovering different meanings for a particular word is fun. Crossword puzzles are challenging, and selecting convincing words to make a point in an argument can be arduous. For something different, I decided to choose one word to discover how many ways it could be used. My choice: the word *time*.

Charles Dickens chose the opening sentence in his book *The Tale of Two Cities*: "It was the best of times and the worst of times." Did it catch on? You be the judge. From here let's continue by having the time of our lives—a time-tested phrase for sure. A clock that hung on the wall in my childhood home had the words *tempus fugit*, Latin for "time flies." True? Also, one can make time, tell time, set time, or take time off. There are time periods, time outs, time limits, time trials, and prime time. I even remember in junior high school typing class typing the sentence: "Now is the time for all good men to come to the aid of their party." The goal was to type the sentence ten times without an error. This took a lot of practice time.

I hope I am not wasting your time, because here's more. Oh, we've all had a bad time, and another time when it was good. Athletes know full well about time trials and using a stopwatch to test the total time of a race. Often one can read about the winners in the next issue of *Time Magazine*. An old adage says time heals. Is this true? And who was it that said, "Time's a-wasting?" Or did you ever sing the song "Time After Time," or "As Time Goes By?"

I must not forget that time is an important element in music. There is swing time, waltz time, 4/4 time, 6/8 time, and even 12/8 time to name a few. Think about this: my metronome beats time and a conductor conducts time.

Oh, how about time zones in the United States? Eastern Time, Central Time, Mountain Time, and Pacific Time all can be confusing if you are not aware of the time differences. As to time zones in foreign countries, Russia has nine.

When learning the alphabet, the letters are said one at a time. Then there are the seasons of the year—springtime, summertime, and wintertime. Why don't we say falltime or autumntime?

A statement from Mitch Albom's fairly recent book entitled *The Timekeeper* says, "Once there was not a word for time at all because no one was counting.". He also added the following: "I found that there are as many expressions with 'time' as there are minutes in a day." So let's see if there are additional ways to use the word time that I haven't previously cited.

We may "pass time" if we have nothing to do, or if we are stalling we usually "take our time." If we are "out of time" it indicates the event is over. Have you ever had "time on your hands?" Why is it on our hands? It is always wise to "be on time" particularly if the situation is important. Is it ever wrong to "waste time?" I'll leave that up to you.

When I think of a clock it tells me my "bedtime", my "breakfast, lunch, and dinner time", and what time to take my pills. It also reminds me of one of my favorite TV programs. I know that 7:00 p.m., five days a week is the time for "Jeopardy" on Channel 7. I can also set my clock/radio to wake me at 7:00 a.m.—my "getting up time". "Time to rise and shine." If I am unable to meet someone for an event, I may say, "Let's do it another time."

Recently someone reminded me of the statement, "Time and tide waits for no man." I know about the tide. It's consistent, never failing. You can count on it. But how many times have you waited for someone and they are late? At this point you are the one who is wasting time in your waiting. Time has been stolen from you.

At this point I believe I have taken too much of your time with this somewhat tongue in cheek recital of *time* words. Oh shoot—just one more: Clocks tell time, crooks do time.

Well, I definitely have come to the end of my time.

So let me end with a poem about the apparent speeding up of time as one gets older. It was written by Henry Twells (1823-1900).

Time's Paces

When as a child I laughed and wept,
    Time crept.
When as a youth I waxed more bold,
    Time strolled.
When I became a full grown man,
    Time ran.
When older still I daily grew,
    Time flew.
Soon I shall find, in passing on,
    Time gone
O Christ! Wilt Thou have saved me then?
    Amen.

September 17, 2012

A ROOM WITH A VIEW

My friend, Virginia Michaelson, lives in West Bloomfield, Michigan. She is in her nineties and basically bedridden, but looks forward in the morning to sit in her wheelchair at the dining table while eating breakfast. Here she looks through the windows at the clouds, the trees, birds, and an occasional dog walker. Here she determines her own weather report, and often she and I will compare California and Michigan reports. After reading the newspaper during this four-hour session in her wheelchair, her caregiver puts her back to bed. Her bed is in the family room that faces a sliding patio door.

She and I have been friends for nearly forty years. We talk on the phone almost every Saturday. Does she complain? Oh, a bit—but then the conversation goes from her football or baseball teams to local and national politics and what she sees through her patio window. She's been feeding the birds for many years. At present birdseed is spread on the patio by her caregiver. Much to Virginia's delight she has attracted more than just birds. There are chipmunks, squirrels, ducks, and even an occasional deer all fighting for their share of the food and water. She recognizes some as returnees, and has given them names. They are all truly her friends.

During the years she has had several cats. These lovely creatures have been her companion and have filled her moments of loneliness especially after the death of Fred, her husband. On many occasions I have heard her call to her calico cat in a loud voice as she and I enter her back door, "Teddy, I'm home. Momma's home."

Why am I telling you about Virginia? It's because I admire her attitude and the ability to value what she has and what she sees and hears. She's loyal to her Detroit Lions football and Tigers baseball teams, and reads the *Detroit News* and the *Detroit Free Press* every day. She has written six books of poetry and composes a free verse poem for her church paper every month. At this point

Virginia is unable to use a pen so she calls the church office and dictates her poem from memory to the secretary, who then types it. Remarkable, I say.

Here is one of her prose poems—it's one of my favorites:

TROUBLES
My troubles are like bread dough
No sooner do I punch them down,
Than they rise up again
And threaten to take over.
What a pity
That I can't bake them,
And eat them
With butter and strawberry jam.

June 3, 2013

P.S. I no longer have the privilege of our Saturday telephone conversations. Virginia died in 2014.

A MOST UNUSUAL FRIEND

Her name is Dr. Elizabeth Reed. She lived all her life in Butler, Ohio in a very large house that had an elevator. Since she was a small child she aspired to be a Doctor like her father who also lived in this large house. Early in her father's practice he made house calls in a horse and buggy. He also inspired Elizabeth's brother and sister to become doctors. Betty remembers going with her father to deliver babies in the surrounding area. At times she would assist. One story she often told was when she was with him and witnessed her first birth. After the birth she said her father handed her the baby, much to Betty's surprise, and told her to bathe the newborn. Her comment to me was, "I'd never bathed a damn baby in my life."

Following her undergraduate years at Ohio's Wittenberg University she entered medical school in Detroit, Michigan at age nineteen. Her photographic memory and natural intelligence gave her an edge in the academic field. Gaining her degree in medicine she returned to Butler, Ohio and set up practice. Like her father, she lived and worked in the family home until her death in 2011.

My husband and I became acquainted with Dr. Betty at First English Lutheran Church in Mansfield, Ohio where my husband was the pastor. He and Dr. Betty immediately "hit it off." She was a Martin Luther scholar, a lover of Shakespeare, and German history, and her own library contained several first editions. She made many trips to the archives in the Mormon Church, Salt Lake City, Utah to research her ancestors and was proud of discovering the family history going back to the 1500's.

Two Dr. Betty stories stand out in my mind involving me. The first was a time I went to visit her in her home. At this point she had given up her medical license but not her privilege to prescribe medications. She and I were sitting in her kitchen talking when without saying a word she got up and left me sitting alone. I had no idea why. When she returned she gave me the following command, "stand up and drop your pants.". She then announced, "I'm going to give you a B-12 shot." She explained that I looked a bit pale. That was it. I didn't question her reasoning but offered her my thanks and my backside.

The second story involved travel. I had made plans to attend a conference at "Spirit in the Desert," a Retreat Center in Arizona where two of my favorite people, Dr. Jerry Schmalenberger and his wife, Carol, were to be the speakers. Dr. Jerry preceded my husband at First Lutheran, Mansfield, Ohio as pastor, and he and his wife were great friends with Dr. Betty. When I told her I was going, she immediately called the airlines and made a reservation to fly with me on the same day.

The conference was exhilarating and concluded in six days. Our return trip was from Phoenix to Midway Airport in Chicago and then on to Cleveland. When we landed in Chicago we learned that we would not be able to continue because Cleveland had had a severe snow storm. All flights had been cancelled. So a taxi took us to a motel. While registering at the motel I suddenly observed our two carry-on bags were missing, and the taxi driver had left. I was devastated since my bag contained my camera, medications, and jewelry. A call to the Lost and Found at the airport proved futile. When I mentioned that my pills were in my carry-on, Dr. Betty asked me what I needed. When I told her she opened her purse and said, "Here, take this."

The next day we took advantage of the motel's free breakfast and made it last all morning. At noon we ate chicken noodle soup from a vending machine. Unbeknownst to me, a telephone call from the taxi driver came to the motel desk asking if anyone was missing luggage. Dr. Betty happened to be standing there and answered the call. He needed verification of ownership which she gave. It proved correct and he delivered the two bags. At this point I knew nothing about the call.

Later that afternoon I returned to the room and found Dr. Betty sitting on the bed. When I sat down she said, "Look around. Do you see anything different?" I mentioned that the beds had been made. She urged me to look again. This time I saw our bags sitting on the desk!!! I immediately burst into tears. My prayers had been answered. Betty told me that the taxi driver said his trunk light was not working so as a result he didn't see the items toward the back. Betty shook his hand warmly and gave him a significant tip.

During the day I made many calls to find flights for our return, and finally made arrangements for Sunday morning. I called my friends in Mansfield who were patiently waiting to hear from us. Joe said, "I'll be bringing the truck because of all the snow. It will travel much better through the snow." When I told Dr. Betty that we'd be going home in his truck, she replied, "Oh, I hope he will bring lots of blankets." I assured her we would not be sitting in an open truck bed—it was not that kind of truck!!! Dr. Betty was a gifted woman, and I relished every moment when we were together. Rarely does one meet someone who makes such a lasting impression. I was one of the lucky ones.

November 11, 2012

A NEW FRIEND

The Northwest Airlines plane was ready to leave the Minneapolis terminal. I had just said goodbye to my mother and uncle after a week's visit. It was always difficult to leave since they were getting along in years. I wondered if I would be returning sooner than later. As I sat looking out the window with tears filling my eyes, a pleasant-looking lady came to occupy the aisle seat next to me. As we taxied down the runway our eyes met and we both said hello. She appeared friendly, and friendly she was.

The conversation soon began with the usual where do you live, and where are you going? I learned that her father had died and she was going for his funeral. Not wanting to invade her privacy, I gave her my condolences. She then said that she was headed for Mansfield, Ohio. I told her this was also where I lived. She said that her father belonged to The United Church of Christ, but her mother was a member of First English Lutheran Church. You can imagine her surprise when I said that my husband was the pastor of that Church. She then said her cousin, Earl Goetz, was to pick her up in Cleveland where we were both headed, and of course I knew Earl as well.

Our conversation turned to Minneapolis where she and her husband were living. She was the soprano soloist in the Presbyterian Church and studied with the same vocal coach that I had when I lived there. Her husband was the principle oboist for the Minneapolis Symphony Orchestra—and again we had friends in common. All of this was a delight and surprise to both of us. Her name was Lee Williams.

Our friendship continued for many years. Lee's mother was in a Mansfield nursing home. I remember attending her 100th and 101st birthdays. One day Lee told me that she and her husband had sold their house on Lake Minnetonka, and would be moving to their boat moored nearby on the Mississippi River. She related how difficult it was to pare down and carefully select the necessary items that would fit on the boat. One day they were ready to sail. When I asked how far they were going? She said, "We will stay wherever we moor and feel comfortable". Finally the word came after three-to-four weeks: Their new home was Demopolis, Alabama. I had to look it up on the map!

Periodically Lee would drive to Mansfield to see her mother, stay at a motel, and call me to get together for breakfast or lunch. I was always excited to hear about their new residence. She said when packing she only took slacks and shorts. But when they had chosen a church to attend she saw that all the women wore dresses or skirts. She had to go shopping. Cloyd, her husband, soon began directing the choir and playing the oboe. She sang in the choir and had joined a book club. They continued to live on their boat even after a couple of hurricanes.

When I think back to our first meeting on that plane, I'm almost positive that if she had had a different seat, we would never have met. Oh, perhaps when I got off in Cleveland I probably would have seen Earl Goetz, her cousin. There may have been a short introduction—but we would not have had the great relationship we experienced through the years. Lee died six months before my move to Sonoma, California.

March 12, 2013

SOMETHING I WISH I HAD DONE

As an adopted child of three months old, you can imagine that I was a welcomed gift for my mother and father since they had no natural born children. As I envision the many questions my parents must have had, and the legal paper work, plus the emotional toll, the day finally came when they held me in their arms. For this reason I realize my care became a high priority.

My mother had a photographer take the first photo. I was positioned leaning against a pillow dressed in a white frilly dress. I wonder if my father took the photo and showed it to his fellow workers. I wonder if relatives came to the house to see this "wonder child"? I have no answers. For the remaining years I was given the best of everything even into my marriage.

As of this moment, I wonder why I never felt or expressed any gratitude. Did I ever say thank you to my parents for choosing me? Again, I have no answers.

As to discipline, I remember as a pre-kindergartner running around the dining room table with my mother trying to catch me in order to give me a spanking. It was soon over when we both started to laugh. I have no clue what I had done that needed disciplining.

Entering my teen years my attitude changed dramatically. I was constantly at odds with my mother. I remember saying hurtful words and shouting a lot. I remember her telling me "not to be so mean." It even lasted into the years of my marriage. I felt she was still controlling me. One example that she was still taking care of me was a Thanksgiving Day dinner. Instead of inviting my parents to dinner at our house, I invited my husband's family. Our house was small, without a dining room, so it became a seating problem. And furthermore, my parents were at our house very often, and it was now time to invite my husband's family. My menu was traditional, and we'd soon be seated when I saw my parents drive up. They came through the back door and set down typical foods for Thanksgiving—turkey, gravy, potatoes, a vegetable and pie all ready to be served. With a quick "Happy Thanksgiving," they left. I know I was not a gourmet cook, but to me at this point I realized she was still running my life.

During the years that followed she and I continued an adversarial relationship until one day in my early fifties. We were at the airport when my flight call was announced. I turned to hug my mother goodbye and without thinking I whispered in her ear, "I love you." It was not a preplanned response. She responded the same. Once seated, I realized this was actually the first time for me to say those three important words.

So, sometimes I wish I had said "I love you" more often and thank you for your love and caring. Is it too late now? Perhaps not! So Mom, if you are listening, Thank you, Thank you, and I LOVE YOU, too.

February 21, 2017

REMEMBERING BERT, MY ONE AND ONLY

The year 1993 was a difficult one for Bert. After four hospital stays from February to July, plus days and nights struggling with the effects of a heart condition called cardiomyopathy, he quietly slipped away at home on July, 17, 1993. Those who surrounded the bedside were his sister Ruth from Minnesota, Pastor Schaefer of our church, Pastor Carl, two friends, and me. A long siege of hospital stays, doctor's visits, and special methods to keep his now enlarged heart to continue beating came to an end. The last couple of weeks he lived still ring very clear in my mind as if it happened yesterday.

The day he came home from the hospital, against the wishes of his doctor, he and I talked about whether this was a good idea. I knew that Bert wanted to be at home. I agreed. Once in the car I suggested we take a short ride through the Ohio countryside, which we had done many times. It was one of our favorite trips. He paused for a moment and then said no. I knew he was tired. As we entered our garage, he slowly got out of the car and carefully walked up the two steps into the family room. After a short rest we began the slow climb to the upstairs bedroom. When we reached the top I asked if he would like to walk into each bedroom and look out the windows. We were fortunate in having great views. As he stood before each window no words were spoken as we both looked at the distant hills, trees, and bright blue sky. He stood for several moments at the last window, then turned to me and said in all sincerity, "That was wonderful."

Jesse and David came to see their dad during his final stay in the hospital. I cannot attest to our sons' feelings knowing that their dad was dying. However, I do remember Bert sitting on the edge of the hospital bed after they had hugged and said their farewells, and sobbing for his own loss. At that point a nurse entered the room and Bert showed his humanness by telling her in a commanding voice to leave and shut the door! She apologized and left quietly as the door softly closed behind her.

For the four years prior to my husband's death he lived a fairly productive life. He was a substitute preacher at many churches in the area. He attended Kiwanis luncheon meetings in the dining room of the local hotel, was a member of the Medical Ethics committee at the hospital, and was an excellent chef in our remodeled kitchen. We went for rides, joined friends for lunch, and had many visitors and overnight guests. He also wrote three books that were published, and several poems that I later assembled in a booklet entitled *Leavings*. He practiced the piano and memorized several new selections—two by Chopin. We also made a trip to Sweden in 1992 together with our son, Jesse, who was a valuable asset as he cared for his dad's welfare. Bert continued working on his dissertation for a Doctorate of Ministry now that his classwork was finished. I remember his comment when asked if he would be able to finish the work. He said: "I don't need a plaque on the wall to say I was smart. The most important element is what I have learned in the process."

Picture 15: Bert signing a book

During this time I don't remember feeling sad. I just refused to think about it. Those last few weeks, I continually made an effort to stay upbeat and at the same time catered to his every request.

Don Beddard, Bert's doctor, was a valuable resource in giving Bert choices for a quality of life with a variety of medications which meant that most of the time he was able to enjoy what he wanted to do and was able to appreciate every day. Yes, there were times (many as I recall) an ambulance siren could be heard in the distance. After he died, the sound of sirens in the distance immediately reminded me of the many times it stopped at our house. I also remember Bert saying "I hear them coming."

One of the decisions the doctor and Bert made was to insert a type of pump under Bert's skin like a heart monitor that would feed his heart medication to keep it pulsating. A nurse came daily to handle the procedure. Putting on rubber gloves she would flush the tubes with saline before injecting a prescribed solution. I watched closely knowing that this procedure was soon to be my responsibility.

It was very important to keep the area germ free. It was then properly covered with a bandage. He was allowed to take a shower but the area had to be sealed with plastic wrap and tape. That was my job. After two weeks the nurse began to teach me the entire procedure. I prayed that I would be able to accomplish the task. With fear in my heart I began. Bert watched me intently as I followed the steps that I had been taught. I knew a mistake could be lethal.

Several times I asked Bert if he would like to record a message. Each time I posed the question he would say, "I'm thinking about it." Then an opportunity came to capture a conversation he was having with a minister friend. I quickly set a small recorder and placed it on the night stand. It ran for about forty-five minutes. It wasn't until later when I sat at the computer transferring his words to paper, when one sentence came as a complete surprise. He said that for the past month he was very, very sad, and emphasized the phrase, "overwhelmingly sad." Once again, I probably was trying to not show sadness and had completely missed seeing it. I left the computer, and cried and cried, not only for myself but for Bert. Why didn't I see any sign of his depression? I really don't know the answer.

I was very proud of my husband. His knowledge and actions of how to deal with people's problems were evidenced over and over. He knew what to do and say at the right time. He would often caution me when I wanted to "blow my top." He knew I'd be sorry for it. One bit of advice he gave me has guided me through the years. "You can't help what you *feel*, but you can help what you *think*. So call your feelings into the court of reason—go with what you know is *true*."

He loved to write prose, poetry, and music. For example, in the 1960's he published a Folk Mass for the Lutheran Church, and later published three books:

The Via Dolorosa: The Stations of the Cross; *I Quarrel with the Lord*; and *Crazy Swedes and Other Wonderful Loons.*

He often listened when I was teaching piano. Later he would give me advice how to handle a particular phrase or practice technique. He was a voracious reader. Several times while confined to his bed he would ask me to read from one of his favorite books, *A Treasury of Great Poems* by author Louis Untermeyer. He would ask me to say what I thought about the reading and discuss it with me. I treasure those moments.

February 4, 2014

WALKING TOGETHER

Would that we could walk together through the dark gates of death and into the blinding light of what joys and bliss we cannot even imagine.

For so we have walked together all these years.

The paths beneath our feet have varied.
    There have been cool, lush grasses of tranquility.
    There have been bright, sunny daisies of innocent joy.
    There have been solemn flagstones of deeply shared insights.
    There have been thistles and weeds of shared sorrows and fears.

But, we have always walked together –

Not we two, but we three.
    For HE who formed us in our mothers' wombs has shared the pathway with us.

Now we three continue together; but only to the point where one must stop and wait while the other two confidently walk through, while the one remains outside.

But HE will return and quietly walk with the waiting one to yet another dark gate; how far away, I do not know.

But, when at last it swings open, there in the burning light, illumined by love, will be the one waiting for the other.

So, while it is yet three, let us walk in confidence, in hope and in the love which has made this side of the gate a foretaste of our life together on the other side.

How good it is that we have always walked together.

How good it is that there has never been another.

How blessed am I that you have so honored me.

                                          Bertil E. Anderson, 1993

THE GRIEF PROCESS

For me the grieving process did not begin immediately. There was so much to do and think about. I made list after list that never seemed to end. Bert's sister Ruth cancelled her return flight and stayed for several days. I was so grateful; for she gave me good advice, and a shoulder to lean on. Phone calls tended to interrupt my tasks but on the other hand it was good to know that people cared. In between times I questioned whether there might have been another medicine or procedure that could have lengthened his life. There were questions about what I should have said or done before his death. Too late now, I said to myself!

In one of my conversations with Bert, I mentioned that I was aware that many funeral services began with the family and a few friends going to the cemetery together with the pastor for the burial service. What followed was a full memorial service at the church. As I described the possibility, Bert kept shaking his head, saying "No, no, no.". I asked why he was against this. His answer was, "I want to be there." The Church was his life and passion. He wanted it to be a full service with communion, one that he had conducted as the pastor during his forty years of ministry. The funeral service was on Saturday, July 24, 1993 at the church, and Bert was there.

A few days later I remember standing alone at the kitchen sink when the reality of Bert's death grabbed me, and I actually shouted, "I'm now a widow." It was a stark reality that he was really gone. Remembering Bert's admonition of how I needed to grieve, I thought, but how do I do that?

The grieving process was not like any that I ever had heard, read or discussed. Not even very kind people who stopped to grieve with me seemed to help. The Bible gave me help, but I still grieved—and it hurt. Books about grief, the Bible, and kind words simply went over my head. I cried more than ever.

One book, however, was helpful: *God in the Dark* with stories that mirrored my experience. A friend, a grief counselor, called asking if she could come for a visit. During the visit she handed me the book and asked if I would read it and let her know if she should recommend it. I agreed. The book was written by a woman who discussed not only grieving, but the difficult experience of realizing that death was imminent. As I began reading I started to cry. With each chapter my crying developed into sobs. Much of what I read mirrored my story. Several months later I reread *God in the Dark* and discovered its spiritual content.

Recently I read the book *The Year of Magical Thinking*, dealing with grief and loss. Joan Didion, author, got my attention with the following quote: "Research has shown that people can adapt to a wide range of good and bad life events in less than two months." The author continued with "[but] it takes the average widow many years after her spouse's death to regain her former level of life satisfaction." In my case I found this to be true. It took only a reminder of my aloneness to trigger tears. Fortunately, I was surrounded by understanding relatives and friends. I slowly began the journey with grief counseling, and continued with prayers to God for strength and guidance. My family was very supportive.

Picture 16: Bert's grave marker

During the many years since his death I've questioned why Bert had to die at sixty-eight years of age. Several days before his death I cried and asked him the question, "How am I going to get along without you?" His answer was so typical of both a minister and a husband. He said, "You'll grieve and you must do that. Then you will go on." It was good advice, and it's exactly what I have done. Thank you, Bert, and thank you, God.

February 4, 2014

THE EMPTY SPACE

*A gentle stillness fills the air,
The hush of one no longer there.
The stillness of the empty space,
The quiet leaving of a grace
Given to us to know a while,
The easy laugh, the gentle smile.*

*The empty hurt, the pain of loss
Will not forever stay like dross
Trying to fill up the empty space
Of one who filled our hearts with grace.
'Tis strange, but wisdom we must gain
Can only be learned by such sad pain.*

*To know how blessed was this friend
We seem to know best at the end
Of all that filled to overflow
The love, the joy, the warmest glow
Of embers shining in the night
That made our friendship safe and bright.*

*And so we walk upon our way
Of what we do and are each day.
The paradox of pain so sweet
To know at last when death we meet
That we have left an empty space
Where once we walked in love and grace.*

*And so to God we give this one
Whose time with us on earth is done.
Whose friendship filled our lives with peace.
Our thankful hearts will never cease
To bless our God that in this place
The hallowed hush of the empty space.*

Bertil E. Anderson, February 1993

A MOVING EXPERIENCE

The thought of moving from one location to another was a bit daunting for me. When such thoughts crossed my mind, I immediately would make a list of difficulties such as how to get rid of items no longer needed, what to keep and/or move, and whether I should stay in Mansfield where I had lived for many years. All these thoughts were pushed aside for another time.

When my husband died in 1993, I continued to live in our house we purchased in 1980 in Mansfield, Ohio. Actually moving was the farthest thing on my mind. I believe this all came from many stories of those who moved too quickly after a death and were sorry for it. So, I stayed put.

Gradually I hired help. First it was for snow removal, followed by seasonal yard work, and grass mowing. However there was much to do in a two story house. It was becoming increasingly difficult each year.

As a volunteer I visited patients from my church at the local hospital. There were at least two-to-three patients per week. As I entered the first room I greeted Bob, the patient, and his wife, Doris, seated near him. During our conversation I asked Bob if I could question him about living in a condo since they had lived in several. I had passing thoughts about moving—perhaps to a condo. He gave me very helpful and useful information. As we continued talking Doris took hold of my arm and said, "One thing I know for sure is that you need to move before you're 75 (years of age)." This hit me like a ton of bricks. I would be seventy-five in four months. Her words made sense. I decided to act.

When I got home I called a friend who was a realtor. She suggested that we go see the builder of the condos within a mile of my house. She and the builder were friends. She made the appointment. Once in his office he said that in three months they would begin building and showed me the location on a site map. I knew immediately I wanted the one where the back of the house overlooked a natural park with lanes for walking. "However," he cautioned, "another couple talked with me this morning and they want the same one you want—but they'll be back on Monday after thinking it over." Then he added, "If you want it you can have it." Immediately I said, "I want it.". I signed the papers, made out a deposit check and that was that.

Now my brain was in overload, and I realized I needed to make sensible plans. As I began looking at all the treasures Bert and I had acquired through the years, some from Sweden, some hand-me-downs, and gifts, I continued to struggle with choices. Knowing that I was moving to a facility that was different from my home, I had to decide what furniture to move. The condo had two bedrooms, a combination living room/dining room, a kitchen, two bathrooms, and a large space downstairs that would function as my piano studio including a large storage area plus a third bathroom. In addition there were many decisions to make while the condo was being built. I thought those questions from the builder would never end. But it was exciting to drive by the house and show my friends how it was taking shape.

I decided to have a sale. I called an auctioneer who came to the house and a date for a yard sale was made for Friday, the day after Thanksgiving. I questioned how many people would be in town since it was a holiday weekend. He assured me it would work, and I signed the papers.

The sale occupied my mind almost twenty-four hours a day as I sifted and sorted what would sell and what should be moved to my condo. I really missed my husband's advice and calming influence. But it was really up to me and no one else. During this time I was teaching piano at home and substituting as an organist on Sunday mornings at various churches. This alone kept me quite busy.

Several friends offered to help me move. With a small truck and lots of back breaking work, the end finally came. The sale was three days away—and I thought I was ready for the auctioneer. Little did I realize how emotional it would be. Thanksgiving was spent with friends, but my mind was on thoughts of the next day's auction. I tried to be pleasant while eating. I wondered if anyone noticed my aloofness, and my furrowed brow.

On the day of the sale I drove to my house and parked across the street. The auctioneer asked me to be there in case there were questions to be answered. Trying to be inconspicuous I entered my empty house through the garage, and sat on the step leading to the upstairs. Through the window I heard the familiar call of the auctioneer and watched as items were purchased, and strangers carrying off my prized possessions. I shed tears when our brass bed, one that had first belonged to my parents. In a few seconds a big chunk of history was gone. I started to sob. I wanted to shout to the crowd, "Please go home. I've changed my mind." Just then there was a knock on the back door. As it opened a voice said, "Helen, are you here? It's Pastor Paul." My weepy voice brought him around to where I was seated and he said, "I've come to give you a hug." I melted in his embrace. After a few comforting words he said a prayer that made me realize I was doing the right thing. After he left I saw him carrying items to his car that he had purchased. Again a God-moment had just happened. It changed my attitude and I said aloud, "Thank you God."

I was now a condo owner in a new neighborhood, and I was actually going to sleep in my new house tonight. I remember lying in bed with three windows directly in front of me watching a full moon move across the sky. It was a clear cool November night. Even though I was very tired after a full day, it kept me awake for a while as I continued watching the moon's path. It was a marvelous sight. As I drifted off to sleep I wondered who lived next door. That would have to wait for another day.

November 11, 2013

JUST ANOTHER SNOW STORM?

It was a cold day in March of 2010. Nothing unusual about that in Ohio, but later in the day a severe snowstorm was predicted. Going to the store and stocking up on provisions to outlast any power outage was a wise decision. That night it began to snow. Around 11:00 p.m., lying in bed, I could hear the wind swirling around the corners of the house. In the morning it was still snowing. The accumulation was more than I thought. However, it truly *was* a beautiful sight. In the morning I looked up the road to the entrance of the condo units. No cars were moving. Good, I thought, I have a free day. No teaching.

The next day a snowplow had made one path up the street in front of my condo. In the afternoon a mail truck was able to get through and left mail in my box at the end of the driveway. As I peered through the front door, the snow depth did not appear as severe as I thought since the wind had made several drifts. I dressed with snow boots, heavy scarf, hooded jacket, mittens, and put a cell phone in my pocket.

As I carefully began my journey to the mailbox, I eyed the drifts to find shallow ones, but had several deep drifts to tackle before reaching my goal. With mail in hand, going back should be easy, I thought. I will step in the same imprints I made going to the mailbox. However, when I started, I soon realized that this was a precarious venture since my boot print was now reversed. It made me unsteady. One more step and down I went landing on my knees. The snow was up to my hips. I couldn't get up. What should I do? Oh, yes, my cell phone.

I took out my phone, opened to the emergency number, looked at it for about ten seconds, and then closed it and put it back in my pocket. My vision of the fire department, with sirens going full blast to come and rescue an old lady stuck in the snow, was not a picture I wanted. There had to be another way. My next door neighbor opened her door, shouted to me an apology that she could do nothing. I agreed. She closed the door.

What to do next? By now my jeans were wet making my knees and legs much colder. I had to find an answer to my dilemma.

Just then I realized two snowplows were beginning to clear the driveways up the street. They were slowly proceeding in my direction, however I determined it would take some time before reaching my driveway. I began waving the mail and shouting. My shouting did nothing against the noise of the plows. I waited. I continued to wave the mail in their direction to no avail.

About ten minutes later the plows had come within three driveways from mine. One of the drivers saw my predicament and drove around, and with a hefty pull, he lifted me to a standing position and walked me to my front door. Close to crying I hugged him and said thank you over and over.

Why am I telling you this story? The answer? This is one of the reasons I moved to California.

September 24, 2013

TO STAY OR TO GO—THAT IS THE QUESTION

I had just spent another Christmas season in San Francisco. It was December 30, 2010 and my family was driving me to the airport for my return to Ohio. I had had a great visit with my son, David, and his wife, Trish; my grandson David, and his wife, Jennie; and my New York grandson Jon, who lives and works as a musician in Brooklyn, New York. As we neared the airport Trish asked me, "Mom, are you getting tired of the snow in Ohio?" I easily answered "yes." At this point Trish continued, "Have you ever thought about moving?" I hesitantly said, "Well, yes." "Would you consider moving to California?" she said. Again I paused and said a quiet "Yes." A further question was "Would you like us to do some research for you in California?" I paused, thought for a moment, and then responded with a tentatively sounding, "W-e-l-l ... Okay."

In early February 2011, David called and asked me to send him information regarding my assets. I mailed a packet of material within a week. Toward the end of the month David called saying that he and Trish will visit retirement homes in Mill Valley and Burlingame. I thought, hmmmm ... do I really want to move to California? Do I want to leave my friends and my house? What will I do with all my stuff? A week later another call came from David reporting on their visit to Burlingame and Mill Valley. Sounds pretty good, I said to myself. He also suggested I come for a California visit in mid-June. Then Jon agreed that I could have his piano that he had left behind in San Francisco. Now that was a big plus. That day there was 7.5 inches of snow. "California is beginning to look better," I said aloud. The next day there was more snow with dangerous ice beneath the snow.

Now it was time for me to talk to my son, Jesse, who lived in New Jersey with his wife, Virginia. I must admit that I was reluctant to call since I was leaning towards moving to California and not to New Jersey. But, also, I didn't want him to feel that I was favoring David over him. When I screwed up my courage and called, he made it easy for me as I explained my dilemma. He immediately answered and gave me the following wonderful answer—"Mom, why would you want to move to New Jersey?" He then assured me that when the time came for the move he would come to help. I was relived and breathed a sigh of relief. He lived up to his promise and was a tremendous help.

I came to California in June and visited facilities in Burlingame, Mill Valley, Santa Rosa, and Sonoma. For me it was a tossup between Santa Rosa and Sonoma. I did not share my thoughts, nor did David or Trish say which they preferred. Sonoma loomed higher the more I thought about it. It was within the city, the architecture was unique, and the people friendly. When I announced that I had chosen Sonoma, Trisha's response was a loud hurrah. That settled it. It was obvious I had made the right choice. Merrill Gardens in Sonoma has been my home since August 11, 2011.

May 29, 2012

THIS WAS MY FIRST (Earthquake!)

It was early Sunday morning, August 24th, 2014. I was comfortable in my familiar twin bed and sound asleep. Suddenly, at precisely 3:20 a.m., there was a loud noise and the bed began jerking heavily. The lamp next to my bed sounded like it was going to crash, and when all this confusion suddenly stopped, I actually shouted "IT'S AN EARTHQUAKE!" I had often wondered what it would be like and sound like if I were to ever experience an earthquake. "So this is it," I said, and I was truly experiencing fear. The clock and lights gave me no information since the electric power was out, and I sat on the edge of the bed trying to find the flashlight in the nightstand drawer. I could tell that I was nervous. I wondered if there would be additional aftershocks, and I felt myself tensing as I got up to walk to the bathroom. When I got back to bed, I curled up in a fetal position and tried to adjust my body to the situation and fell asleep.

The next thing I knew someone was shining a flashlight and calling my name asking if I was okay. I called out "yes" and asked who it was. "It's Karen," was the answer, and I responded "Thank you, thank you" several times. Knowing that I was being cared for came as a calming gesture, and I was able to sleep again.

When the power returned my radio gave me the story of what had happened. It was devastating to learn throughout the morning the severe damage to the neighboring city of Napa. Fires, buildings near collapse, stores showing empty shelves with their contents scattered on the floor, and roadways severely buckled. I listened for about half an hour before getting up to check the rest of my apartment. Yes, it was obvious there had been an earthquake.

As I looked I saw through my patio door my heavy iron plant stand tipped over on the deck with the contents tipped out but unbroken. Inside, my attention turned to my curio cabinet. The doors were open and several items were tipped over inside with additional pieces on the floor. An angel lost part of her lute she was holding. I was relieved when several precious pieces were unscathed. Power was restored and I felt safer in the daylight and listening to television.

Since a few days have passed since the earthquake I have had time to think about what has happened. First of all an earthquake could be the end of life for some. It could be me. Secondly, for some in certain places an earthquake is fairly common. Japan comes to mind. In Ohio when I first told of my plans to move to California, the common response was, "I'd rather live in Ohio than to be in earthquake country." My response usually was that I'd take my chances, remembering the scary severe weather Ohio has faced at times. Retro-fitting for buildings seems to be a good thing, and it's good I live in a wooden structure and not one built with bricks. Lastly, I now know what it is like to be in an earthquake. I don't like it except I now feel like a "real" Californian.

August 26, 2014

WHAT ONE YEAR HAS TAUGHT ME

In four days, I will have lived at Merrill Gardens in Sonoma, California for one year. After visiting several other facilities, I signed the necessary documents for an apartment on June 30, 2011. I returned to Ohio and had the month of July to sort and pack, and say my goodbyes. I left Ohio and moved into my apartment on August 11, 2011.

During this past year I have become aware of many changes in my life and lifestyle. As I look back over my life, there have always been changes and new lessons to be learned. I'm fairly certain, however, that I have had to make more changes and have learned more new lessons this year than over my entire adult life.

The following list, in no particular order, tells what I have learned and or experienced in one year:

- How wonderful it is to live near family.
- The joy of meeting new people and hearing their stories.
- The challenge of learning the names of the residents.
- To choose and participate in many opportunities, e.g., exercise, games, movies, presentations by doctors, trivia, musical programs, trips, etc.
- How to bowl with the Wii game.
- How to set up the Wii game for bowling.
- To learn another new game—Wii golf.
- The joy of not having to cook—and being served three meals every day in the dining room.
- To appreciate the many kindnesses from the MG staff and dining personnel.
- That I do not miss my car.
- The shortest route from my apartment to the dining area.

- To be satisfied with less.
- The joy of having my laundry washed, dried, and neatly folded and returned the next morning.
- Floors vacuumed and/or mopped, minimal dusting, and removal of garbage.
- How to de-clutter.
- To be grateful that I will never live through another snowstorm.
- To appreciate having a fine piano on which to play in my apartment and a grand piano in the MG living room.
- How to deal with losing a resident through their moving or death.
- The discipline of remembering to press the red button each morning to let the staff know I am okay.
- The discipline of setting aside some "down time" for quiet reading, thinking, and prayer.
- At this point I'm wondering what additional items will be on the list at the end of next year? I sincerely hope the list will increase.

August 7, 2012

                        *   *   *   Follow-up   *   *   *

After four years, a few more things I have learned:

- How to be on time for a trip. (Got left behind once.)
- That I cannot be involved in everything. (Make choices.)
- To appreciate the wait staff even more.
- The appreciate the steady attendance and participation of the residents at the "My Story, Your Story" weekly sessions.
- Everything has the right to change—how to live and accept the change.

September 22, 2015

CHOICES CALL FOR DECISIONS

Every day we all make choices. Some choices are easy, and some take clear thinking before deciding. For other more serious problems one may seek professional help. For the easy choices we usually follow a pattern, something we have done the same way for a long time. For instance what to eat, what to wear, where to go or do, for these choices it almost happens automatically. For choices that are a bit more difficult, we may go with our "gut" feeling. I think this is called intuitive thinking. I'm not sure exactly how this works. Do the results always turn out to be the best choice? Again I'm not sure. For those who turn for help from professionals, one must still be convinced before deciding to act, and then we often have that nagging feeling that there still may be a much better choice. At one time I was reminded by my husband to be careful when giving advice. He said, "You know, the person may just take it."

One day my mother called me to help her with a problem. She had her name on a waiting list at a retirement facility in Minneapolis, and a call had come to say there was a room available. She called me in Ohio and asked "What should I do?" I hesitated because I did not want to tell her what to do but wanted to allow her to make the choice. So I said "Mom, you have two choices; either you go or you stay where you are." "What if I go and do not like it?" she said. My immediate answer again was, "You have two choices, either stay where you are or you leave." These were simplistic answers, of course, but I quickly added that if she decided to accept the offer of the room, I would come and help her move. After more telephone conversations she made a decision to move, and I fulfilled my promise to help. It proved to be a good choice.

For us who live in this facility we have easy choices. We can sit where we like in the dining room and have a choice of meals from a menu. Our alarm clock is set or not set as to the time to arise, and we choose which activities to attend. Also we have four choices as to the size apartment that would be suitable. We then decide what to bring with us from our former residence and for overflow there are hallway storage areas if necessary.

Now, contrast all this with those who are in prison. It is a well-known fact that people who are incarcerated have a very difficult time adjusting to the "outside world" once they are released. In prison all of their activities followed a strict schedule. Meals (no choice of menu there, by the way), showers, exercise, a variety of classes, work schedules, and lights out, are precisely timed. All of this presents a huge problem when they have done their time and are released from prison. Since they have not acquired the skill of making choices they may flounder in this their new world that does not mirror their previous time in prison. But if they are fortunate to have a support system upon their release, a family, a group home, or some other means, they may learn to make the right choices. If not, they usually get into trouble and return to prison.

On another level let's talk about health. For many illnesses there are diagnostic tests such as x-rays and CT scans, followed by treatment hopefully to return us to good health. Further, we have the choice to follow the advice of doctors and other professionals or ignore their advice altogether. I have found it easy to tell someone they should call a doctor if they have a problem. However, for me to be told to contact a doctor, I procrastinate. So wouldn't it be great if an intelligent person invented an instrument like a barometer that would make wise choices for us? And then again, would we sit there and think, are there any other options? May I have another choice please? So for the present, I plan to keep my brain active in order to be able to make good decisions. But most likely I'll probably still look for other choices.

October 9, 2012

IT'S ALWAYS BEEN A QUESTION

So, how did I enter this world on June 4, 1927? Actually I do not know. All I know is that my birth mother could not care for me and as a result allowed me to be adopted at the age of three months. My adopting parents signed the legal papers, and with that I became the daughter of Edwin and Adelia Hoffman and given the name Helen Rowene Hoffman. My mother wanted to name me June because I was born in June, but my father strongly objected. He said the reason was that my Swedish grandparents on both sides of the family would call me "yune" (the "j" is silent in Swedish). He wanted a name that they could pronounce so it had to be Helen. My middle name, Rowene, was my mother's choice. Why my parents could not have children was also a mystery, but I never broached the subject with either mother or father.

Mother said that she told me of my adoption when I was quite young, but true to form I did not remember it. On one particular occasion some children were teasing me about being adopted as we walked home from school. I immediately ran into the house crying telling my mother what these mean kids had said about me. Her response was "I told you a long time ago about your adoption." I also remember at this point it hurt. I thought, "How could any mother give up her child?"

A couple of months before I was married, mother told me a few details about my adoption and said that she had some papers that I could have if I ever wanted to find my birth parents. During her haltingly difficult attempt to explain she started to cry. She then showed me a well-worn brown leather envelope with a ragged ribbon tied in a bow to hold it together but never opened it for me to see.

Before my wedding in 1949, Mother sent for my birth certificate to the Hennepin County courthouse in St. Paul, Minnesota. When it arrived I saw that it had no evidence of my birth parents. However, it functioned fully as a legal document.

I've often wondered about my decision of not trying to find my birth parents. Also I have questioned who do I look like and do I have any sisters or brothers. At this point I have to leave these questions unanswered.

After my father died in 1973 she brought up the subject again. She said she wanted me to have this information, and told me that my father was very much against giving it to me since they had promised secrecy to my birth parents. So I elected not to pursue it any further. I could see that it was still quite painful to her, and I did not want to hurt my adoptive parents. I knew that the reason for the adoption was done in love, and that she and Dad had dedicated me to God, and promised to raise me in the faith of the Church. I realized that my life to this point could not have been better.

When mother entered a nursing home in 1981, she insisted that I accept the leather envelope tied with that ragged ribbon. I have since opened it a couple of times, but it didn't really give me much pertinent information to help locating anyone. As a result at this point, I thank God for parents who accepted the challenge of raising a child not their own but making their own. That's love beyond measure.

June 28, 2015

ALL IN THE FAMILY

Relatives are an important part of any family, especially if the relationship is congenial and everyone actually likes one another. In my case, my husband's sister and brother were good examples. Bert's sister, Ruth, met Marvin Lindstedt at Bethel College in St. Paul, Minnesota, the same college that Bert and I attended. We got married the same year—1949. Ruth and Marvin left five years later as missionaries to the Philippine Islands with their three children, Peggy, Karen, and Steve. Peter and Beth were born later. Bert's brother, Arne, married Joyce in 1951 and baby Mark followed. Arne spent many years overseas in the Air Force.

Picture 17: The siblings—Arne, Ruth, and Bert Anderson

Since our families were separated by miles, and sometimes by years, our together time was very important. We cherished the occasion when we could arrange a get-together. There were never any hostilities, only laughter, hugs, and stories, and a game or two of our favorite card game, Kings in the Corner.

Now the years have passed and all three men are gone. Three widows remain. We three share a common experience. Bert, my husband, died in July of 1993. His brother, Arne, died in August 2011. And the following year, Marvin, died in April 2012.

Picture 18: Ruth, Joyce, and me.

Marvin's immediate family decided to join together this week, one year later (April 2013) to celebrate his life and remember him. I wanted to write something to add to their remembrances so I wrote:

In my mind's eye I observed Marvin listening to his family's conversation. He would smile, and one would know that he was pleased. This was his joy. This was his family.

He was a quiet man, a deep thinker, and very generous in many ways. He had a good life, one that gave him pleasure since he was fulfilling God's plan serving as a missionary in the Philippine Islands. He had a faithful wife who was his true partner. In addition his 5 children fulfilled what one would call a houseful. Marvin's form of discipline was entirely by example, propelled by love. Having known him for over 60 years, I can honestly say I was happy to be a part of the Lindstedt family. Marvin and I shared the love of music especially the classics and the swing music of the 50's and 60's.

I also can speak for Bert, his brother-in-law (my husband). Often when we were all together, the two men (one Baptist, the other Lutheran), would share ministerial experiences and the theology of today. They never argued—they respected one another's opinion.

There is so much more that I could add, but I'll simply say:

I loved him dearly . . . especially his short table prayers!

Since that event, Marvin's wife, Ruth, died in August (2014). Today as I write there are only two of the original couples: Joyce in Duluth, Minnesota, and me in Sonoma, California. But this is the pattern of life. Separated by miles; yet still bonded together as family.

Picture 19: Marvin and Ruth Lindstedt, Helen and Bert Anderson

I too, will leave this earth. How soon no one knows except my Maker. Hopefully my legacy will be a book of my stories mostly written about family and friends and written for those who might enjoy reading them.

April 9, 2013

CHAIRS

Recently I wrote an essay about the word *time*. It was interesting to discover how many ways we incorporate the word time in our writing or conversation. Well, I found another word that challenged me in the same way. The word is *chair*. So let's have fun and play the word game.

Think about it. What kind of a chair first comes to mind? For me it was the rocking chair. Let's hope it is a comfortable one with a pillow on the seat. For a mother trying to quiet a crying baby it is often the answer. A high chair and later a potty chair are good to have for a very young child. If you are royalty you sit in the King's or Queen's chair. If you have back problems you look for a comfortable chair, one that supports your back. In the Merrill Gardens dining area many chairs are available so you can choose the best fit. (New chairs that were all alike were added in 2014) An arm chair is an age-appropriate one that allows you to stand up easier. In that same vain there are wheel chairs, both electric and self-propelled.

For those who have been on a cruise no doubt you sat on the open deck in a deck chair. Did you fall asleep or were you taken with the ocean waves and its deep blue color splashing on the side of the ship? In nice weather you may be seated in a lawn chair or a beach chair. In the woods it probably would be a camp chair, sometimes called a stool, and the beach chair would be resting on a warm sandy shoreline.

I can think of two rather tall chairs both having to do with sports. One is at the beach and the other at a sporting event. Can you picture what they are? The first one is a tall chair for a lifeguard, and the other is a high wooden chair for a referee at a tennis match. I can understand why these chairs are so tall. It is necessary for the lifeguard to be able to survey the waters he is guarding, and the referee must be able to be fair as to whether the ball is out or in the designated space.

At this point I decided to check Google for additional types of chairs even though I still had several on my list. On Wikipedia the top announcement regarding chairs gave this figure: there are 52,900,000 entries. It added the following statement. "There are as many types of chairs available that an entire book could be written on the subject.". So, do I want to continue this quest? Not really except to list several that I thought about previously such as: swivel, overstuffed, captain's, ski-lift, straight-back, barrel, wingback, director's, dentist's, office, Adirondack, and on and on.

However there is one type of chair that I have left to the last. It is one that I would never want to sit on, and am sorry when I learn someone was forced to be seated on it. It is the electric chair.

Okay, one more thought. I have seen drawings of people in the Stone Age being seated on the ground or on large rocks or tree stumps. Did they call it a chair? I wonder if they were alive today would they be bedazzled by all the choices we have on which to sit?

But now for some fun—can anyone give me a good definition of a chair?

December 11, 2012

WHY SHOULD I WRITE MY STORY?

I must admit that I have never written anything significantly worthy before coming to Merrill Gardens. Oh, perhaps in college I had assignments, but certainly nothing to keep or frame. It wasn't until a group of us here at Merrill Gardens got together and began thinking about the possibility of starting a writing club and the idea took root. The idea was presented at the next Town Meeting for all the residents and it was to be called "My Story, Your Story.". This was January 2012. Because I was in on the planning I felt obligated to write a story for the first official meeting.

So, I sat down in front of my computer, and sat, and sat, and my brain told me nothing. What was I to do since the first meeting was the next day? I am now admitting that I dug up an old article that I had written several years ago to submit to the *Reader's Digest* but never mailed. I thought it was pretty good, and after all who would know in this new group when it was originally written. I certainly wasn't going to tell at the first meeting of our story group that it was not a new story, and I believe I got away with it.

Why am I telling this now? I think it is because I want everyone to know that writing isn't always easy. However, at this point in my life, after writing 90+ stories, I also want it to be known that it does become easier. One bit of encouragement came from one of my favorite authors, Anne Lamott who said when she was asked the question about how to get started writing, "you must first sit your butt on a chair."

I'm sure for all of us somewhere in our past history there is a story waiting to be told. You may not think that any little incident in your life is worth telling. Then again you may have led a fascinating life, but if you don't become a storyteller no one will ever know about it, especially your family. Also those of us who have lived to seventy, eighty, and ninety years of age, we have experienced many things that no longer exist such as living without electricity, The Great Depression, or life on a farm. Or you may have immigrated to the United States from a distant land. There must be a story connected with these adventures. When you finish your first bit of writing, you'll be glad you told your story and so will your family. And for the rest of us seated here, we'll also be delighted.

Believe me! It's true.

June 11, 2013

AND SOME WONDERED IF IT WOULD LAST

The official beginning of "My Story, Your Story" was on February 7, 2012 when twenty-one people crowded around tables in the Card Room. One of our own Merrill Garden residents, David Nagle, gave a presentation about ways to write stories. He encouraged all of us to begin thinking about our past and to jot down ideas and then put it together in some order. Many of us deemed the first meeting extremely successful. There were lots of completed stories, verbal stories, and just plain talk. It was good to hear many positive comments following the session. A few months later we moved to the Rec Room with chairs placed in an oval shape. This allowed those who had a hearing deficit better clarity.

Most of the credit for its beginnings is credited to Dibbie, a Merrill Gardens resident. She explained that it was a great event in her previous residential facility and how it operated. She stressed that it should be fun. Louise, Steve, Dibbie, and I began to put it together and a pitch was made at the Residents Town Hall Meeting describing what it was all about. The four of us became leaders, each taking a turn to chair the session. When Louise found it necessary to bow out sometime later, Dan was asked to fill in.

Since then we have met for forty-seven weeks—February 7, 2012 through January 28, 2013, and only taking time off for September 11, Christmas Day, and New Year's Day in 2012. The average attendance has been sixteen with the maximum of twenty-four.

Sadly we will soon be saying "so long" to Dibbie since she is moving to Atlanta, Georgia. She has been an inspiration to all of us with her many stories. Her quick explanation for not writing her stories was because of poor eyesight. Nevertheless, it did not deter her from telling her stories. She told them all as a seasoned storyteller—and all of them usually made us laugh. Many of us remember the story entitled "A Date with a Murderer" and "Seeing Lucille Ball Riding a Pink Elephant."

So to you, Dibbie, as you move to a new residence in Atlanta, we wish you God Speed. And remember—when you become the impetus for starting another My Story group in Atlanta, you'll have all those wonderful stories you have told us here in Sonoma's Merrill Gardens. To you, Dibbie, we all say a big thank you and how much we will miss you. And for all the rest of us, we join together and say:

"HAPPY 1ST ANNIVERSARY". . . let us eat cake!

February 5, 2013

ANNE LAMOTT

With all the books in the world and their corresponding authors, one sometimes has a list of favorite authors and tends to read their works before exploring new ones. I have such a favorite. Her name is Anne Lamott. She is a Californian, born in Marin County, lives in Tiburon, and has become somewhat of a cult figure. She is a *New York Times* bestselling author, a past recipient of a Guggenheim Fellowship, and an inductee to the California Hall of Fame. In addition she is a "down to earth" person with a bit of salty language, funny, and open about her failures, and successes.

One Saturday night my family and I went to the Uptown Theater in Napa, California to hear Anne speak. I was thrilled that I had the opportunity to hear her in person. As we entered the theater I saw her in the lobby at a table signing and selling her books. I looked at her, and I felt like a teenager staring at a rock star. Timidly, I moved toward the table. She looked up at me and I blurted out, "I've read *Traveling Mercies* three times." She smiled and at that point I'm not sure what she answered.

She would be talking about her most recent book *Help Thanks Wow*. It's a quick read though one can ponder about a serious truth on each page. It is unlike any book on prayer that I have ever read. It makes sense, and has the potential of being read over and over to allow certain truths to take root.

Bird by Bird was the first of her books I read. In it, she tells about her young son who had a school assignment to write about birds. He was fussing and fuming and complaining that he just could not get started. Anne's father was standing nearby and finally exclaimed, "Just start with bird by bird." To me it was a book about how to begin writing. Her first bit of advice? "Sit your butt on a chair."

My next read was a curious one: *Traveling Mercies*. On the flyleaf it said, —"A chronicle of faith and spiritually that is at once tough, personal, affectionate, wise, and very funny." I loved it on one hand, but on the other hand felt guilty for liking it so much. She was so different from me, but I could identify in almost every respect. Before *Traveling Mercies* she wrote *Operating Instructions*—another down to earth book about raising children.

In a recent *Time Magazine* article Anne Lamott was asked the following question, "You're a grandma now, so the inevitable question arises, Can you still pull off the dreadlocks?" Her answer: "I've always had a policy with my family: You get to have your hair, I get to have my hair." No questions asked. On the stage at the Napa theatre, her appearance was less than stylish. She wore a pullover shirt with jeans and a scarf around her neck. Her signature dread locks made her who she is—unpretentious. I looked less at what she wore and paid more attention to what she said and much of what she said produced applause, laughter, and "aha" moments.

Two additional books I have read are *Grace (Eventually): Thoughts on Faith* and *Plan B: Further Thoughts on Faith*. These two books describe how she handled or failed in life's difficult situations. These books are truly a worthwhile read. She has also written some novels—*Blue Shoes*, which I read, and *Rosie and Crooked Little Heart*.

Writing is her profession. This means appearing and speaking at many venues and book signings. At the conclusion of her talk that lasted one and a half hours, she answered questions from the audience. One woman asked for advice for herself as a potential writer. Anne quickly pulled out a pen from her back pocket and said, "Always carry a pen with you. You never know when an inspiration will hit." She also said that "Writing is like driving with the headlights on—you can only see just ahead of you but you always get there."

What will I do with all this inspiration? I hope to continue writing; not to become famous, but to fulfill my wish to leave something of value for my family that tells a bit about who I am.

December 4, 2012

EMIGRANTS

Several years ago I read four books in a series entitled *The Emigrants* written by Vilhelm Moberg, a Swede. It is a fictional story depicting Swedish families making the decision to leave their homeland, followed by their preparations for their travel around the year 1850. I was interested in these stories since my grandparents and my husband's parents were Swedish emigrants.

During the summer of 1974 we made our first trip to Sweden. We were both interested in finding family birth places and visiting surviving family members. It was a successful trip, since we came away with many stories and photos to show our respective families here in the United States.

My husband was able to walk in the house where his father lived, and with tears in my eyes, I saw the house of my grandmother. I cannot describe the feeling. It was from this farm she left to live in The United States.

As we left the house and got in our car, Bert stopped, got out to dig out of the dirt a good sized stone, and picked a small flower. Later he gave them to my mother properly mounted with the words "These items are from the road your mother trod on her way to America." Mother and I both wept.

No doubt emotions ran high for those who left the homeland but also for those who remained. The father in the story said, "I must go outside and behold my sons' funeral procession" as the family watched the son leave his homeland.

One memento I have is a wooden trunk made by my grandmother's father. The trunk was made for her to carry her possessions for her long journey by ship to the United States. It is made of wood, approximately 24 x 18 inches, by twelve inches deep, has a curved lid, with her name, Louisa Hager, spelled with nail heads on the rounded cover. I suspect her father was in tears as he pounded those nails knowing he most likely would never see his daughter again.

The remaining books in the series are *Unto a Good Land*, *The Settlers*, and *Last Letter Home*. Also, an award winning film was made with Max van Sydow and Liv Ullman entitled "The Emigrants". A film worth seeing and the books all good reads.

October 15, 2013

HIS NAME IS PAUL

Paul Gilger is an American architect, set designer, and playwright. He is an unusual kind of guy—simply put, a multi-talented man who has accomplished more in his life at age fifty-nine than most. I met him several years ago in Mansfield, Ohio when he was visiting his parents whom I had known for several years. He was born in Mansfield, worked as an architect for a few years after graduating from Cincinnati University and later moved to San Francisco. Recently I saw his set-design work at a production of "Camelot." It was unique since it incorporated film on the back wall to enhance the Elizabethan architecture.

One of his greatest accomplishments was crafting the works of Jerry Herman of "Hello Dolly" fame into a stage musical with a cast of six people. He titled it "Tune the Grand Up" but later changed it to "Show Tunes." It features the songs of Herman in story form with songs, costumes and bits of dialogue. I saw this performance in San Francisco on New Year's Eve in 2002 and Jerry Herman was in the audience. It also has been playing in Japan for several years. He also designed an industrial light and magic film studio for the famous film maker, George Lucas. Paul lives in Santa Rosa, California.

His other passion is the famous Lincoln Highway, the first transcontinental highway. The highway begins at Times Square in New York and ends 3,649 miles later at Lincoln Park in San Francisco. In addition he is the chair of the Lincoln Highway Association National Mapping Committee. He recently stated "I'm a big fan of the Lincoln Highway, so I have dedicated ten years of my life to it." He updates the map continually whenever new information is found concerning road improvements and alignments. He participated in a trip on the Lincoln Highway to celebrate the 100th anniversary of the complete mapping of the highway. One group left from San Francisco and the other left from New York City with a plan to meet midway in Kearney, Nebraska. The New York crowd on the east tour started on June 22, 2013 in Times Square and Paul led a tour from Lincoln Park on June 23. It took one week traveling about 250 miles a day no faster than 55 MPH.

The drivers chose their own car. There were two Packards, a Tucker, Model A Fords, Model T Fords, Porsches, Lincoln Continental convertibles, plus campers. There were also home-built vehicles and Volkswagen "Bugs." As tour leader, Paul drove a trusty Mustang convertible. When any car broke down during the trip, and that happened often, the entire entourage would wait while mechanics in the group assessed the problem and made repairs.

There is so much more to this story, but I will leave it up to Paul to tell the next chapter the next time we are together. And I, for one, am thoroughly interested in what it is about the Lincoln Highway that has resonated with so many people.

October 15, 2016

SECURITY AND INSECURITY

A recent *Time* magazine cover read—"Homeland Insecurity" followed by "Do we need to sacrifice our privacy to be safer?" This got me thinking about how life has changed over the years as I looked at the subject of Security vs. Insecurity.

When I was a child one of the safeguards was to lock the doors when we went on vacation, but when at home leave the doors unlocked during the day. At night my father would check all doors and windows before going to bed. There was never anything that gave me pause to be afraid until I learned that he slept with a revolver under his pillow. My mother hated this. In all the years we lived in this house there was never an incident to warrant the use of the revolver.

Another safeguard my parents used before going away was *not* to tell me where or when we were going. They were afraid that I would "spill the beans" and the whole neighborhood would know. When the car was packed and the house was securely locked, Dad would drive around the neighborhood looking for me. When I was spotted, he would call to me and Mother would sweep me into the car. With a wet wash cloth and clean clothes I was made presentable to travel.

Today in the USA there are more guns than ever, especially assault weapons. For me, the use of an assault weapon has no redeeming qualities. To combat this problem one of the answers has been to put up surveillance cameras. It seems that more are being erected daily. In times of war, our government has often restricted personal freedoms in the name of national security. In the recent episode of the Boston Marathon bombers in April 2013, cameras came to play an integral part in the capture of the two culprits responsible for this horrific deed. Also, it was a personal camera that prompted detectives to agree that the two pictured young men were the ones the authorities were looking for. This time cameras really proved their value. I am no authority to say what has been done by the US or how this affects our privacy, but I do not like the idea of having to be afraid. Like Linus' blanket in the "Peanuts" cartoons, many children have a blanket that brings comfort when they are afraid. What do grownups do to feel secure? Is this why some carry guns?

I now ask what makes you feel safe? Or, what makes you feel unsafe? Here is a personal example: Last week when I came home after 10:00 p.m. to my Senior Residence, I expected to use the telephone outside the front entrance door to ask someone to come to open the door. I was really surprised when the door opened automatically. As I walked by the front desk, there was no one to greet me, and no one within voice range. This made me feel insecure. As I wound my way down the hall toward my second floor apartment I was cautious and uneasy until I was safe inside my apartment.

As a teenage driver, I remember my heart beating fast with the sense of impending danger as I pulled up to our detached garage at night, left the car running while I unlocked the door, and then pushing the button to open the garage door. As it began to lift, the streetlight made scary shadows, and my imagination saw too many frightening possibilities. Once inside the house, my insecurity quickly flipped to relief when I saw Dad half asleep in a chair waiting for my arrival. Now I was completely safe—especially since I knew he had a revolver. What's your story? What makes you feel secure or insecure?

July 9, 2013

I LOVE GOOD NEWS

It is quite evident that most people like to hear good news. It makes us happy. It makes us utter words of joy. It makes our day. In today's world, however, newspapers and television appear to cater to bad news. Wars, strikes, horrendous accidents, deaths, and fire and weather storms appear daily in the news media. I guess this is what sells. I admit I read most of it, or at least the headlines and then determine what to do with the information. If it is a local paper, I may check if the stories are about anyone I know. This also goes for obituaries. I often admire writers who are able to capture a story with a clever headline that propels one to read the complete story. One I distinctly remember was in the *Jersey Journal* on the front page in big bold letters: MAYOR'S WIFE GOES UNDER THE KNIFE. No need to guess what this story was about.

Last week I wrote a story about getting a new iPhone. To bring you up to date, I have gained more operational knowledge. It's fun to receive a call, bring up pictures of the family vacationing in Hawaii, and check the weather, or set the alarm. But the best of all joys came this evening, Monday, July 29. My phone rang (it's a funky tune)—I answered and the caller said, "Hi Grandma. It's Jon calling from Hawaii." He's my grandson who lives and works in New York City and is vacationing with his family and his girlfriend. Of course I was thrilled to hear from him.

We talked about a minute and then he broke the news—"Molly and I became engaged today!" This was really good news, primarily since I have chided him several times about not waiting too long before he popped the question. In fact, I told him about my grandmother, who posed the following question to my boyfriend; "Are you going to marry Helen or are you just going to monkey around?" Bert told Grandma yes, so the joke was that my grandmother knew he was going to ask me to marry him before I did. This was not the case for Jon and Molly—today it was for real! This was truly a Good News Story for me.

I wonder what would happen if in our conversations we would share good news in an effort to thwart all the bad news we hear daily. In my mind I seem to remember that there actually was a newspaper in the United States that decided to print only good news stories and events. In checking Google, to my surprise there are a great number of newspapers with good news themes. Congratulations to those who dare "swim up-stream" and give us Good News. Check it out at www.happynews.com.

July 30, 2013

P.S. Molly and Jon gave birth to their first child, a boy, Henry Christopher Anderson today, March 31, 2018. Oh happy day.

BE MY GUEST

How many times have I signed my name in a guest book at a memorial service, or a wedding? I think a lot. And I wonder about the origin of these books? And further, what happens to these very personal items after a few years? Do people keep them accessible or are they tucked away in a drawer or in a box of photos stashed in the attic. My guess would be these memory books are not read very often and maybe never. Today I had guests here at my residence. We ate in the private dining room. My two cousins, Ruby and Virginia came from Elk Grove, California, together with their cousin, Betty Jean from Santa Ana, plus Betty Jean's friend, Shirley, from Phoenix, Arizona. At one time we all lived in Minnesota. As you may suspect our conversation centered about our lives in that great state.

Following lunch here in our private dining room, we walked outside along the courtyard and up the stairs to my apartment. My cousins knew I was writing stories, and knew that I looked forward to someday have a published book. When they asked me to read a story I chose two. Of course I could have gone on and on reading more, but decided that might be boring. I was also asked to play the piano. I took advantage of the opportunity and handed them a guest book to sign while I was playing. After they left I picked up the guest book to read what they had written—and then something wonderful happened. As I began to read and continued to read I ended up reading the entire book, stopping to savor each name and associating an incident or two with a familiar face. The first pages were names of people who attended our 40th wedding anniversary on September 3, 1989 at First English Lutheran Church, in Mansfield, Ohio. All these signatures covered the first seven pages. Looking over the names I was struck by how many people are no longer living. Oh, the loving memories of all those wonderful people.

As I continued reading, I saw Lola had signed her name on February 1, 2004. Lola was a professional cook who had studied in France, and at one time had her own classy restaurant. I was nervous before she arrived. What would she think of the menu? When she arrived she immediately walked into the kitchen, sat on a stool and watched me as I tended the pots. I was nervous. At one point she walked over to the stove, lifted the lid on the meat dish, and then asked if I had any liquor. She chose a bottle from a box in my pantry and proceeded to change the flavor of the main course dish. With a couple of quick stirs it was time to serve the meal. Everyone raved about the food. During the meal there were the usual compliments that one expects. When the party was over, and we said our farewells, I picked up the guest book and began to read. I was anxious to see what Lola had written. She had written: "GREAT FOOD!!!"

Reading on there were several names that immediately flooded my mind with stories. One was Phil and Marilyn, who made my house their home when they came from a distance and needed a place to stay while visiting in and around Mansfield. They had signed the guest book on each occasion. (Phil served as Associate Pastor together with my husband at First English Lutheran, Mansfield in the early 80's.)

Then there were a number of foreign visitors from Japan, Sweden, Africa, and Russia each with great stories to tell. In addition I had forgotten two signatures that once again made me smile. There was Sandra Mahek who wrote: "Just here for grandkids piano lessons—a rare treat." On another day there was the following message from her grandson: "Nick Mahek, aka your student. It's great to have you as a teacher." Now those are words that a teacher likes to hear. So I've decided to continue to keep my Guest book handy. It's a future source of many memories, and a good read.

October 6, 2014

IS THERE A BOOK IN MY FUTURE?

Ever since the first session of "My Story, Your Story" I have had thoughts of someday assembling material and producing a book about my life. At the time it admittedly was a lofty dream but it seemed not only possible but also probable. That is until recently the day came when I decided to actually begin the process. Now I am faced with the nuts and bolts of how to begin. To date I have written over ninety stories plus nine pages of parts of my history. To put it all together seems arduous and messy, involving long hours and more writing and seeking help from those who know something about it. But this one thing I know, I am ready to begin.

My first effort was to find suitable containers to hold the chapters that I have written with enough space for pictures. Do I use hanging files, accordion pleated cases, or seek help from the Staples store or the Internet to find yet another method? The next job is how to choose the order of my material and where to start. Do I begin chronologically with "I was born in Minneapolis, Minnesota" or do I just assemble stories in a random mode? Will this become clear as I proceed? My son suggested that I first try writing a table of contents and perhaps this idea may present a clearer outline as I move chapters in and out of their spaces. This may work. The other idea was to use sticky notes on a white board and move them around to come up with a suitable outline.

An additional necessity is to set up a work area in my apartment. This is when I wished I had my previous house that had lots of space. At present I have a large 1-bedroom apartment that affords me a place for my piano in the space designated as a dining room. In that same space is a drop-leaf dining table, computer desk, small bench, and a printer cabinet with space below for supplies. Ordinarily, it all works. It appears that the dining table opened up will be the largest work surface and easy to reach with my swivel desk chair. The biggest problem is that I hate having a mess. I like things tidy. It's obvious I'm going to have to change and get used to things being out of order.

Articles that I have read on the subject of leaving a legacy for one's children and grandchildren make the point that family history will be a benefit to family members. It is obvious to me at this point that someday I am really going to be able to hold a book in my hand I have written. I am now committed to the task. And then again—I may at some point before it's all over find it necessary to be committed to another kind of institution.

January 14, 2014

STUFF AND NONSENSE

Once again I'm thinking of words that fascinate me. This time the operative word is *stuff*. Oh, there may be some nonsense as the title indicates, but I have given you fair warning! It all started yesterday passing a few storage units that line the halls where I now live. Often I hear how the units are stuffed with items the residents couldn't leave behind when they moved. How does this happen? Here's my story.

As a child my closet was stuffed with lots of toys and games along with my clothes and shoes. Every few months Mother would decide to organize my toys and games and get rid of items that I no longer played. What a mess. But finally everything was in boxes and neatly stored on shelves or taken to the attic. Next was how to deal with yearly birthday and Christmas gifts, and where to put the new stuff. This problem continued year after year.

Following our wedding, my husband and I moved from my childhood home to an apartment. Now it was my stuff and his stuff and very little storage space. We put storage boxes under the bed, in closets, and even used some as an end table covered with a cloth. A few years later we moved all our stuff to a house. Oh, how wonderful to have all those extra closets and even a basement to store all our stuff. It didn't take long before the closets were stuffed with more stuff. Then David was born and he created a whole lot of new stuff. Suddenly the house seemed smaller.

Four years later we moved to Rock Island, Illinois where my husband would be attending Augustana Seminary. An old three-bedroom, two-story rental house in Rock Island, Illinois afforded us more room. Our growing boy had his stuff; we had our stuff; two college students who rented a bedroom had their stuff; and the house was soon overstuffed. Three years later we moved to Portland, Oregon. My husband was on a one year internship at a church, and we rented a small furnished one-bedroom apartment. We didn't need a lot of stuff so we only brought items that fit in our car such as a broom, mop, a carpet sweeper, few pots and pans, some clothes, and toys. Actually we managed quite well without a lot of stuff. Once again we returned to Rock Island, Illinois and two years later after Bert's graduation and ordination, we moved to Jersey City, New Jersey. Our new house, a parsonage, had a spacious attic, a large basement, two bedrooms, kitchen, dining room, living room and den. It didn't take long before the storage places were occupied. We were accumulating more stuff.

Every time we moved to a different house, (there were four), our possessions grew proportionately. In 2011 I moved from Mansfield in Ohio to Merrill Gardens in Sonoma, California. Here the scene changed dramatically. Since I was living alone in Mansfield in a two-story, three-bedroom house, all decisions were left to me. Now I was moving to a one bedroom apartment. As I sat in front of what seemed like hundreds of boxes my choices became more difficult. How could I part with all the photos of trips, letters from friends, scrapbooks, paintings, gifts, etc.? Since everything had to be ready to ship in a month, I decided to make four piles—stuff to move, stuff to sell, stuff to give away, and stuff to trash. This worked. Did I make the right choices? It doesn't matter now. I am content with what I have—and the best part? I do not need to rent a costly storage unit.

I must tell the story about Bert's mother who moved from Chicago, Illinois to Minneapolis. It seemed logical since two of her children, Ruth and my husband, Bert, were living in Minnesota. At first she stayed with Ruth and family and later moved to an apartment. Her last home was a Senior Residence in St. Paul. With each move her possessions shrank. When she died the sum total of her belongings were in a trunk, and it was not full. It only took a short time for Bert and his brother, Arne, to empty it. (Daughter, Ruth, and family were serving as missionaries in the Philippines at that time.) As I sat there I realized my mother-in-law had done us a favor. I quietly said thank you, Mom, for considering those of us who remained.

As for me I did take a few precious things—items that are gifts and had value, and remembrances of people I loved. Now I'm pondering giving them as gifts to family members next Christmas. The question is will I have second thoughts? Time will tell.

February 19, 2013

WHEN THE WELL RUNS DRY

My mind is a blank. Actually that is not true. What's true is that there are no particular thoughts going through my brain, and as a result there is nothing for me to write about. So why am I sitting at my computer trying to write about nothing? I guess it's because I'm hoping that something will suddenly gel into a story, and I will be able to tell that story for this week's story time. So far nothing is working.

So how about remeniecing? Oh, shoot! I can't even spell remmeneicing. (My computer just told me it's spelled *reminiscing*.) Forget that. How about copying a worthwhile article to share with the group? As I looked at my watch I realized "My Story, Your Story" group is meeting in four hours, and before that I have a meeting and lunch, and furthermore the quotable articles I have read are not handy.

At a recent speaking engagement by Anne Lamott, one of my favorite authors, she shared her response to the question of how to get started—"I always tell them first of all, sit your butt on a chair." Okay Anne, I have done that. Now what? At this point it appears that I am still back to square one. But just then an image appeared! How about thinking about past Labor Days.

Labor Day! Now my brain is beginning to bring up several images. Immediately I thought of past Labor Days. It certainly was an important day. But more important was that school started the next the day. Pencils, notepads, erasers, and also a new pencil box were purchased and ready to go. Every year a new dress and new shoes was a certainty. After all it was a special day. Also Labor Day was the last day of my vacation. Driving home from Grandma's farm or our cottage at the lake was the end of traveling for now. It often was the first subject talked about on the first day back to school. If there was a parade downtown, I do not ever remember attending. Pictures in the daily newspaper usually had an adequate synopsis. Actually I do not remember much about the reason for having a holiday called Labor Day. To me, for years, it was always the end of summer. In a month or two the snow would fly in my city of Minneapolis, Minnesota, and then in four months it would be Christmas.

The yearly calendar offers many holidays. These days are opportunities for family get-togethers, vacations, and time off for workers. Here I'm reminded of the saying "But a woman's work is never done." Think about it. Mother is usually the one who prepares the food for a picnic, packs the suitcase for a trip, and tidies the house before leaving on vacation while Dad sits patiently in the car. Of course it was his job to fit our luggage in the trunk.

Well, I'm not going to push my luck by trying to add another paragraph. At least as simple as these words have been, I now have a few words to speak aloud. I hope for next week that my brain will supply the contents of a worthy story, and I won't have to work so hard. Oh, I'm reminded, today is our wedding anniversary that happened sixty-five years ago. I love you and miss you, Bert. You are now resting from your labors.

September 2, 2014

THE HOLIDAYS

December holidays sometimes make me crazy. Last night I lay awake trying to organize my thoughts and made gift lists in my head. Did I accomplish anything by doing this? Absolutely not! In the morning I couldn't remember much of what I planned. This type of behavior has been a problem for me over the years. I remember being cajoled by my husband to stop thinking so much and start doing something. I think I want everything to come out perfectly, showing I know how to plan and then come up with gifts that are extraordinary.

My biggest problem is attempting to give everyone that perfect gift. I often buy something during the year thinking that it is a perfect gift, and when the time comes to wrap it, it just doesn't seem right. At present I no longer have a car so this means no more shopping like before. Even when I scan magazines for ideas, I can't make up my mind so I end up with no decision. There's always a gift card, of course, but that seems so impersonal. I have, however, purchased gift cards as a last resort.

For years in our church we've honored the season of Advent. It is a time of preparation for the coming of the Christ Child. The Advent Wreath, with its four candles representing the four Sundays before Christmas Day is a prominent symbol and is most often placed in the chancel close to the Altar. Each succeeding Sunday a candle is lit. Often what it said to me is that I am not ready for Christmas. However, Christmas will come whether I am ready or not, which is a lesson about the faithfulness of God.

Lately I have had conversations with my friends who have told me they no longer buy and send gifts. How is this done? I say to them. Their answer—they just stopped. My gift giving includes relatives on the East Coast, Sweden, and here in California. Some gifts need to be mailed. Again the problem for me is how to get to the post office. In 1950 I started writing an annual Christmas letter. A positive side of doing this is that it is now a collection of yearly events. I plan to continue writing the annual letter, and using it as a reference for my book. It's a good thing.

There are four family birthdays in December. Our son, David, was born December 13, 1951. Next, was his son, David (my grandson), also was born on the 13th of December. There was no question, he had to be named David. Then this David had a son born on December 5, named Nate (my great-grandson, Nathan). Now add one more birthday and its Nate's maternal grandfather, Paul, whose birthday is December 12. Once again we will gather in the private dining room where I live for the third year to celebrate all these birthdays. Result? More gifts to consider!!

I remember when I was about twelve years old, taking the streetcar together with my best friend, Gladys, to a hardware store on Lake Street to buy Christmas gifts for family. I had one dollar to spend given to me by my Mother. She also gave money to Gladys. As we walked into the store there was a table arrayed with shiny glassware that immediately caught my eye. I circled the table several times before choosing a divided pickle dish that was edged in gold (okay, so it wasn't gold). Perfect, I thought, never considering Mother had several pickle dishes in her dining room cupboard. I counted my money and with the remaining coins I bought my father a tie. Gladys spent the dollar on gifts for her entire family. She bought handkerchiefs for each of her three sisters, and something for her two brothers.

Through the years my gift list has grown considerably, plus sending a newsy Christmas letter and cards. Once again, I am asking myself is this the year to call it quits? But then I wonder, "If I stop will people think I'm dead?" The jury is still out.

November 25, 2014

MUSINGS

What do I do when I attempt to find a subject to write about and nothing grabs my attention? I'm sitting at my computer wondering how long should I sit here? Will the muses hover forever, or have I come to the end of my storytelling? Oh, there are thoughts that rush past my brain, but I would certainly name them unworthy. Oh well, I guess that's it. But then. . .

How about this?

I was asked to be included as a Wii bowling team member for a tournament next Thursday, the 31st of January. J.B., our leader, was gathering names for a drawing soon to be held. Four names would be drawn out of a hat—and that would be it. I gave J.B. a strong and firm answer—and that answer was NO. I definitely did not want to be in the drawing. His response was "I'll put your name in," and he walked away. Guess what? On Monday's daily sheet of activities, there it was in bold print: TEAM MEMBERS are Goldie, Helen, Alicia, and Marie. What didn't J.B. know about the word NO? What do I do now? Do I start practicing like mad, or not show up? Hmmmm. . .

This got me thinking about times when I have not been willing to do something and found out later that I missed a golden opportunity. Several Merrill Garden trips come to mind. I'm sorry that I missed the trip to see the Norman Rockwell collection of prints. Too bad. It happened. I missed it. And then as a child, why didn't I jump off the diving board to prove that I could? Or volunteer to take part in the school play, or run for office in high school? Is there something in my brain that suggests I should say no? According to the many brain/games and brain presentations I've heard here at Merrill Gardens, our brain only does what we tell it to do. Oh, oh, I really didn't want to hear that. It appears that I often say no because I do not want to fail. Since I am very competitive, mostly in sports, I try to be the best. When I enter a competition I see myself wining. Now, let's look at the next bowling tournament again.

The tournament is in two days. I haven't been practicing like I should if I planned to be on the team. In fact, I can count on one hand how many times I've practiced since the last tournament. As a musician I would never perform in a concert without a suitable amount of practice. Did this enter my mind when I told J.B. no? You bet it did. So what do I do now? I guess I'll stay tuned and see what happens. In a couple of days or less I'll know the answer.

What would you do?

January 29, 2013

RELATIVES

There is something reassuring about having relatives—especially if everyone gets along. I guess I've heard too many stories of fractured relationships where family members have not communicated with one another for years. I often wondered what happened that would cause such a serious rift. To me this is very sad. I can honestly say through the years there have never been any angry lengthy separations in my family. In fact during my growing years I remember my mother talking on the phone every day with her sister-in-law. They were very close. My father, after returning from a trip, and even before taking off his coat, would call his brother, and say, "Hello Captain, we just got home." I'm not sure why he called him Captain. He was his younger brother.

Beside his two brothers on the farm, my father had two brothers that lived in Minneapolis. Each had children—Victor had four girls and one boy, and his brother, Bill, a girl and a boy. As you can well imagine being an only child I had made to order fun with my cousins. I remember Virgie and Margie, my older cousins, treating me to a make-over including hairdo and make-up. I felt like a princess; so grown-up. Years later Marge and her fiancée were married in the family backyard, and I sang "I Love You Truly" through an open window, accompanied on the piano by my husband.

During the depression my aunt and uncle who had the five children had it more difficult than my family with only one child. Often my mother would pack up my outgrown clothes and whatever else was not being worn or used to help ease their crunch. I've often heard the story told by one of my cousins that to them it was like Christmas, as they all pulled at the many items in the box hoping to find something that appealed to them. This made me feel good.

Also there is something that is rather difficult and a bit hard to explain. When the families were together it gave me such a strong sense of belonging. Maybe as an adopted child it made me believe that I *really* belonged. It seemed so right to be together as one big family. When the women were in the kitchen discussing recipes or washing dishes, the men were talking about future hunting trips, and we kids were playing indoor games or running in the yard.

This all added to my feelings that everything was all right. Also, I wonder if the adults found it helpful during this time to forget about the war, the money crunch, or whatever problems they may be facing. To share food and hugs seemed to be the glue that held the family together, besides the fact that they actually liked one another.

Picture 20: My 90th birthday party

I can honestly say this family scenario of getting along has traveled down through the years to my present family, which includes a variety of faiths, nationalities, and of course ages. It has now come down to the fact that I am the Matriarch, a title I absolutely adore. As I look at my great grandchildren, grandchildren and children plus all the in-laws, it gives me peace to know that this family will always be one great big family—where peace and love abide. For this I daily give thanks to God.

April 7, 2015

IT'S ABOUT "LIFE"

Here I go again. I guess it's my passion for words and their meanings. This time I have chosen the word *life*. Actually my brain was working on it when I was sleeping, and as soon as I awoke, I immediately thought of several "life" words all having to do with water. I got up quickly, and jotted down the following:

There are life boats, life vests, and lifeguards, who throw lifelines to those who are unable to rescue themselves. Next came items when one is at sea that are life threatening such as sharks, storms, and losing sail. If one has a working cell phone, this can be a life support system that will guide you to a safe harbor or the nearest shoreline, or maybe being miraculously rescued.

Then there's the familiar saying—"Life is like a bowl of cherries." I guess it means that most of life is sweet and good. Well, we all know that sometimes it can be the pits!! All along there are ups and downs during our lifetime. When things are not going too well, we often hear someone say, "Well that's life!"

Most likely our parents encouraged us to have a purpose in life. This meant our lifestyle should be circumspect and have no reason to be ashamed of what we have done, and to choose wisely in all things. Sometimes parents, if they were able, bought life insurance for us. I still have it. Who knows, it may save my life if I need it, or even help someone else's life at some point. At my death, my immediate family, grandchildren, and great grandchildren, plus my nieces and nephews may be grateful for the payoff from my life insurance. That is if I am blessed with a "long life."

I used to like reading and looking at the many pictures in *LIFE* magazine. I'm sorry for its demise. I wonder what actually happened to the magazine titled *LIFE* and was it all about LIFE? "Life" indicates living, being alive. Would it have been too difficult to continue finding interesting stories of people who were heroes, or had remarkable lives, which would have kept the magazine alive? Oh, shoot—I need to stop this useless chatter and get on with my life before it ends in the pits.

One further question—"Do you know where your lifeline is and what it means"? Read on. . . .

LIFELINE MEANINGS:
1. If line swoops down to about an inch above the base of the palm, it shows life expectancy of about seventy years for women, and sixty-to-seventy for men.

2. Lifeline, long and deep = vitality and health. a) short line—strong and deep; able to overcome health problems. b) short and shallow—have tendency to be controlled by others.

3. Extra lines = doubled means great vitality.

4. Swooping lines = great strength and enthusiasm (plus improved love life).

5. Lines straight = limited exploration of love—and very cautious.

6. Line extends to middle of palm = life consists of a lot of traveling.

7. Chain linked line = allergies, physical and emotional problems.

8. A donut = hospitalization as a result of some sort of accident.

9. A break = changes in life style, an accident or illness.

10. Crossing lines = worries or danger.

Do you believe any of this?

June 24, 2013

A TOAST AT JON AND MOLLY'S WEDDING

It is truly an honor when a relative or dear friend asks you to give a toast for their scheduled wedding. But before I tell you what I said, I must first tell you this story.

While I was in college in Minnesota, I was dating a young man who also attended the same college. One day my boyfriend made the suggestion that we offer to "grandma sit" my mother's mother so that she and my dad could have an evening off. Grandma was bedridden and my mother had full responsibility for all of her care—night and day. She really needed a change from her daily routine.

You also must understand that Grandma only spoke Swedish. My mother and dad also knew the language. In addition, Bert, my boyfriend, also spoke Swedish. Both of his parents were born in Sweden.

So the evening was arranged. My parents left, and Bert and I were sitting in the living room talking, when Grandma called out from the bedroom, "Bertil, kom hit." Translation: Bertil come here. So Bert entered her bedroom, and leaned down to listen to what she had to say. She said, "Det är en sak som jag vill veta." Translation: There is one thing I need to know. Then she added, "Skall du gifta med Helen eller skall du bara monkarunt?" Translation: Are you going to marry Helen or are you just going to monkey around?

Bert assured her that he was not just monkeying around—and that he intended to marry Helen. Of course he did not tell me this story until after he proposed marriage.

This story came in handy when grandson David, Jon's brother, was courting Jennie and he never seemed to get around popping the question. It seemed like years. Actually, it was years. So I finally told him my grandmother's story. Within a year there was a ring on Jennie's finger.

Then came the day when my grandson, Jon, introduced Molly to the family. From the moment she walked through the front door, she immediately headed for the kitchen and introduced herself. I was impressed. With her friendly and bubbly personality, I wanted to make sure that Jon would not let her get away. So again my grandmother's story came in handy. And it worked. The proof? Jon and Molly were married on June 28, 2014.

Now, I give you dear readers, the privilege to use this story if the situation warrants it. Remember the words "Are you going to marry _____, or are you just going to monkey around?"

So here's to the newest married couple in our family, and to all of you who have read this story. "If the shoe fits", may good luck and a long life be with you.

Picture 21: Jon and Molly's Wedding

June 28, 2014

MITCH ALBOM

Writing my first book has been time consuming and emotional. As I thought and searched my memory, story after story began to actually become a reality. Since I am now living in a retirement facility filled with mostly active people, I find that I want to play games or participate in classes rather than actually sit down and write about my life. I'm supposed to be retired, but story after story soon became a reality, and so I keep going.

I like to read. On the first page I can tell whether I care to continue reading. One such book was one that captured my imagination immediately on page one. I was hooked. The author was Mitch Albom. The book was titled *Tuesdays with Morrie*. I couldn't believe that someone could write such a riveting story. It had suspense, purpose, personal interest, sympathy, and humor. I thought to myself, who is this man? Soon another bestseller was published entitled *Have a Little Faith* and my response was the same. Another winner! Again, I wondered what makes him so readable. The third book I read was *The Timekeeper*. This time I wanted to discover what made him tick, and here's what I discovered.

Mitch Albom was born in 1958 in New Jersey. He graduated from Brandeis University in Massachusetts with a bachelor's degree in Sociology. He started as a sports writer that won him national fame. During this time he worked in the music industry and enrolled in Berklee College of Music in Boston, Massachusetts studying jazz. To keep afloat he played jazz piano in nightclubs in Boston and in Europe. Later, journalism became a pursuit and he wrote for several newspapers, which propelled him to earn a master's degree at Columbia University.

At one point he heard about the serious illness of his favorite Professor, Morrie Schwartz at Brandeis University, who had ALS (Lou Gehrig's disease). Feeling guilty that he had not continued their friendship as they had vowed to do, he decided to pay him a visit and found his visits were consistently on Tuesdays. He visited him to the end of his life. The book *Tuesdays With Morrie* was the result. It soon became No. 1 on the *New York Times*' Best Sellers list, and not long after was made into a movie.

Now add to the list the following titles: *For One More Day*, *The Five People You Meet in Heaven*, *Fab Five*, *And The Winner Is*, plus a stage play, "Duck Hunter Who Thought He Shot An Angel." This is a library that's worth reading.

A few facts about Mitch Albom:
- Albom's books have sold over 33 million worldwide.
- 10% of profits of his book *Have a Little Faith* go to Hole in the Roof Foundation. This foundation helps refurbish places of worship that aid the homeless.
- He founded seven charities in Detroit and Haiti where he operates an orphanage and mission.
- He has a daily radio call-in program in Detroit.
- He writes a daily sports column.
- He is working on his next book.
- He is fifty-five years old and married.

Here are two Albom quotes:
- *"For years I wrote in my basement. More recently I graduated to one floor above to an office with all my books and music and—ta-da!—a window."*
- *"Anyone who tries to write a memoir needs to keep in mind that what's interesting to you isn't necessarily interesting to a reader."*

Perhaps this is the case for me as I continue to write one word after another. As to whether anyone will be interested, time will tell from my first page.

May 7, 2013

A DIFFERENT KIND OF JOURNEY

Part 1:
After my last exam by my primary physician, Dr. Yong Liu, on March 19, 2014, I was given a directive to have a mammogram before my next appointment. Shoot!!! I didn't want to do it. Let it go, I thought. I then asked to myself, didn't Dr. Beddard and Dr. Wynn in Mansfield, Ohio say it really wasn't necessary at my age? Or was it a personal matter, and I could have the exam or choose not to? Again it did have something to do with my age; after all I was in my late 80's.

My next appointment with Dr. Liu was scheduled for June 4. Since this was my birthday, I mused, "Shouldn't I be celebrating my birthday instead of going to the doctor?" What would she say if I told her that I elected not to have the mammogram? After all, she can't force it on me. When I finished with my argument the jury in my head said, "Go ahead, have the mammogram." I called for an appointment.

The Women's Imaging Center building on Perkins Street in Sonoma looked clean and non- threatening. It was May 16. I pushed the door open and announced my arrival at the front desk. She handed me several pages and instructed to fill in the information. It seemed to take forever. When I finished a young woman cheerfully said, "Helen Anderson? I am ready for you." I wanted to say, "But I'm not ready for you." I was told to remove everything from the waist up and don a silly looking gown. It made me smile as I checked my image in the mirror. I was ushered into the examining room and positioned for the test. Oh well, I thought, this will soon be over. Little did I know how wrong I was.

Before I left the Women's Imaging Center I was told that I would receive a letter from a radiologist with the results. Since this was Friday the 16th I suspected I would hear the next week. Monday, Tuesday, Wednesday passed and no word.

Later that afternoon I received a telephone call. The message: "Please report back to the Imaging Center for another mammogram followed by an ultrasound at the hospital. A nodule was found in the right breast." What's up, I wondered, but dutifully I agreed to be there on Friday, May 23. This time the radiologist reported a biopsy was necessary. The date for the biopsy was set for the 30th of May.

The biopsy procedure was interesting. I listened to the conversation between the radiologist and the nurse, and could see the screen as the work was progressing. It wasn't a picnic, but I was able to relax. When it was over I got dressed and left with my faithful daughter-in-law, Trish. She suggested stopping at Whole Foods for supper items. Now I really had questions. What's going on? I then began to purposely strive to think positive. After all, it could be benign.

It was now June 4—my birthday, and of all things I had an appointment with Dr. Liu, my primary care physician. Or course I was nervous because she was going to tell me what my mammogram, ultrasound, and biopsy tests revealed. As I entered the room the nurse did the usual weight, blood pressure, and temperature readings. Then I was alone. I picked up a magazine pretending to read, but it was difficult to concentrate. The door opened and Dr. Liu asked the usual question, "How are you?" I immediately answered, "Nervous." "Nervous about what?" she said. "About the report," I answered. She sat down and began to flip the pages in my file. It seemed to take an eternity. Finally her finger followed the pertinent paragraph, and she looked up into my eyes and said, "The tests showed the nodule to be malignant."

Those words hit me like a bolt and tears trickled down my cheeks. Dr. Liu leaned forward, touched my knee, and let me have my moment. In about thirty seconds I looked up at her and said, "Okay, what's the next step?" She told me about two doctors who are experts in the field: Dr. Elboim, a surgeon, and Dr. Stanton, an oncologist. To me the word oncologist underscored the fact that I have cancer, and I needed to make the call for appointments.

When I got back to my apartment I immediately opened my computer, started an e-mail to my family, and wrote the following:

> *I just received news that all the tests indicated a malignant nodule in the right breast. Please know that I am at ease with the diagnosis. Please be the same. MOM.*

There were immediate answers with words of encouragement and promises from family to be there for me. I felt loved and cared for. Now I needed to make those calls to the two doctors.

The appointment with Dr. Elboim was scheduled for June 10. Trish, my daughter-in-law, agreed to drive, and we headed for Santa Rosa. The doctor's offices were directly across from the Memorial Hospital. As we entered the building I was struck by the clean lines of modern architecture, neatly spaced green plants, and appropriate artworks. For a moment I forgot why I was there. At the desk I was given many forms to fill out.

A nurse came to usher us into an examining room. I answered more questions plus submitted to the usual vitals. When she finished, Marlene Lennon, a nurse practitioner, went over information in a large notebook for me to keep and refer to. She shared and explained graphs, diagrams, and procedural items pertinent to my case. Trish took notes. Finally Dr. Elboim came in, pulled up a stool, and shared more information. When I heard the words describing the tumor as "non-invasive" and "slow growing", Trish and I shared a "thumbs up." The final decision was to schedule a lumpectomy operation for July 10 at the Sonoma Valley Hospital. We breathed a sigh of relief. We can now celebrate the wedding of my grandson, Jon and Molly, his bride to be, on the weekend of June 28, 2014. Yeah!!!

It was a good thing to have a wedding to temporarily ease my thoughts about my surgery on July 10. Thanks to my surgeon, Dr. Elboim, who said, "Go and enjoy your family and the wedding. I'll see you after it's over."

Part 2:
Journeys come in all shapes and forms. A journey can be traveling without a specific destination, or a preplanned tour designed by a travel agent. Another trip may be to obtain family history as we did in Sweden, or simply starting out on a Sunday afternoon and discovering something beautiful and new.

Our pre-planned journey on June 28, 2014 was to attend Jon and Molly's wedding. The setting was Woodside, California. While several musicians (all horns) played the music for the bridal procession, my attention was drawn to a deer that stopped as though he was listening to the music. Also I saw a squirrel settle on a tree branch to watch the event and then scamper from one tree to another. The band increased their volume as Molly, the bride, began the aisle walk accompanied by her mother. Molly's father died when Molly was two years old. With four groomsmen on one side, and four bridesmaids on the other, the scene was complete as the junior bridesmaid, ring bearer, and flower girl slowly walked to their appointed spot. She and her mother embraced when they reached the stage, and Jon, the groom (my grandson), and Molly stepped forward to face Molly's uncle, Judge Kane. His words were carefully chosen to introduce the subject of marriage. Several people spoke before the bridal vows were said. At that moment, I observed something interesting. Molly, an actress by profession, and Jon a musician, each one very comfortable on a stage, had a handkerchief handed to them to catch their tears. Their actions were completely unscripted. So were mine.

Throughout the weekend there were new people to meet, family moments to relive, and lots of good stories. Something new for me was the "cutting of the pie." Yes, instead of the usual tiered wedding cake they had a variety of pies plus ice cream. Why didn't I think of that for our wedding? For sure, in my time, that would have "hit the fan," so to speak. Many of us stayed at the Stanford Hotel, in Menlo Park on Saturday night. In the morning we met for a brunch. Then it was all over except for our memories. At this point I started to count the days until I will have another adventure on the 10th of July.

July 4, 2014

SURPRISE, SURPRISE

There have been a number of surprises in my life that have left me speechless. But the one that outdid them all happened two days before my 80th birthday, June 4, 2007. My family from New Jersey had told me that they were coming to Ohio to celebrate my 80th together with my California family. We would all go out for dinner and that was fine with me. About 3pm the doorbell rang and it was Jesse and Virginia, my son and his wife. There were hugs and kisses all around, and as we sat down to visit, again the doorbell rang. I went to the door and to my surprise there stood my Swedish son, Lars and his fiancée, Maud. They had flown to New Jersey from Sweden and had come with Jesse and Virginia but had gotten out of the car a block before my driveway. I was speechless. It was a joyous and tearful surprise.

Another surprise was when Bert and I were engaged to be married and again it was my birthday. Plans were made to have dinner with another couple. When they arrived at my house, Bert handed me a large gift-wrapped package. When I tore off the paper it revealed a bright blue decorated step-on garbage can together with a dustpan and brush to match. I didn't know what to say. I heard my mother gasp. Bert suggested that I look inside the can and I found a beautiful corsage. His comment—"I knew we'd need a step-on garbage can. I couldn't pass it up." I had to agree although the initial shock was still hovering. Truly this was on a different surprise level.

My third example happened this week. My grandchild Nathan is nearly 1.5 years old and the novelty has *not* worn off. Each visit brings a new ability and/or action. Every opportunity to be with him is a pleasure I cannot measure. Nathan's maternal grandmother, Roslyn, is a professional photographer, which means that I have been supplied with the latest "cute" pictures throughout his young life. However, the latest set of pictures is a priceless collection. Roslyn has put together an ABC book that is unique. Each picture depicts one letter of the alphabet together with Nathan. The surprise? I now have an ABC book of my very own!!

May 21, 2013

WHO IS MY NEIGHBOR?

In the many places we've lived we have always had neighbors. I'm talking about the next-door kind. Many of these folks bring back good memories, and others, well. . . I'll leave that unsaid. In the Bible we read verses that admonish us to "love our neighbor", and also it adds for us to love ourselves. I have to admit that loving our neighbor is not always easy to do. It depends on many things. Is the neighbor reachable? Does the neighbor respond in kind? Are there barriers that make it more difficult? I would like to think that a neighbor does not have to only be persons next door, but anyone we meet such as co-workers, people in organizations, our church, friends, etc. I guess what I am really talking about is "civility". Why can't we all live peacefully regardless of differing opinions?

This being said, I'd like to think more about some neighbors that actually lived next door. We've moved many times so of course, each time there were new people to meet. One family that comes to mind lived next door in Mansfield, Ohio. Our moving day was hectic. The movers needed instructions where to place the furniture, the pictures, the odds and ends, and what to do with the boxes and boxes and more boxes. About midday I heard a knock on the back door. When I opened the door there was a nice looking lady holding a plate of newly baked blueberry muffins plus a pitcher of iced tea. With her cheery "Welcome to the neighborhood," I knew immediately we would be friends, and this was true for nearly twenty years before I moved to a condo.

In Jersey City, New Jersey the house we occupied was owned by the Church. It was on Culver Avenue, a very long street with approximately twenty houses stretching up a slight hill to Hudson Boulevard, the main thoroughfare. (It was later renamed Kennedy Boulevard.) All the houses were separated by a narrow driveway to a garage. I remember that we were the only non-Jewish family on that street. To our right was Doctor Solomon and his wife. To the left was an older couple. He was a pharmacist. These two families were the perfect example of gracious neighbors. The men often had long conversations over the backyard fence, and the women were equally friendly.

When my husband developed a severe nose infection, Doctor Solomon came in every day to check on him and prescribed the necessary medication. He cautioned him to be diligent in taking the medication since if the infection was left unattended it could travel to his brain. The doctor's action was entirely a neighborly one. He refused every offer we made to pay him.

David had many Jewish friends. One day when he came home from school I noticed his eyes filled with tears. I asked him, "David, what's the matter?" He hesitated but then tearfully said, "All my friends have maids and we don't." I consoled him with a firm hug and offered the following advice, "David, tell your friends that you have a maid, too, but just don't tell them it's your mother." With that he seemed satisfied.

As to other neighborly people my stories could go on and on. However, in a nutshell let me tell you about two more. I remember the little older lady who lived next door to us in Tenafly, New Jersey. Her soft knock on the door would often bring a newly baked item, or a jar of jam that she had just sealed. She always refused to come in, but I was welcome at her door anytime. I enjoyed sitting at her table drinking a cup of tea and listening to her stories.

When Bert was on internship in Portland, Oregon we lived in an old house that at one time was owned by one family. It was a stately mansion with two huge pillars standing erect on each side of an impressive front door. The present owner had fashioned the house into several apartments. We had three rooms on the second floor: a living room, bedroom, and a tiny kitchen. One drawback was that the bathroom (toilet only) was down a long hall and was shared with two other families. The owners were very friendly. Our son was a bit skittish about the dark hall leading to the bathroom so he would run fast each way. He was seven years old. Evidently these footsteps were heard downstairs. One day at our doorway was a bag of candy and a note to David asking him to please run quietly. This was a lovely way to handle a problem.

Two years later on our way to Seattle, Washington for Bert's ordination, we stopped in Portland to visit our happy year on North Marshall Street to see the house that was our home for one year. The owners were still there and were happy to see us and we them. I'll never forget these gracious neighbors who helped make our year so pleasant.

Now that I am living in Sonoma within a community called Brookdale with 173 residents, I have many, many neighbors. Remembering names can be a "brain game" giving the brain a workout. It is easy to remember who lives in the apartment across the hall until someone new moves in. One difference from the previous places I lived, no one has ever brought me any blueberry muffins.

October 14, 2014

IT'S OVER

The date of July 10, 2014 for my surgery loomed over my head for weeks and as it got closer and closer my mind raced as to what it would be like and what it would reveal. I wondered if it was the same for others as they waited for this life-changing event. I guess the unknown factor is the culprit. It plays tricks on a person with many dubious outcomes that boggles the mind. Oh, if only we could know the outcome ahead of time. No, I take that back. That would be worse.

The various steps leading to the event with a series of revelations seems to be much easier to handle. Factoring the advice one gets from friends and relatives, I tried to believe all they said will be true. And if the good wishes and the assurances of "you'll be just fine" could be believed, I probably could have sailed into that operating room dancing on my toes and singing Sinatra's "That's Life" at the top of my lungs. But each step of the way came and went and the mind and body prepared for the next stage. I prayed for peace of mind. I prayed for the hands of doctors and nurses who were there to do their best. I thanked God for the assurance that I was in good care. I thanked God for family, especially my daughter in-law, Trisha, who was with me to all appointments. David came the day of surgery. It was fortunate that Trish had the summer days available. She was a schoolteacher. In addition, my neighbor, Joan, checked on me daily.

So, how did it turn out? After the surgery (lumpectomy), a visit to the oncologist laid out a picture of what he saw as the best treatment. He assured me that radiation or chemo was not necessary. He then opened his computer, typed in all the known factors, i.e., height, weight, age, etc. plus the medical data from the radiologist and surgeon. Like magic, three medication possibilities appeared on his screen. From there we talked about each one. Based on clinical data over twenty-year period, it pointed strongly that I should be on Anastrozole. This medication attempts to catch any loose unseen cancer cells.

I asked him how long I would be on this regimen. His answer? "Five years.". "Okay," I answered. Then I reasoned that I am going to have to live five more years in order to see if the medication worked. That would be July 2019. Sound like a good plan? I think so. I'm going for it.

July 2014

THIS IS MY BOX

The Christmas opera, "Amahl and the Night Visitors," written by Gian Carlo Menotti, is the story of the three Kings who come to Bethlehem to locate the child that Herod the King desperately needs to find. On their way the kings enter the house of a mother and crippled child and find them experiencing extreme poverty and hunger. At one point in the story the kings, in their dazzling garments, are seated and each one offers a gift to the child. One king sings about the box he carries: "This is my box; this is my box. I never leave without my box." (If you are not familiar with the entire story, I urge you to look for it.)

Today I have a box and would like to tell you about it. It is unique. It is like no other box that I have ever seen. It is not a jewelry box, a gift box, or a toolbox. It does not hold cigars or cigarettes, and it's certainly not a breadbox. One could name several other kinds of boxes such as a "wood box," a box full of logs to keep a big iron stove ready for use. I remember seeing this in my grandparents' kitchen.

By now you should realize that I love word play. Let me have my fun and name a few types of boxes. Does anyone remember the pet name for an accordion? It has been called a squeezebox. Can you visualize it? And by the way the large and/or small organ often found in churches has been dubbed "a box of whistles." When you see all those differing lengths of pipes with air being forced through them the description fits.

Does my box contain Jack? If you wind the side crank and sing "Pop Goes the Weasel," suddenly you'll meet Jack as he pops out of the box, but he's not in my box. Also, there are penalty boxes, mailboxes, and if you are in an arena, there may be two men ready to box. Each one has boxing gloves to fight to the finish. Have you ever received a gift that began in a big box that opened to the next size box, and as you continued to open box after box you finally found the gift in a little tiny box? Frustrating, yes, but it was usually worth the effort. Okay, I've had my fun. Now let me tell you about the box I own.

This box has been in the family for many years. Its primary use was to store men's celluloid collars during the early 1900's. I believe my grandfather did just that.

On top of the box is a small oval container made out of metal and lined with satin. It depicts Christopher Columbus with three men and is verified by the word *Columbus* on the inside cover. This little box is presumably for the studs that connected a collar to the shirt. My father had this box on his dresser, and my husband also had it on his dresser. Bert used it to store his white clerical collars. Today it is an accent piece in my living room. Inside I have stored some sewing equipment and buttons. No collars. My intention is to ask my friend Milena to clean it and attach the two metal designs at the corners that had fallen off. I agreed and anxiously awaited the restoration of my precious wooden box.

January 22, 2013

RIVALRY

Let's start with the definition: Rivalry is a competition for the same objective or for superiority in the same field. In some instances rivalry is good. It promotes discussions, albeit sometimes heated, but on the other hand it affords a good bit of fun. It is bad when it turns to hatred and becomes violent. We've all seen both kinds of rivalry in action.

One area of rivalry that is ever present occurs in sports. It is difficult to live in an area and suggest you are cheering for an opposing team. Sometimes you are labeled as a traitor. The team to root for is usually very evident when you see team lettered jackets, caps, bumper stickers, and flags. The stores are saturated with these items. Watching a game on television and searching the stands is also easy to ascertain which team is the home team. Team colors give it away.

All this became a problem for my husband and me when we moved to Michigan. We soon were caught up in the blue and gold (or as they say, maize and blue) for the University of Michigan. No matter where we went, eventually some reference would be made concerning this team—and how great they were. The loyalty was fierce. We, of course, joined in with our cheers. We were also cautioned to not confuse the University of Michigan with that other lesser University, Michigan State.

Several years later we were contemplating a move to Ohio. A church issued a call to my husband to be the Senior Pastor of First English Lutheran Church in Mansfield, Ohio, a city of about 150,000. Bert was invited to Mansfield to come and discuss the possibility of agreeing to be their pastor.

When he returned after an overnight visit he told me the news about what he had heard and seen. A couple of weeks later we were both asked to come. When we arrived we were wined and dined and were asked a lot of questions. During the conversation we were told about the great Ohio State team—colors red and white. On our next visit we met with the church council, and the following evening we were welcomed as the new pastor's family at a "Fastnacht"—a celebration of Mardi-Gras. Here we were presented with identical jackets. You guessed it. They were the red and white jackets of Ohio State. The next day we settled on the purchase of a house.

At this writing I am in California and find my loyalty has shifted to the Giants, the Warriors, and the Forty-Niners. But while we were still in Ohio, it was very exciting to be a rooter for the Giants when they won the World Series in 2010. My San Francisco family was ecstatic. Little did I realize that in a short time I, too, would be living in California. I moved to Sonoma on August 7, 2011, with my loyalty to the basketball, football, and baseball teams solidly secure.

September 25, 2012

COMPETITION

I wonder? Is one born with a gene for being competitive? It would appear so in some cases. Look at children playing games. Many times there is a child who must be the winner, and if this doesn't happen, he or she sulks, claims someone cheated, and may even walk away. As a personal note, I may have been that child at times. I remember often wanting to be the leader, call the shots, and in addition be the undesignated referee.

It started in school with recess games. If it was baseball, I wanted to be chosen first when sides were chosen. It was really upsetting to be chosen last. Sometimes I wanted to be the pitcher. In fact I practiced at home by drawing a square on the garage door. Then with underhanded pitches I'd try to hit the bulls eye (a strike). In college I played basketball. It is played entirely different today. We played only half court and since I was tall, I was the center. I practiced free throws often and got pretty good at it.

I remember on one occasion in a chemistry class I was asked to leave the room when a prank had been played on the professor. Even though I had nothing to do with it, I laughed as the professor turned around and saw the contents of the empty beaker he had been describing. A student in the front row had dumped it in the sink. Not knowing who was guilty, the professor pointed his finger at me and shouted "out". I dutifully picked up my books and headed for the gym since I knew it was empty. I practiced free-throws. I was alone, had no competition and enjoyed every minute being a champion. At least I didn't have to endure the chemistry class.

Another occasion happened in our driveway in Tenafly, New Jersey. There was a basketball hoop attached to our garage where Jesse and a couple of friends would play. One day I asked to join a game called Around the World. As I remember, one began by shooting three perfect free throws and then moved on to first base. If these shots were successful one would go to second base, and then on to third. Finally if all the shots were made without any misses, it was necessary to again make three perfect free throws. Well, I did it to the cheers of the boys—except Jesse, who to this day insists that I stepped over the line on the last free throw. By the way, Jesse and his friends were all on the high school basketball team!

I'm somewhat embarrassed to admit that the urge to toss something, a wad, a pillow, or a sock into a waiting container is really strong. The greatest urge is in a restaurant. A water glass and a tiny piece of a paper napkin just had to be tossed. Of course I have to consider the type of restaurant and those I am seated with. At home in my apartment, I have three throw pillows leaning against a larger bed pillow. Across the room is a waiting chair. The goal is to get the three to land and stay on the chair. It is tricky since they are often inclined to bounce onto the floor. If I am successful I clap my hands and say "Good Job." If one jumps to the floor I say something else.

I have to admit at the age of eighty-eight, the tossing of objects is still fun. It may be childish and silly, but who cares. I hope I will still be able to do it for several more years.

June 20, 2015

WHERE DO THE SUMMERS GO?

Summers are easy things to lose. For me, the days pass swiftly from June to September and are, for the most part, a blur. Sure there are memories of pleasant days or trips, but unless one keeps a diary these are essentially forgotten. Now add ten, twenty, or more years to this equation, and we are left with very few complete stories. Oh, of course, we may have photos or letters that call up our memories, but the swift passing of events are difficult to bring to mind unless there is a collective conversation on the subject that prompts a story.

Ever since the beginning of the "My Story, Your Story" group, I have begun remembering more and more because of hearing similar stories from others. For instance when the subject was about games children played during the summer, it prompted me to recall as a child playing outside no matter what the weather. It was easy to gather a gang of kids in the evening to play games. My house was on a corner, and the street sign and light pole made it a perfect meeting place. A favorite game was "I will draw a frying pan; who will put the wiener in?" This essentially was a game of Hide and Seek. During the day we often made a tent with blankets over a clothesline and this became a house, a hospital, a school or a secret meeting place. If it rained we sailed paper boats along the curb in the water heading for the street drain. If it thundered or there was lightening we were called inside.

In Minnesota, the temperature in the summer could reach 100 degrees or more. Mother would open the windows and doors in the morning as soon as she got up, and as the temperature rose she would close them and pull down the shades. There was no air-conditioning. A couple of fans circulated the air. I remember having heat stroke, and Mother putting a cool rag over my eyes and making me lie in bed for a couple of hours.

Heat didn't seem to bother my father. I can still see him leaving for work in a full business suit, long sleeve shirt, tie, and vest, and a hat, of course. There was no air conditioning in his office.

During our first year of marriage we rented an apartment. Our days were full of study and teaching as we worked to finish our Bachelor of Music Degree. In the summer the apartment was closed up all day and into the evening. My husband got an idea to fill our bathtub with cold water before we left in the morning to aid in cooling the rooms. The first evening about 8 p.m., we came home, opened the door and immediately were hit by hot air. The bathtub water plan had not worked. Bert raced to the bathroom to open the window over the tub forgetting it was filled with water. With sopping shoes and socks, he decided to scrap his idea.

Then there were the summer events such as the Fourth of July. It was the biggest one and plans were usually made in advance for a picnic, choosing a perfect place outdoors in a park or near a lake. It usually included getting together with relatives. Here again I really cannot recall attending any outstanding July 4th celebration, or watching a parade. As for birthdays I have a birthday book to remind me of these events.

What I am trying to say is that much of life's stories are not always completely forgotten; they are really hidden in a part of our brain, and hearing someone else's story triggers our brain and like magic, a new long lost story is remembered. But maybe that's a goal more easily spoken than achieved. At present where I am living, everyone has stories, and so I'm anticipating that hearing more stories will prompt my brain to remember my many untold stories. Time will tell, but I do have high hopes. Actually it has just happened.

September 4, 2012

SCHEDULES

Ever since birth, one's lives have been on some sort of schedule. As a baby the schedule was simple. There was a feeding schedule, sleeping schedule, diaper changes, and comforting to name the basics. As I grew the schedules became more involved until we were knee deep in one sort of schedule after another that sometimes numbered more than I could accomplish.

I have been making to do lists for many years. It has helped me keep track of what needs to be done. There is real pleasure to cross off the item that I've done. Yes, and I have been known to add an item to my list in order to have the thrill of crossing it off. And yes, it is really a thrill. It means that I am keeping my life in some sort of order. For me an ordered life is far better than chaos that occurs when too many items are waiting to be tackled. This was most certainly true when I was much younger. Later the clock and the calendar were my guide. Appointments, shopping, meals, bills to be paid, vacation, and teaching schedules had to be front and center in my mind in order to be on top of my game. Did I always keep things running smoothly? Of course not, but at least most of the "to do" items were eventually tackled.

Now I am retired. There should no longer be long to-do lists as before. It is a time to enjoy life, take an afternoon off, sleep late, skip breakfast, and you name it—the day is an open book. But what has happened? From the day I moved to Merrill Gardens in 2011 my life has been scheduled—some days more so than others. The Daily Sheet prepared by the Activity Director keeps me aware of what's happening each day in the building. I'm glad I do not have to make up my own list. Now that's not quite true because I still have bills to be paid, doctor's appointments to be made, transportation scheduled, get to meals on time, decide and write stories for "My Story, Your Story", and morning exercise sessions. But one thing that is not scheduled is working on a jigsaw puzzle. This happens most often in the evening when everyone has disappeared to their apartments. Here I am isolated from everyone and everything. It is a time to relax. I say, "More time for jigsaw puzzles and less for long to do lists."

October 29, 2013

CINDY'S STORY CONTINUES

One day while gathering material for my book, I happened to find a slip of paper that said, "Cindy's cell phone." I looked at it and then set it aside. During the next few weeks this information kept showing up, and once again I laid it down. Then on Friday July 31, 2015 I called Jesse and said that I had found Cindy's telephone number, and I'm wondering if I should call her? His immediate answer was, "Yes, Mom, absolutely!" No doubt he was identifying with the scene when he decided to remain in New Jersey when Bert and I moved to Michigan, and we lost track of him. Even though this happened many years ago it is still a fresh memory for both of us.

Finally I picked up the phone and punched in the numbers. A young sounding voice said, "Hello". I asked if she was Cindy. "Yes," she answered. "Well, this is Helen Anderson." There was an immediate response. "I'm so glad you called. I've been looking for you for the past two weeks." She said her searching even included checking obituaries. All during the conversation she kept saying how happy she was that I called. Our conversation was mainly catching up after so many years. It was nice to learn that she had been to Sonoma's famous ace track. That was before my move to California. She talked about working for Xerox Services at home. Sometimes she goes into the office, she said. She and her husband live in Stroudsburg, Pennsylvania.
I was interested to hear about her children, Caroline and Robert. "Caroline is a doctor working towards certification as an anesthesiologist." I thought how could this be? The last time I saw her, she was a cute, shy, little blond girl—and now she's a doctor? Robert was two years older, going through those difficult teen years—and now he has an Engineering degree? But then I remembered Cindy was very intelligent. She was also a very nurturing single parent. It all made sense.
We exchanged phone and cell phone numbers and addresses. Before we ended our conversation I said I hoped she would be able to visit me in Sonoma. That would be a great gift.

August 2, 2015

IT'S ABOUT GUS

Who is this new handsome waiter at Merrill Gardens with the gorgeous eyes and beautiful smile? This is the question a number of residents were asking when he first appeared in the dining room. I, too, wondered, so I decided to find some answers. One day last week I asked Gus' permission to interview him and this is what I learned.

His full name is Gustavo Garcia. He is 21 years old. He was born in Spain. When he was one year old he, his parents, and two brothers and two sisters left Spain for Mexico and settled in Tonaya, Jalisco, Mexico. It was here that he learned to fish, to hunt deer, iguana, and birds. To him it was not a sport but a necessity for food for the family. His uncle taught him the correct use of guns and how to fish.

At the age of twelve, the family with their green cards moved to a farm in California. He started sixth grade without knowing one word of English. He lived with his grandmother while attending junior and senior high school. When I asked him how he learned his morals and manners that are so evident in his present behavior, he quickly gave credit to two of his high school teachers. This is where he claims to have learned to be a good citizen and to have respect for his elders and for the elderly. His school grades were superior throughout. He said that at this point in his life he has learned more than he ever envisioned.

At present he is taking a Biology class in college. He intends to first study to become a nurse, and then go to Guadalajara University in Mexico for his medical degree and become a doctor. The reason is that tuition at the Guadalajara University is considerably less than in the States. He is really interested in neurology—what causes strokes, brain trauma, etc., and he hopes to pursue this discipline. He will be the first person in his family to go to college. At present he has Federal Student Aid from the US Government.

Gus stated that he feels very close to people here at Merrill Gardens. He felt deeply about the death of resident, Jack Frey, attended his funeral, and commented what impressed him the most was when he read all that Jack had accomplished during his life. He also was so sorry to learn of the loss of Frank Rugebregt's wife. He said "I am religious," and that he prays to St. Mary, and added "I am a Christian."

To make some additional money to add to his Merrill Gardens earnings, he works as a DJ at Zumba Classes on Saturdays. (Zumba is an exercise class that uses salsa, merengue, and other types of Latin music.) It is obvious to me that he will let nothing stand in his way to obtain his goal. I, for one, wish him God Speed and Good Luck on his journey to not only become a doctor but to make a difference in the world.

P.S. The reason I decided to include this story is that it typifies the majority of our work staff who are either Mexican, from the Philippines or a South American country.

August 27, 2013

A TRIP TO THE ER

It was Saturday. I awoke at 6:30 a.m. with a heart problem. They call it A-Fib. As I pondered the irregular heartbeats, I was concerned. Since this had happened before I assumed it would go away. It didn't. I got up, washed, dressed, and left for breakfast. In the elevator my head began to whirl, and I sat down in a chair after getting off the elevator. In the dining room I met my friends, Mary Lou, David and Cece. I told them about my problem and felt some better after having my usual oatmeal, orange juice, milk, rye toast and decaf coffee. Marylou walked with me toward my apartment and urged me to take it easy.

At 10:00 a.m. there was a class called "Brain Games" with Marilyn Barnes. The time came. I didn't go; I still was not feeling all that good. At noon I met Gene for lunch and was joined by Hannah. I ate a light lunch of fish and rice, cottage cheese, and peaches. Back in my apartment I sat on the sofa and contemplated what I should do. My heartbeat was still very irregular. I read my Bible selection for the day and then turned on the television while finishing the crossword puzzle. The irregular heartbeats continued. Finally at 2:00 p.m. I called son David, who with Trish, were at their Glen Ellen home about twenty minutes away. They came immediately and took me to the ER in Sonoma. There was a flurry of monitors attached, and an IV put in place. An x-ray was taken and nurses monitored all the systems. I found it interesting to listen to all the conversations going on so the time went by quickly. Close to 5:00 p.m., a doctor came in to inform me that my heart now had a steady beat. I also was dehydrated. He signed the necessary papers and I was released.

When the paperwork was finished, I dressed and met Dave and Trish who had been waiting three hours while I was being cared for. I expressed my concern that their afternoon was wasted, but at this point I felt really good.

The best part of the day's activities was that after my release from the emergency room, the three of us went to a Thai restaurant in Sonoma and had a great dinner. That was "icing on the cake" after an afternoon of uncertainty.

February 9, 2013

WHAT'S ON THE MENU?

Having been raised in the Midwest in the 1930's and 40's, my taste in foods came from a rather limited menu of beef, pork, chicken, and occasionally fish from the many lakes in Minnesota. This was pretty much our family's standard fare for our evening dinner. There was lots of gravy, homemade biscuits, in-season fruits, and desserts full of sugary stuff. Mother always set a nice table and to this day I can smell the aroma of some of my favorite meals.

Thanksgiving was traditional with turkey and all the trimmings, but Christmas Eve dinner harkened back to an old Swedish tradition. We always had Lutefisk, a cod fish served with a cream sauce. I hated this meal since it smelled funny, but if I wanted to open my presents after dinner, I had to eat this dreadful item— maybe not all of it, but at least one small taste. My family always had several helpings of this horrible fish.

At present, living in California, I began to think about how this area has a completely different menu, either in a restaurant or as a guest in someone's home and how it has influenced me. There must be a general rule of some sort that one has to have a cupboard filled with boxes of pasta. There's pasta plain or with butter, pasta with many different types of sauces, and pasta with—you name it. At first I wanted to ask, "Where's the beef?" but my mother taught me to be polite. Vegetables in Minnesota were always peas or carrots, sometimes green beans, or beets, either plain or ones called Harvard Beets. Asparagus rarely appeared on the menu. As to fruits—there were fresh strawberries only in the month of June, followed by fresh raspberries, peaches, apricots, and pears. In July, watermelons appeared and a variety of apples in the Fall. In my childhood I never heard of guavas, plantains, different colored melons, or jicama.

Since coming to California I have eaten an array of new foods—some I like and a couple I plan never to eat or order again. The new foods I now eat with pleasure are: fresh crab, tamales, Thai foods, barbequed vegetables, pesto, figs, calamari, and items on a good Chinese menu including green onion pancakes. I also like Mexican food if it is not too spicy. Never had it in Minnesota! As to my present no-no list and listed in no special order are: artichokes, Brussel sprouts, and sushi. I could also live without avocados, and dim sum.

I am completely at sea when it comes to choosing a good wine. Wine was never served when I was young. But now living in northern California, I have no excuse. As a result I have had to make mental notes when dining out, with the attempt to learn the names of good red and white wines.

By no means are all the items listed "cut in stone." Who knows maybe I'll be brave and try again to see what everyone is raving about when eating sushi.

March 18, 2014

DEALING WITH CHANGE

I once saw a poster that said "CHANGE HAPPENS." Looking back over the years I realize that everyone goes through many, many changes. I was no different. Some changes are monumental such as death of a loved one. Then there are common changes like changing jobs or moving to a new location. Some changes are superficial: changing clothes, changing directions, and plain old changing your mind.

At this point in my life I have encountered a new change: buying and trying to learn to use an Apple iPhone. The mechanics of learning something new at my age is obviously much slower than it used to be. I accept that fact. Following the purchase of the iPhone, I was given a quick tutorial at the Verizon store by my son and daughter-in-law who both have iPhones. It all seemed so logical. How wonderful to be able to accomplish so much with this little black box. Then I went home and began the quest of using "this little black box" on my own. The difficulty was trying to remember what they showed me. I remembered how to turn it on. Up came "The Home Page". Wow—all those icons permitting me to roam and discover what they contained: messages, calendar, music, phone, mail, maps and weather, to name a few. This is going to be fun, I thought. But then I roamed too far. I was completely lost. The only thing to do was to turn it off and begin again.

The next thing I tried was to send a text message. I've envied people who text. As I watch their fingers race across the keyboard, I wonder, will I ever be able to do that? So I decided to try. A note to my financial advisor read, "Got new phone. Can't get money." I pressed Send and "poof," it was on its way. Oops—I forgot to sign it. I knew no way to retrieve the message, but knowing my age I surmised he would realize it was me. So far I haven't heard from him.

When I purchased my previous cell phone I received a booklet with explicit directions for its total usage. I used it often and found my way quickly. This time I got a very small pamphlet. I guess Verizon assumed that most people already know a lot about cell phones.

The staff where I live have answered several of my questions. So far they have been very helpful. However, I can soon see them going the other way when they see me coming. I've tried to think about the fact that using this new device is good for my brain, but does my brain have to struggle so hard while using it? Something else I'd like to know – Why do young people adapt so easily to these complicated devices? I wonder if someday I'll also conquer the total use of "this little black box?" No doubt by that time there will be a more complicated one.

July 23, 2013

HELP, HELP

Is there anything more frustrating than using modern equipment that requires know-how and quick thinking and you don't have either of these attributes? I speak of the use of today's cell phone. Actually, it isn't so much the phone but what the voice says to you after initiating a call. First of all, you have to inform a faceless programmed voice to answer this question "If you want to continue in English press 1." Once again there is a list from which to choose. At this point nothing on the list fits your needs. Starting once again another list is given with the same results and the voice announces, "You will now be connected with an agent; the wait will be fifty minutes.". During this time loud music bombards your ears, and is interrupted every thirty seconds with more information you do not need. At this point I want to scream. Several times, "We are so sorry for your long wait" is said only to keep you waiting longer. In the meantime my battery is being robbed of its precious minutes.

Oh, how I long for a telephone operator named Marge who would answer my call and sweetly ask, "How may I help you?". Let's face it—those days are gone.

The purpose of my call was finally accomplished after eight attempts to reach the Social Security Administration. It is now 3:30 p.m. and the deed is done. When I complained how much trouble I had getting through, the operator's first excuse was that it was my cell phone. "Next time," she said, "Use a landline phone." Then she added that the Social Security Administration offices were in the process of installing new equipment and that she had lost several calls herself. Did I feel sorry for her? I did not.

During the many times I was waiting for a call back from an agent, with my phone glued to my ear, I worked a couple of puzzles on the computer, and then with my right hand I began pecking out this story.

By chance I clicked on my horoscope and this is what it said:

Recent events have you feeling like you're walking on a tight rope and you're troubled about how, exactly, you're supposed to make it through. Remain calm and remember to be open to possibilities instead of tightening up in fear, and you'll have an epiphany that will result in a much-needed upsurge of courage right when you need it.

Ok—so what was my epiphany? Beats me, but you can bet I'll be looking for that courage if I ever need to call Social Security again.

August 20, 2013

TIME OUT- FOR A TIME

How quickly one's life can change! I had no premonition or warning that before the day ended, I would be dealing with a catastrophic event. It was November 10, 2015. The day began as usual with breakfast in the dining room, exercise at 9:00 a.m., and then back to my apartment to review my notes for the Residents' Council meeting at 1:00 p.m. As the president, I needed to be ready.

The council meeting ended at 2:50 p.m. I was satisfied that the council had worked together and much had been accomplished. I stood, turned, and my foot tangled with a couple of chairs behind me. Suddenly I was on the floor. I remember feeling the impact. It took my breath away for a bit. At this point, with a goodly number of people watching, I thought about the many times I'd performed in front of crowds as a musician but it was never like this. I knew that I should remain immobile, knowing I definitely would be taken to the hospital. The paramedics came. There were questions that I needed to answer and different devices attached here and there on my body. Fortunately it was only six blocks by ambulance to the Sonoma Valley Hospital. My friend, Anita, came to keep me company in the emergency room. She was a God-send. David came at 10:00 p.m. In the meantime there was a flurry of nurses and questions to be answered. After several x-rays the report indicated that I had two fractures of my pelvis, and a fractured left arm. A doctor told me I should be thankful that it was not a hip fracture.

Nearly six weeks later I was released, not completely back to normal, but I knew I had had good care. I was confident that I'd soon be functioning as before. Little did I know about how slow the healing would be. First a wheel chair was the means of getting from one place to another. Then came many sessions of physical therapy including a balance class.

As I thought about my time in the hospital I began making a list of what I had learned as a patient. Here is my list:

TEN THINGS I LEARNED AS A HOSPITAL PATIENT
(11/10/2015 - 12/16/2015)

1. If you have any degree of modesty, forget it, you'll never need it.
2. Don't try drinking water from a cup while lying flat in bed.
3. When a caregiver says, "Okay, roll to the left," endure the pain because biting her/his head off is not appropriate.
4. Stop imagining what the newly announced procedure will be. Because of progressive discoveries, you will always be wrong.
5. Always order coffee (or Ensure) for the next meal. It most likely will be the best item on the menu.
6. You will never have a significant amount of sleep. Someone will always disturb you for "blood samples," "pills," "blood pressure," or the use of a bed pan or commode.
7. Do not pretend to be sleeping when you hear the occupational or physical therapists coming. They are the best people to hasten your recovery.
8. The disappearing call button is often missing when you need it most.
9. Always say or think "Yes, I can do" what the therapists ask of you, even if it seems impossible.
10. Always remember to say "Thank you" for each procedure. They will be pleased knowing you appreciate their work.

Also—praying often to God with thanks for the guidance and progressive strength.

If you have been in the hospital for any length of time, perhaps you would like to make you own list. It takes away some of the pain, especially when the bills begin to arrive.

January 25, 2016

TIME SAVING GADGETS

In my 85+ years of living on this planet, there have been thousands or maybe millions of items invented claiming to be time savers and enhancements. All of these inventions made it necessary to move into the future and buy the latest gadget. Let's look at a couple of inventions. In the housekeeping department, a precursor to the electric washing machine was the washboard. We were told that the washing machine used less elbow grease, and the job finished in less time. The dryer soon followed. I'm fairly certain that not many would want to go back to the washboard era.

Another invention is the cell phone, a tiny box that has capabilities far more than I could ever imagine. My son told of a time when he lost his way while driving and asked his phone, "Where am I?" In a couple of instants the answer came back. What else can a cell phone do? First and foremost it is a telephone with mechanisms to quickly dial without punching in the numbers. In addition you can play games, listen to music, get answers to your questions, text message, take photos, send e-mails, film an ongoing event, and receive calls. It is a datebook, a calendar and has weather information. You can pay your bills and do your banking. All this takes place within a small mechanism that fits in your pocket. Who imagined this when we saw Dick Tracy use his indestructible wristwatch as a phone so many years ago?

Today I watched a demonstration on TV of a small computer screen that can be attached to one's glasses (on one side) and operated by a cell phone. Are we so busy that this gadget is one that everyone will see as a "must have"? At this time the cost is excessive. I'll be interested to see if it becomes popular. In addition there is also the capability of building your own cell phone from a kit.

There are always those who see the down side of progress. A quote by Albert Einstein caught my eye when I read the following: "I fear the day that technology will surpass our human interaction. The world will then have a generation of idiots."

Perhaps an issue that needs to be discussed is whether the world's population is separating itself from discourse with "must have" gadgets? Personally, I miss an old-fashioned gab session. How about you?

April 23, 2013

OUT WITH THE OLD, IN WITH THE NEW

An old bearded man dressed in a white robe carrying a scythe, and a baby in a diaper are iconic pictures as we turn the calendar for a New Year. These images have been around for a long time. It tells us to accept the New Year and leave the old year behind. It's over. Done! Finished! Nothing can stop it. Nothing can call the year back. This got me thinking about other things in our lives that bear a similarity.

Let me list a few:
1. **Fashion**: Fashion designers do just that. They design items that set the trend for a period of time, usually with a new look. This follows with the old being replaced by the new. Occasionally one sees hints of the really old reappearing. Perhaps it's in our closet hoping to be worn again.
2. **Moving**: Most of us who have moved have had to downsize. It was a matter of choice what to keep and what to discard. Some folks found it difficult to part with some items and made room for those items in a large or small storage unit. Others perhaps started life anew and left behind or gave away outdated stuff.
3. **Resolutions**: The New Year seems to be the perfect time to make changes in lifestyle or location so we make resolutions. These resolutions can be one of many choices. For example: Losing weight, learning a new skill, writing a book, or being more kind to one's neighbor. How long one keeps a resolution is a subject for another time. (I don't remember making a resolution.)
4. **Laws**: It's the job of the US Senate and The House of Representatives to enact new laws for the betterment of society. Some laws take effect with the change of the calendar. Again out with the old law and in with the new. A huge change for the masses came with the banning of smoking in public places. I wonder about Obama Care. Will it survive and be beneficial? I hope so.

5. **Location**: As one ages most of us have had to make changes. One's work often was the reason to move, or maybe it was failing health. Where I now live, I have made new friends. Have I discarded the old? Certainly not! My relatives and a number of priceless friends are important to me so I telephone or write notes hoping to keep abreast of what's happening in their lives. It may be difficult to let go of the old, but at some point a choice needs to be made.
6. **Manufacturing**: Companies are continually telling us that they have made a better "mousetrap." Automobiles, in particular, advertise improvements and design to entice the public to get rid of the old and buy the new. But isn't it interesting that antique cars are sought after and purchased at a much higher price.

Undoubtedly there are many more examples of getting rid of the old and accepting the new, but when I spoke of "friends" in this article, I was reminded of the simple song/poem: *"Make new friends. Keep the old. One is silver, the other gold."* This is a good example of not discarding the old when encountering the new. I guess one has to be flexible in most situations. I sincerely try to do this since I do not want to be known as that old Fuddy-Duddy!

One additional childhood memory of New Year's Eve is my father taking out his rifle and placing bullets in the cartridge. Why? What was he preparing for? He certainly wasn't going hunting. It was a tradition (maybe just for him) to stand at the curb, and exactly at the stroke of midnight shoot several rounds in the air. Standing alongside my dad was my dog, Birdie. She, of course, loved to be outside, but the moment Dad started shooting she would run in circles. Being a hunting dog she frantically tried to find the prey that should be falling to the ground. Finding nothing she would be so disappointed as if she failed to complete her duty. Now I often wonder if this activity of my father was solely his idea, or were there additional shooters celebrating the New Year, and was it actually dangerous, and, I wonder what happened to the bullets.

At this point I am reminded of going with my friends to the neighborhood Lutheran church on December 31. They were members. I was not. (I was a confirmed member of First Covenant Church in downtown Minneapolis where my parents were members.) At the Lutheran Church we would all gather in the Fellowship Hall for games and snacks. We all looked forward to this event. It was great fun.

At approximately fifteen minutes before midnight, everyone would gather in the sanctuary for a time of reflection. It was important in this quiet atmosphere to think about the past year and to be in a repentant mood. Five minutes before midnight everyone would kneel, silently pray, and promise to be a better Christian in the coming year. It was very sobering to then hear the sound of bells, fireworks, and shouts at midnight and realize a new year had begun. What would the New Year hold for me? Now at age eighty-eight, I look back through those years and am amazed how my life has evolved. I never could have imagined the life I have lived. Today, as I write, I thank God for the experiences and those who have impacted my life. And I must admit I still think about my life as a Christian when I hear the midnight bells and fireworks, and wonder if I'll celebrate one more New Year's Eve.

January 7, 2014

MUSIC, MUSIC, MUSIC

Since the age of four music has been a significant part of my life. My first piano lesson actually began on November 9, 1931 with Mrs. Soderlind who came to my house for a half hour lesson once a week. Thanks to my mother I still have the lesson plans my teacher wrote for each week. During that first day I was acquainted with the seven letters of the alphabet and how it corresponded to the keyboard.

Every year a piano tuner came to our house. On one visit, he listened to me play and then tested my ability to identify notes on piano while facing away from the keyboard. He told my mother that I had perfect pitch. He said it was an ability not everyone had. To me it was a natural condition.

As I grew in stature and musical ability, I loved to play but not necessarily practice what was assigned. Now and then I would intentionally skip practicing for three or more days. One day I was unprepared for my lesson, so I decided to go to the candy store. As I came down the alley chewing on my purchase, I was met by my mother and Mrs. Soderlind coming toward me. I learned a valuable lesson that day—that is, to "face the music." Mrs. Soderlind stayed and I had a lesson that proved more pointedly that I had not practiced. Another day I came to play the piano and found it locked. When I complained my mother said that if I didn't practice there was no need to keep the piano open, and it would be locked for two weeks. After a couple of days I begged to have it unlocked but she kept her word. To me this was torture. After two weeks I cried and begged and promised to do better. The piano was then unlocked.

When I turned thirteen, Mrs. Laura Ford Gierre became my next teacher. Her studio was downtown at the Minneapolis Musical College. The year was 1940. She was very strict so my keyboard ability grew as a result. I played in many recitals and made a couple of recordings. I often played for choir rehearsals at my church and school, and played piano solos for many events.

In college I met my future husband, Bert, who was also a good pianist. The year was 1947. We both studied with the same piano teacher, Mr. Bergman. We became a two piano team and through the years concertized before and after marriage. We both taught piano. Bert also had perfect pitch.

After Bert's death in 1993, I had the opportunity to study jazz with Tom Croghan, a classically trained pianist, who was a retired OB-GYN physician. I was sixty-eight years old. My thinking was that it would be fun and easy since I was able to play by ear. How wrong I was. One time I complained that Tom was freezing my brain with all the scales and chord progressions I needed to learn. I kept on trying and little by little some things began to make sense. It also made me realize how much there was to learn in order to play jazz. I couldn't just copy it by listening and duplicating what I heard. I had to own it.

Unfortunately my teacher developed a brain tumor and died three years after the diagnosis. Many of the tunes that I play today are arrangements he gave me. I will forever be grateful for the opportunity I had to further my musical education with Tom and to know a bit more about those who skillfully play great jazz, like my favorite jazz artist, Oscar Peterson. Tom frequently chided me that he was waiting to hear me play *real* jazz—but that never happened. What I learned was many new jazz riffs, a sequence of jazz chords, but I never was able put it all together. You can't say I didn't try.

Tom had many friends in the jazz field. He often had them come to Mansfield for Jazz programs at the Renaissance Theatre. I was always in the audience. It was a pleasure listening as they interlaced their jazz expertise with one another. I even remember showing my enthusiasm by using my finger whistling skills and doing it often. Each time they came I was totally enwrapped in the music and clapped enthusiastically on beats 2 and 4—something I learned in our home in New Jersey when Norman Edge, our friend, who played double bass in the Morris Nanton Trio. I was really into it—eyes shut, and clapping on beat 1 and 3 when he turned to me and softly said "Helen, Jazz is accented on the 2nd and 4th beat." I was grateful for the advice so I didn't continue to look like a complete nerd.

My grandson, Jon, while a student at New York University mainly studying jazz, told a story that happened in one of his classes. The professor had been playing recordings of various jazz artists in order for the students to learn to recognize personal styles of the artist. At one point he began to play a record of the Morris Nanton Trio—saying that the students should not even try to guess who was playing, since they would never be able to come up with the right answer. Jon did speak up and named the group much to the amazement of the professor. When asked how he knew, he said that his grandparents knew the trio personally, often played their records, and at one time had the trio in their home. Those records were passed on to Jon's father—thus Jon heard it as a little kid and remembered. Now I was impressed! Jon is now a very successful pianist in his profession. He and his wife, Molly, a budding actress and playwright, live in New York City.

My piano skills have served me well here where I now live. Every Wednesday, for the cocktail hour, I play the piano attempting to please the audience with music they recognize and perhaps with sing-a-longs. As I write this story, I once again am thankful to my mother and dad for all the encouragement they gave me to continue practicing. I can't imagine the total cost for all those years of lessons. Certainly during The Depression it must have been a sacrifice. Thanks Mom and Dad. I wish I had thanked you more.

April 12, 2015

PRACTICE, PRACTICE, PRACTICE

I've read that it takes 10,000 hours of study to become an expert. If you studied one hour per weekday, it would take forty years to reach that goal. And if you studied full time, i.e., eight hours per weekday, it would still take five years to reach 10,000 hours. In other words, to succeed at anything, be it sports or business, or whatever, it takes practice, practice, practice.

During my early years I often heard my mother chide me and say, "You need to practice the piano in order to get better." This was usually followed by, "You know, practice makes perfect." I didn't mind playing the piano, but actually practicing my lesson was often boring and hard work. But is the old adage "practice makes perfect" always true? I say no! To me a better way to complete the phrase is to add the word perfect—"perfect" practice makes for perfection. Slow careful and repetitive practice is the secret that brings resounding results.

According to Google the term "practice makes perfect" has been traced back to the 1500's and is attributed to John Adams. It is considered a proverb. My guess is the phrase goes back even farther from the Latin term *uses promptos facit*—use (or practice) makes one ready; i.e., practice make perfect. Recently, I came across a quote by the world famous pianist Ignace Paderewski (born 1860): "If I don't practice for one day, I know it; if I don't practice for two days, the critics know it; if I don't practice for three days, the audience knows it."

Through the years a phrase I often heard was "practice what you preach." In other words, "actions speak louder than words." This is sometimes harder to deal with particularly when there are serious problems that need to be solved. Most often this calls for educated professionals to aid in recognizing what the problems are and how to solve them. These professionals have practiced their discipline and continue to study in order to maintain their expertise.

Doctors and lawyers are said to have a practice. I believe here the word practice is used to give the seeker confidence of getting the best advice concerning his or her health or wealth. A doctor may have chosen to maintain a family practice.

Another use of the word practice is in the phrase choir practice. It would be an unusual choir that would ever consider performing without many, many practices.

In sports there are always practice sessions in order to build muscle and strength to perform well. Recently I have been watching basketball. I'm always amazed when three-point shots are made. These do not come easily. To score a three-pointer, I would venture a guess, no, actually I could not even guess, how often these shots have been practiced.

What about target practice? I remember going with my father as he practiced shooting clay pigeons—and hearing the familiar word "pull" being shouted and then seeing the object flying through the air. If he was successful the clay pigeon would break apart and fall to the ground. He needed to do this in order to be a better shot when hunting.

How well I remember having practice tests in school in preparation for the real test the next day. Often the teacher would say, "Take out a piece of paper and number from one to ten." The questions were from the lesson we had been studying. This gave us a clue what needed to be reviewed.

One last thought on the word practice: one should always practice good behavior. Hey, Mom, how am I doing?

October 22, 2013

RECITALS AND BUTTERFLIES

I have played in many recitals in my life. My first piano teacher had one recital each year. It was held at the Leamington Hotel in Minneapolis, Minnesota. The large room had marble pillars, beautiful floors that looked like marble, and long beautiful draperies that hung to the floor. A grand piano was positioned in front of chairs that were arranged in two sections with a center aisle. I was five years old, had a new dress, a bow in my hair, and a few butterflies going on deep inside. There were printed programs. Mrs. Soderlind made a few announcements and then the program started with each student taking their turn. When I heard my father clear his throat and shift his position, I knew it was my turn to perform.

On our way home, my mother always reminded me of my mistakes unlike my father who usually patted me on the back and told me I did well.

My next piano teacher taught at the Minneapolis Musical College in the city. It was a two story building and had a small stage and a recording studio alongside. In order to be well prepared for a recital I was required to make a record of the two piano selections that I would be performing. This caused the same butterflies. My parents would attend but my recital outfits now omitted the bow in my hair. Because I had advanced I was often asked to perform at church and school where I experienced less butterflies.

In college there was no real stage except for a raised platform. Bert, my boyfriend, and I soon became a twosome and performed duets for programs and events. The butterflies were almost non-existent because our attention was on sounding like one piano, and we had fun practicing and performing.

We then transferred to McPhail College of Music in Minneapolis to earn our degree. McPhail was a three-story building with a recital hall on the third floor.

Again I was on a stage, but the butterfly syndrome was more severe because there were over forty music teachers at this school, and one could be assured many of them would attend and know the music being performed. At the end of our junior year Bert and I married.

Graduation was held at a local theater one year later on a very large stage. I was on the program and it was time to begin. The orchestra was in place, and as I walked on the stage the applause began. I bowed deeply, sat down, adjusted my long gown, and wiped my hands with a lacy handkerchief. I then looked at Bert, who was at the second piano, for assurance and courage. The orchestra was ready, and with my nod to the director the music began. My butterflies, at this point were having a field day. When I finished I bowed, walked off the stage and was called back for a second bow. Had my butterflies disappeared? No. They were literally jitterbugging.

Following graduation Bert and I concertized as a two piano team. We were asked to go on a concert tour and agreed to take it on. However, I became pregnant and so the deal was cancelled on the advice of the doctor.

After a few years, I began giving private piano lessons again followed by scheduled recitals. This led to discussion with students about dealing with butterflies and learning how to bow properly. It was my conclusion, because of my past experience, to have student recitals at least two or three times a year. The last thirty years of teaching it grew to four or five. The result was that the students' butterflies lessened considerably. They learned that the more you perform the more confident you become.

Here at my Sonoma residence I play for an hour every Wednesday afternoon for the Wine Social. And guess what—no butterflies. The reason? I believe it is because everyone is so kind and complimentary. I play music I love and ones the residents seem to recognize. Sometimes they sing along. How lucky I am to have this opportunity. However, I still have to practice and be prepared so those dreadful butterflies do not return.

December 18, 2012

TREES

Joyce Kilmer in his poem entitled "Trees" captured poetically a lovely picture of his love for trees. I particularly like the final verse:

> *"Poems are made by fools like me,*
> *But only God can make a tree."*

As I thought about the different kinds of trees that I have seen in my lifetime I began to focus on their differences and when and where they existed. First were the two maple trees that graced my front yard when I was a child. They afforded the necessary shade in the hot summer, and gave opportunity for climbing for my friends and me. The branches were reachable and supportive. (We often sat up there as a hideaway and called out to passersby.) In the back of the house five regal Lombardy poplars stood like sentries guarding the garage.

At my parents' cabin on Ruth Lake in Emily, Minnesota there were woods that teemed with lovely white birch trees interspersed with large and small fir trees. Our son, David, would often bring pieces of birch to show his friends. The fir trees all looked like potential Christmas trees.

In our travels to the West Coast I saw my first palm tree. As we continued north we drove into the giant redwood forest in Northern California. Yes, we did drive through the wide opening in the famous giant redwood tree. I remember the aromatic fragrance of these ancient wonders. Years later I walked the paths of Muir Woods in California's Marin County and was again awed by the immensity of the trees and learned more of the park's history.

In 1980 we moved to Mansfield, Ohio. There we learned about the Buckeye tree and cautioned that the seeds were poisonous. However, people collected buckeyes making necklaces, art pieces, and unique decorative objects. Stores often carried delicious Buckeye candies. The candies consisted of a dark chocolate base and a light chocolate center. Recipes are available, but be aware, they are tricky to make. The famous Ohio State University football team is known as The Buckeyes.

Outside my apartment window there is a beautiful tall magnolia tree. It was one of the reasons I chose my current second-floor apartment. At first I would check to see if there were any blossoms. I soon learned that the blossoms appear one at a time, and each one lasts for only two or three days. This gave me more time to admire the tree and watch for its milky, white flowers to appear.

Here is a pleasing poem from Ilan Shamir entitled "Advice From a Tree":

> *Dear Friend,*
> *Stand Tall and Proud*
> *Sink your roots deeply into the Earth*
> *Reflect the light of a greater source*
> *Think long term*
> *Go out on a limb*
> *Remember your place among all living beings*
> *Embrace with joy the changing seasons*
> *For each yields its own abundance*
> *The Energy and Birth of Spring*
> *The Growth and Contentment of Summer*
> *The Wisdom to let go of leaves in the Fall*
> *The Rest and Quiet Renewal of Winter*
> *Feel the wind and the sun*
> *And delight in their presence*
> *Look up at the moon that shines down upon you,*
> *And the mystery of the stars at night.*
> *Seek nourishment from the good things in life*
> *Simple pleasures*
> *Earth, fresh air, light*
> *Be content with your natural beauty*
> *Drink plenty of water*
> *Let your limbs sway and dance in the breezes*
> *Be flexible*
> *Remember your roots*
> *Enjoy the view!*

October 2, 2012

QUOTES

What did they say?

There are hundreds, maybe thousands, of books of quotations of famous people and those unknown.

On my shelf is a book titled, *A Dictionary of Musical Quotations*, by Crofton and Fraser. I purchased it for use in my profession as a musician. An example is by J. S. Bach, written as an epigraph to his *Little Organ Book* (1717) where he wrote, *"For the glory of the most high God, alone ... and for my neighbors to learn from."*

Going through this book of quotations cafeteria style, has been a rollicking event. It gave me bits of history, reminders of forgotten personalities, humor, poetry and love. I read about Ludwig van Beethoven, stone deaf in his later life. He was reported to have said, *"I shall hear in heaven."*

James Galway, the famous contemporary flutist, was noted to say, *"I got to try the bagpipes. It was like trying to blow an octopus."* This really made me laugh.

Also, Richard Benchley's statement about Opera is a classic. He said, *"Opera is where a guy gets stabbed in the back and instead of dying, he sings."*

I found a person this week that fascinated me because of the enormity of quotes from his famous *Little Red Book*. It was Chairman Mao Zedong, leader of the Chinese Communist Party from 1964-1976.

I submit the following four quotes from Mao:

> *"To read too many books is harmful."*
> *"Political power grows out of the barrel of the gun."*
> *"In waking a tiger use a long stick."*
> *"I am a lone monk walking the world with a leaky umbrella."*

Most of us remember the following quote, *"Ask not what your country can do for you—ask what you can do for your country,"* a statement made by John F. Kennedy, the newly elected President of the United States in his inaugural address in 1961.

And who could forget President Ronald Regan's famous speech in 1987 at the Brandenburg Gate, Germany, where he proclaimed, *"Mr. Gorbachev, tear down this wall!"*

Such quotes stay in our minds for years because of the seriousness of the events. And then sometimes we remember a famous saying such as *"Damn the torpedoes, full speed ahead,"* but do we recall who said it. (It was Admiral David Farragut.)

From there I began to think about statements made by my parents, my husband, and others. One from my husband that I shall never forget and has proven valuable is—*"Be careful when giving advice. They may just take it."*

I will always remember what he said to me two days before he died when I asked the question, "How am I going to get along without you?" He said, *"You will grieve, and you need to do that. Then you will go on."* Good advice, for sure, and I carried those words together with God's Word all through the years.

I ask myself, am I saying helpful, loving, and/or informative words that will give courage to someone in need? It's a tall order, but in my way of thinking, it's what the world desperately needs.

Finally, I leave you with words from a short speech by Robert Kennedy at the home of South Africa's first black president, Nelson Mandela, in June 1966. Years later, President Obama, while visiting Mandela's cell where he was held for eighteen years, quoted Kennedy's famous words:

> *"Each time a man stands up for an idea, or acts to improve the lot of others, or strikes out against injustice, he sends forth tiny ripples of hope, and those ripples build a current which can sweep down the mightiest walls of oppression and resistance."*

November 4, 2013

WILD FIRE

It was near 5:30 a.m. on Monday October 9, 2017 when I heard a knock on my door. I said "Come in," and heard the familiar voice of Karen, the Director of Brookdale. She entered my room to explain that we were in danger of the encroaching fires and needed to prepare for a possible evacuation. She handed me two large plastic bags into which to place any valuables to be saved. The fires were not yet a threat to the town of Sonoma but the smoke was thick, dangerous, and made it difficult to breathe.

Not sure what to do, I called Bean. "Wallet, money, medications," he replied. When Sandy (my caregiver) arrived, we began packing a suitcase. After packing, I told her that Bean would come at 3:00 p.m. to take me to San Francisco. The Epsteins had accepted me as a house guest for a day or two. Once the smoke cleared I would go back to Brookdale.

On our way to San Francisco, there was evidence of fire—pasture land, once cattle fodder was now blackened; and cows standing in groups on small patches of green. Skyward, there were hazy reddish clouds, and around us were occasional sights of fire. Cross the Golden Gate Bridge, a turn on Lake Street, and we arrived at the Epsteins' home.

My eyes immediately were drawn to the many stairs up to the front door. Step by step, with Bean and Paul, I was easily inside.

Their living room was my haven for the next few days. That evening, the whole family was together at the dining table. Roslyn, a gourmet chef, laid out a delicious meal together with love, family, and calm, all in my new temporary home.

The fires were raging in California in the North Bay with the appearance that it would be contained and not be a threat to Sonoma where I live. Still I watched the devastation in Santa Rosa and mourned for their losses and the evacuations with one sad story after another. I remarked to myself about the selflessness of the reporters who stood amidst the burning rubble speaking to those who had lost their homes. And the brave first responders risking their lives to save thousands of people.

My return to Brookdale was delayed day after day as the fires worsened and the smoke got worse. The rest of Brookdale (Sonoma) had been evacuated to another Brookdale location in Santa Cruz where people were sleeping on cots in hallways and every kind of available room. I felt lucky to be with family in San Francisco.

The following days were varied—especially meals. Several different soups—leek and potato, split pea and ham. Night time was unusual. I slept with my clothes on, sans shoes, on the sofa with two pillows and a cozy comforter. My walker is close by for bathroom night journeys. Dinner time was varied—always with some relatives joining in. Even Jon, from New York City, came on Thursday and returned the following Monday.

Let me tell you a little about the fire. It started Sunday night, October 8, 2017, as a few small fires. But high winds rapidly spread the fire over huge areas. On Sunday and Monday, the many small fires merged into five massive fires, which were moving at 100 yards per minute. Bean and Tricia's home in Glen Ellen was destroyed that first night.

As that week wore on we watched the fires approach Sonoma. What was previously unthinkable now looked all too likely—much of Sonoma was evacuated in anticipation of fire engulfing the town. Its beautiful town square, its famous wineries, and the homes of over 11,000 residents were all in the paths of two raging fires.

Whether Brookdale Sonoma would survive the encroaching raging fires, ran through my mind. Were the treasures I possessed going to survive—my pictures, artifacts for my book, plants, piano, and music? At this point there was no answer.

By midweek there were over 8,000 fire fighters from 350+ different agencies, including from Oregon, Washington, Canada, and even from Australia. Air tankers full of fire suppressant began arriving. As fires converged on Sonoma from both the north and the east thousands of fire fighters set up around the town. They bulldozed fire breaks, poured fire suppressant from low flying air tankers, raced from block to block as high winds blew burning embers throughout the city, and fought for every foot of land. By Sunday they had saved the town! The danger to the town had passed and the evacuation order was lifted on Monday.

Most residents of Brookdale returned Monday afternoon and I returned on Tuesday. As you can imagine, we all had stories to tell.

April 27, 2018

WALKING IN CIRCLES

"Walking in circles" is an expression for being lost or confused; that is, ending back at the beginning and not finding what one was looking for. A dog is a good example of an animal who will circle an area several times before lying down. Also, when a person is in distress, he or she may pace in a circular path. Another example that quickly comes to mind is of a maze with a rat trying to find his way through a series of pathways with only one way out. But I would like to look at another type of circle called a labyrinth, in which one deliberately walks in a circle for the purpose of meditation and/or relaxation.

My focus on a labyrinth is a spiritual one. First of all I learned that there are 4,200 spiritual labyrinths in 75 or more countries. The objective is always the same—centering one's mind on God or personal peace and tranquility as you slowly walk the prescribed pattern laid out on a flat surface, be it indoors or outdoors. Grace Cathedral in San Francisco has both indoor and outdoor labyrinths. There is one as you enter the main doors, and has scheduled times for use. On the outdoor grounds, the labyrinth is used around the clock.

LABYRINTH FACTS:
1. It has only one circular path—there are no tricks; no dead ends like a maze.
2. It takes thirty minutes to walk it properly.
3. While walking slowly, one should reflect, pray, meditate on peace within oneself, your community, and the global family.

PURPOSE:
1. Purgation—(Relaxing) letting go of details of your life.
2. Illumination—(Receiving) when reaching the center, stay as long as you like reflecting on your life.
3. Union—(Reversing) retracing your steps in stage three by joining God, and healing forces.

I remember seeing labyrinths in several places. One that impressed me the most was at Chartres Cathedral, fifty miles southwest of Paris, France. The church was constructed in 1145 and then reconstructed over a twenty-six year period following a fire in 1194. It is known worldwide for its beautiful stained glass windows that depict biblical stories. The labyrinth is imprinted on the floor as you enter and is intended as a spiritual pilgrimage, and a tool for prayer, spirituality, and meditation. It is about a journey, not a destination.

An additional labyrinth I experienced was at a retreat center named "Spirit in the Desert" in Carefree, Arizona. This one was quite different because it was laid out on land with the path lined with stones following the universal pattern. A local Boy Scout troupe did the labor work.

There is an obvious connection between the brain and walking a labyrinth. As one pays attention to the direction and follows the pattern in rows, the mind begins to release tension and reality becomes more obvious. If there has been stress, it is lessened. If there are life questions to be answered, answers may be waiting depending on the concentration of the walker.

It is obvious to me that a labyrinth is a gift to the masses if it is walked meaningfully.

September 10, 2013

DO WELLS EVER RUN DRY?

One day you are eight-nine years old—in fact, it's true for a whole year. And then you go to sleep one night and upon waking, your year just increased to ninety. I've thought about turning ninety. It really didn't bother me, until the family began talking about it and preparations of how to celebrate were in the works.

The rhythm of life is a natural slowing of physical and mental abilities—eyesight, walking, forgetfulness, including a day when some bit of food remains on your clothing after lunch. A five-week stay in the hospital after a severe fall makes one subject to all the routines of regaining your strength. But enough of that. What can I do?

I can think! I can read, and share stories with my caregivers and Brookdale friends. But now do I dare mention something that takes up much of my time? The answer is CONSTIPATION! Everyone seems to have this problem at some time, but it truly is a personal issue. Or is it? The subject has to be shared with someone—but with whom? Doctors don't have much patience. The summation of my question was answered by one of my doctors: —"Remember, it is only garbage in and garbage out." I wanted to hit her with my bedpan, but instead I changed doctors.

Once again at home I was faced with another "My Story, Your Story," and needing to find a story to present. At this point in my writings, I expressed frustration concerning the possibility of coming to the end of ideas to write about. After all I had been without computer access for over five weeks. Then I said to myself, "You can't quit that easily. How about dealing with the title?" I concluded that the title "Will the Well Ever Run Dry?" needed to be dealt with.

Where is this well of ideas, and how do I access it? Does anyone have the key? All through my life there has been one story after another—and I've written very easily. Now at ninety years of age, my thinking process has slowed a bit and I have to rely on a well of ideas that has truly begun to slow. The nearest event from which to extract a few scenes was June 10, 2017, the day of my birthday celebration held at the home of Bean and Trish (family) in Glen Ellen. To prepare for this big event, I headed for the beauty shop. While under the dryer I fainted and knew nothing until on a gurney heading to the hospital. Fast forward after multitudinous tests and urgings to stay at Sonoma Valley Hospital I left for Brookdale. With a change of clothing, a washcloth to my face, and a dash of lipstick, I was on my way to Glen Ellen. When I walked in facing the crowd, I apologized for being late and enjoyed hearing the singing of Happy Birthday.

The party was a blast—delicious food, a huge birthday cake, and speeches. The day was ending when suddenly I awakened to the sound of ER boots. Once again I had fainted. It was 7:30 p.m. Once again the familiar tests were applied and the familiar sounds of "NO" coming from my lips. I refused to go to the hospital. The outcome was later determined that a certain medication was too strong.

Well, the question "Do wells ever run dry?" is truly a good question. Just live long enough and there will always be something to talk about. It has been proven to me. Have I convinced you?

July 18, 2017

A FINAL WORD

Whew! My story could go on but I'm tired. Naturally, this book has left a number of stories untold. You see, the original intent was to tell selected happenings as they came to mind often as part of our weekly "My Story, Your Story" meetings.

If you don't find your name or what would have been a great story please know it was not intentional to leave it out.

The next few sentences are directed to my three great-grandchildren: Gabriella, Nate, and Henry, with a heads up to their parents.

Remember the important things and the silly things, the big events and small enjoyments, the highs and the lows. Write them down, share with others, and pass them on to your children. They will all become part of the river of memories from our family that flows to the future.

Helen Anderson

April 28, 2018

THE PRAYER OF SAINT FRANCIS

Lord, make me an instrument of your peace.

Where there is hatred, let me sow love.

Where there is injury, pardon,

where there is doubt, faith,

where there is despair, hope,

where there is darkness, light,

and where there is sadness, joy.

Divine Master, grant that I may not so much seek to be consoled as to console,

to be understood as to understand,

to be loved as to love,

for it is in giving that we receive,

it is in pardoning that we are pardoned,

and it is in dying that we are born to eternal life.

PICTURES

Picture 22: Grandma Nelson - 90th Birthday

Picture 23: Grandma Nelson - 90th Birthday

Picture 24: Grandma Nelson and me, 1928

Picture 25: Grandpa Nelson and me, 1928

Picture 26: Grandpa and Grandma Hoffman – 50th Wedding Anniversary

Picture 27: Grandpa and Grandma Hoffman with their five boys. My dad, Ed, is in the middle of the back row.

Picture 28: Edwin Hoffman and Delia Nelson – Wedding

Picture 29: Edwin and Delia Hoffman – 50th Wedding Anniversary

Picture 30: Bert's father – David Elias Anderson

Picture 31: My Dad – Edwin L. Hoffman

Picture 32: Dad hunting rabbits

Picture 33: My childhood home in Minneapolis. 5300 – 44th Avenue S.

Picture 34: My dad Ed, my son David, and one big fish!

Picture 35: Here I am at 2 ½ years old.

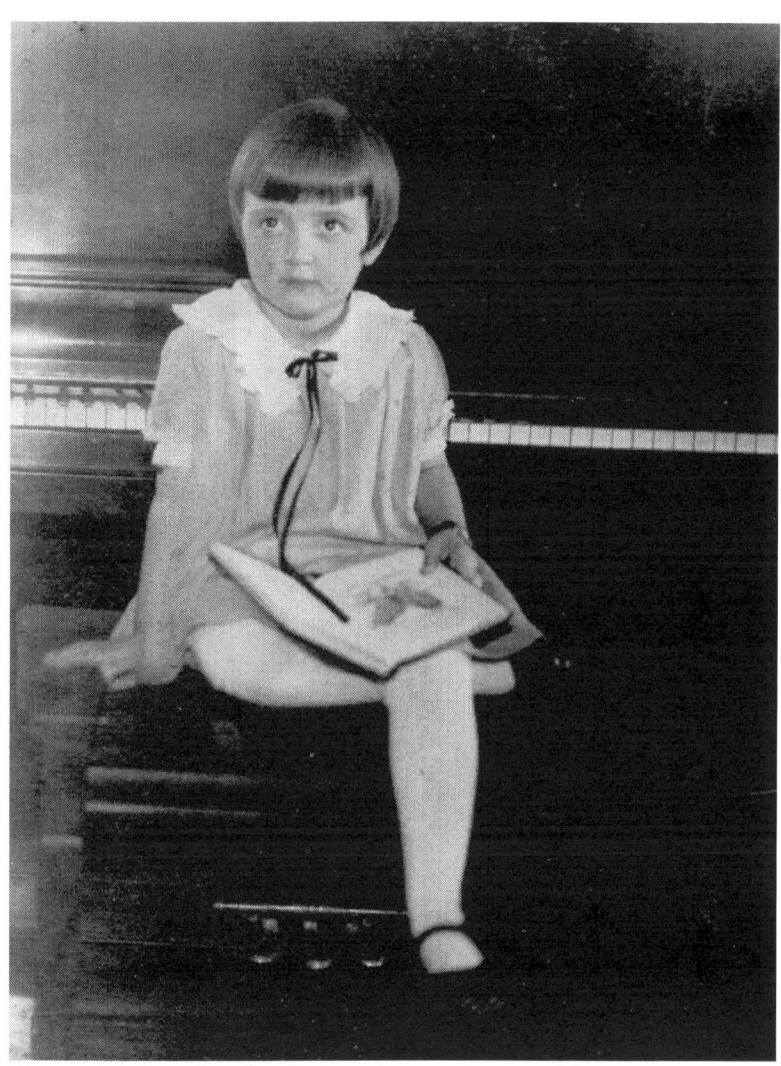

Picture 36: I'm already playing piano at 4 years old.

Picture 37: Gladys and I standing in a tub of water. Can you guess why?

Picture 38: A birthday party. Can you find me in the back row?

Picture 39: Gladys, me, and friends.

Picture 40: Here I am at age 13 years

Picture 41: Confirmation May 25 1941 at First Covenant Church

Picture 42: This is from a movie my dad took.

Picture 43: Sulking on the porch.

Picture 44: Edwin and Dee Hoffman, Helen, Eva Anderson, Bert

Picture 45: Bert and me in 1950

Picture 46: Rock n Roll! Halloween fun.

Picture 47: Dave and Jennie's Wedding

Back Row: Me, David (Bean) Anderson, Jon Anderson, Andrew Epstein (Jennie's brother)
Front Row: Trish Anderson, Barb Mahon (Trish's mother), Dave Anderson, Jennie Anderson (nee Epstein), Roslyn Bannish (Jennie's mother), Paul Epstein (Jennie's father)

Picture 48: No one recognized me in this Halloween outfit

Helen's Opus 1

Picture 49: Four generations of Anderson: Nate, Dave, Me, Dave (Bean)

Picture 50: Bye Bye

TABLE OF CONTENTS

PROLOGUE	i
ACKNOWLEDGEMENTS	iii
IT WAS ALL MY GRANDMOTHER'S FAULT	1
GLADYS	11
GRADE SCHOOL MEMORIES	14
PLAYTIME GONE WRONG	20
PERFECT PITCH	22
HOW I LEARNED THE SWEDISH LANGUAGE	24
LIFE ON THE FARM IN THE 1930's	26
MORE THAN JUST A FARMER	30
AND THEN THERE WAS ARVID	33
A GREAT FOURSOME	37
ANOTHER QUESTION—TB	39
FINICKY CHILD	41
DEER HUNTING VACATION	42
MY FIRST DOG	44
THE GREAT DEPRESSION	46
TONSILS	48
PUZZLES, PUZZLE ME	50
MY MOTHER'S FAMILY STORY	52
WHAT WOULD JESUS DO?	55
NYAH NYAH NYAH	57
HE CALLED ME "PATSA"	59
SIXTH GRADE	60
GOOD FRIENDS, GOOD FUN	61
ATTICS I HAVE KNOWN	62
OLD FASHIONED PICTURE TAKING	65
MONEY	66
MY DAD	67
GOOD ADVICE FROM DAD	71
MY FIRST ADVENTURE AWAY FROM HOME	72
MINNEHAHA SINGERS	74
MY FIRST UNFINISHED PIANO PIECE	76
THE MAN BEHIND THE MUSIC—Dmitri Shostakovich	77
AIRPLANE ATTRACTION	78
MY FAVORITE COLOR—AND WHY	80
MY TEENAGE YEARS	81
MY VERY FIRST JOB	83
GOOD KID/BAD KID	84

A PROVERB: TRUE OR FALSE?	86
SOULMATE	89
BERT'S CHILDHOOD	92
BERT'S WAR YEARS—1942-1945	94
GOOD NEIGHBORS	97
ONE MORE STUPID THING I'VE DONE	99
DAVID	100
A BIG MOVE—TO ROCK ISLAND	102
CHANGE HAPPENS	104
LET'S HAVE COFFEE	107
AN UNEXPECTED TRIP	109
TRAVELING WEST	111
LIFE IN PORTLAND, OREGON 1958-1959	114
A BIRD TALE	117
THE JOURNEY BACK	119
ON NEEDLES AND PINS	121
A PASTOR'S WIFE	123
LEARNING FROM THE BEST	124
WHO ARE TODAY'S HEROES?	126
I CAN'T DANCE—JUST ASK ME	128
A FOOLISH MOVE	130
CAUGHT IN THE ACT	131
A NEW WORD	133
LOOK BEFORE YOU LEAP	135
A CAMPING TRIP TO REMEMBER	137
JESSE	140
MY THREE UNUSUAL SONS	142
ADDING ONE MORE—CINDY	144
CINDY'S STORY CONTINUES	148
A LETTER—GRANDMA TO GRANDSON	150
SWEDEN, HERE WE COME	152
LEARNING A NEW SKILL	154
KENNETH JEWELL CHORALE	156
DID WE MAKE A MISTAKE?	158
PARTNERSHIPS	161
BOGIE, A DOG TO REMEMBER	163
FAMILY TRADITIONS	165
MUSIC KIDS SAY AND DO THE DARNDEST THINGS	167
MAKING A WORTHWHILE DISCOVERY	169
FIRST ENGLISH LUTHERAN CHURCH, MANSFIELD OHIO 1980 -1989	172
"SAINTS ALIVE"—A MUSICAL	181
TWO STUPID THINGS I HAVE DONE	184
OH NO, ANOTHER WORD HUNT	185
A TRIP TO REMEMBER	187

LARS	189
PHEW! HOW DO SWEDES EAT THIS STUFF?	191
TOO LATE, TOO BAD	193
A CANDLE HOUSE SURPRISE	194
IT'S ABOUT TIME	196
A ROOM WITH A VIEW	199
A MOST UNUSUAL FRIEND	201
A NEW FRIEND	204
SOMETHING I WISH I HAD DONE	206
REMEMBERING BERT, MY ONE AND ONLY	208
WALKING TOGETHER	212
THE GRIEF PROCESS	213
THE EMPTY SPACE	215
A MOVING EXPERIENCE	216
JUST ANOTHER SNOW STORM?	219
TO STAY OR TO GO—THAT IS THE QUESTION	221
THIS WAS MY FIRST (Earthquake!)	223
WHAT ONE YEAR HAS TAUGHT ME	225
CHOICES CALL FOR DECISIONS	227
IT'S ALWAYS BEEN A QUESTION	229
ALL IN THE FAMILY	231
CHAIRS	234
WHY SHOULD I WRITE MY STORY?	236
AND SOME WONDERED IF IT WOULD LAST	238
ANNE LAMOTT	240
EMIGRANTS	242
HIS NAME IS PAUL	244
SECURITY AND INSECURITY	246
I LOVE GOOD NEWS	248
BE MY GUEST	250
IS THERE A BOOK IN MY FUTURE?	252
STUFF AND NONSENSE	254
WHEN THE WELL RUNS DRY	256
THE HOLIDAYS	258
MUSINGS	260
RELATIVES	262
IT'S ABOUT "LIFE"	264
A TOAST AT JON AND MOLLY'S WEDDING	266
MITCH ALBOM	268
A DIFFERENT KIND OF JOURNEY	270
SURPRISE, SURPRISE	274
WHO IS MY NEIGHBOR?	275
IT'S OVER	277
THIS IS MY BOX	279

RIVALRY	281
COMPETITION	283
WHERE DO THE SUMMERS GO?	285
SCHEDULES	287
CINDY'S STORY CONTINUES	289
IT'S ABOUT GUS	290
A TRIP TO THE ER	292
WHAT'S ON THE MENU?	294
DEALING WITH CHANGE	296
HELP, HELP	298
TIME OUT- FOR A TIME	300
TIME SAVING GADGETS	302
OUT WITH THE OLD, IN WITH THE NEW	304
MUSIC, MUSIC, MUSIC	307
PRACTICE, PRACTICE, PRACTICE	310
RECITALS AND BUTTERFLIES	312
TREES	314
QUOTES	316
WILD FIRE	318
WALKING IN CIRCLES	320
DO WELLS EVER RUN DRY?	322
A FINAL WORD	324
THE PRAYER OF SAINT FRANCIS	325
PICTURES	326

PICTURES

Picture 1: Here I am at three months old	5
Picture 2: The Nelson Farmhouse in Milaca	29
Picture 3: Uncle Arvid	36
Picture 4: Birdie and her puppies	45
Picture 5: My Dad - Edwin L. Hoffman	70
Picture 6: Wedding. September 2, 1949	91
Picture 7: I'm the one in the carriage; not the one holding up the fountain	115
Picture 8: Jesse, David (Bean), Lars, and Me	143
Picture 9: Cindy with her children Caroline and Robert	146
Picture 10: It was wonderful to see Cindy and her children again.	146
Picture 11: Installation Sunday at First English Lutheran Church, 1980	173
Picture 12: Lucia and her court	175
Picture 13: We are looking good!	182
Picture 14: Can you see the can of Surströmming on the table?	192
Picture 15: Bert signing a book	209
Picture 16: Bert's grave marker	214
Picture 17: The siblings—Arne, Ruth, and Bert Anderson	231
Picture 18: Ruth, Joyce, and me.	232
Picture 19: Marvin and Ruth Lindstedt, Helen and Bert Anderson	233
Picture 20: My 90th birthday party	263
Picture 21: Jon and Molly's Wedding	267
Picture 22: Grandma Nelson - 90th Birthday	326
Picture 23: Grandma Nelson - 90th Birthday	326
Picture 24: Grandma Nelson and me, 1928	327
Picture 25: Grandpa Nelson and me, 1928	327
Picture 26: Grandpa and Grandma Hoffman – 50th Wedding Anniversary	328
Picture 27: Grandpa and Grandma Hoffman with their five boys. My dad, Ed, is in the middle of the back row.	329
Picture 28: Edwin Hoffman and Delia Nelson – Wedding	330
Picture 29: Edwin and Delia Hoffman – 50th Wedding Anniversary	331
Picture 30: Bert's father – David Elias Anderson	332
Picture 31: My Dad – Edwin L. Hoffman	333
Picture 32: Dad hunting rabbits	334
Picture 33: My childhood home in Minneapolis. 5300 – 44th Avenue S.	334
Picture 34: My dad Ed, my son David, and one big fish!	335
Picture 35: Here I am at 2 ½ years old.	336
Picture 36: I'm already playing piano at 4 years old.	337
Picture 37: Gladys and I standing in a tub of water. Can you guess why?	338
Picture 38: A birthday party. Can you find me in the back row?	339
Picture 39: Gladys, me, and friends.	339

Picture 40: Here I am at age 13 years — 340
Picture 41: Confirmation May 25 1941 at First Covenant Church — 340
Picture 42: This is from a movie my dad took. — 341
Picture 43: Sulking on the porch. — 341
Picture 44: Edwin and Dee Hoffman, Helen, Eva Anderson, Bert — 342
Picture 45: Bert and me in 1950 — 343
Picture 46: Rock n Roll! Halloween fun. — 344
Picture 47: Dave and Jennie's Wedding — 345
Picture 48: No one recognized me in this Halloween outfit — 346
Picture 49: Four generations of Anderson: Nate, Dave, Me, Dave (Bean) — 347
Picture 50: Bye Bye — 347

Made in the USA
Middletown, DE
02 August 2018